The Politics of Women's Liberation

**Winner of the American
Political Science Association Prize
for the best Work
on Women in Politics**

The
Politics
of
Women's
Liberation

A CASE STUDY OF AN EMERGING SOCIAL MOVEMENT AND ITS RELATION TO THE POLICY PROCESS

Jo Freeman

Longman
New York and London

For Cathy and Jenny

Preface

THIS IS A BOOK ABOUT SOCIAL MOVEMENTS, public policy, and feminism. Therefore, it seems only reasonable to tell my readers why and how I became interested in these concerns. What follows is a personal intellectual history of the influences in my life, and my responses to them, which led to this manuscript.

I have always been a very political person. I was raised to believe in God and the Democratic party and I gave up on the former (at age twelve) long before I became disillusioned with the latter (in my mid-twenties while living in Mayor Daley's Chicago). Consequently I was a ready recipient for the heady atmosphere of the University of California at Berkeley where I spent four of the most important years of my life (1961–65). They were also among the most important years in the life of this country, during which the death knell was rung on the cold war and the firebell of alarm was sounded by the civil rights and the student movements. I was very much involved in these movements—first in the Bay Area and later in the South working on voter registration for the Southern Christian Leadership Conference—and thus very much concerned with the issues they raised: civil disobedience; the nature of political change; protest as political action; the obligation of the citizen and the role of government; the limits of political space; movement organization, participation, and impact; the meaning of social conflicts and crises; and the appropriate response of the political system to dissidence within it.

Thanks to the educational open-mindedness as well as the intellectual stimulation of some of my professors, I was able to draw on the inspiration of my political activities to write the best term papers of my undergraduate career, and thus to know the joy that can come when action and thought can unite and each can enhance the other.

It was while I was doing this research, during my senior year, that I first began to speculate on the potential sources of new movements in the near future. I smile now at the hubris of such speculation—only time and more education have made me aware of how inadequate my intellectual tools really were—but the consequences stayed with me for years. The next major movement in this country, I felt, would be one of women. (I also forecast a movement of the elderly but have been less satisfied with its accuracy.)

This conclusion compelled me to think about the possible implications of such a movement's demands (which have proved far greater than I ever imagined) and my own relationship to it. These thoughts in turn forced me to confront my own real prejudices against women. I was one of the many girls who internalized an individualistic version of what Betty Friedan was to call the "three-sex theory": there's men, there's women, and there's me. Thus it was quite possible for me to share the socially accepted prejudices against women without ever drawing the appropriate conclusions about my own inferiority. I was all prepared to be the classic "exception"; pitying but not understanding those poor souls snared in the web of sexism without ever seeing the ways in which my own life had been channeled from birth.

I spent the next few years consciously wearing down my negative feelings about women without ever thinking about their implications for myself. It wasn't until 1967 and 1968, when I first experienced direct discrimination and had the context of the emerging movement in which to evaluate it, that I finally understood women's discontent on a gut level and not just in my head.

The story is an old one; thousands of women have lived it. My career choice at the time was journalism and I had put in several months of underpaid apprenticeship on a local Chicago community newspaper. After accumulating a substantial file of stories and photographs, I assaulted the local media. If they had simply told me I wasn't good enough I might have accepted their judgment and gone to journalism school, but the level of sophistication about sex discrimination was very low in those days. I was bluntly told, before I opened my file, that all the papers had a quota of no more than 5 percent women on the city desk and there were rarely any openings. When I questioned this limit, the reply was that women couldn't be sent to cover riots. (I never quite got up the courage to ask why they thought rioters would be more likely to attack white women than white men, since they certainly weren't refusing to hire the latter in favor of black reporters.)

During the next few months of answering ads and signing up at employment agencies I experienced the many subtle and not-so-subtle forms of sex discrimination for any job paying more than that of a clerk-typist. Time and time again I was told that, despite my competencies and the then high need for skilled personnel, I could not be offered a good job because I would soon leave it to get married (or to have a baby, or just to leave). Initially I felt I could persuade interviewers of my "exceptionality." Other women might leave but not I. My record spoke for itself. Only slowly did it dawn on me that they simply didn't want to listen. The fact that I was female obscured everything else. I might be an exception in my own eyes, but to the world of potential employers, I was a walking stereotype. After months of having this reality drummed into my head I finally realized that there was no individual escape. Some women might have it better than others, if the circumstances were right, but the prejudices against all women affected the lives of every woman. Gradually, the hot, persistent flame of anger, with which most feminists sustain their dedication, began to burn within me.

When I finally did get a job as assistant editor on a trade magazine—at secretarial pay—I experienced discrimination all over again from the inside. A reiteration of my observations and conclusions would be trite in 1975. Suffice it to say I saw the handwriting on the wall. Perceiving few opportunities for women and many women contending for them, I turned instead to one of the classic channels of upward mobility—graduate school. Fortunately it was a good year for women applicants. Not only was fellowship money at its peak, but Selective Service had recently ruled that enrollment in graduate school was no longer a draft exemption—frightening admissions committees into feeling that giving money to men was a poor investment.

It was at the University of Chicago that I became interested in public policy. I had wanted to study social movements, but the only faculty members in the school interested in that subject left within a year of my arrival (I had to organize a student seminar to find people to talk to on the topic) and my assigned adviser was into public policy. Skeptical at first, I finally realized that public policy provided a different perspective on the same issues I had always been concerned with. I was interested in social and political change. I saw social movements as the primary vehicle by which this change was brought about, by pressuring the system from the outside. It eventually penetrated my protest-schooled skull that policy was the means by which government stimulated, responded to and/or curtailed social change. To study movements without studying policy was like studying a coin without ever turning it over. Unfortunately, few students of either discipline had come to the same conclusion, so I was left with a fairly empty field to wallow in or cultivate. This book is the result.

During these years I had my antennas tuned to any possible signs of female revolt. In 1966 I picked up many tremors, but none that led to more than a few sporadic meetings and outpourings of personal discontent. I first read of the National Organization for Women—with feelings of delight and relief—early in 1967 in a newspaper interview. My letter to the interviewee was never answered. Nor were any of the other five letters I wrote during the next year to the other NOW addresses I read or heard of in varying places. Clearly something was happening, but I couldn't find it. My frustration grew. I thought of organizing a group myself, but felt I lacked both the contacts and the resources. That summer I applied for a student fellowship at the Institute for Policy Studies in Washington, D.C., which supported many social-change activities. I said I wanted to organize women. The interviewing fellow told me he saw no potential in that, and my application was denied.

That same summer I made contact with some New Left women who were beginning to reevaluate their status in that movement, and within the next six months we had organized the first independent women's liberation group in this country and created one nucleus of what was to be the younger branch of the movement.

I think I was the only person in that group who really believed we were organizing a new movement (at least the others have told me this since then) and not just another New Left constituency. Thus, from the beginning I made it a point to *watch* what was happening. In my past political activities I had been so caught up in the activism that I had not had the time or distance to observe. I had acquired many questions about the origins, structure, and impact of movements, but never the data to provide the answers. With this new movement I had another chance, and I didn't want to lose it. I wanted to be an *observer* as well as a participant.

It was not an easy movement to observe. It was diffuse, uncoordinated, with few communications organs and, except for NOW, held no national meetings. Adding to these difficulties was an intense suspicion in the younger branch of anyone admitting to studying the movement. During the first few years this branch was still tied to the New Left and thus often affected by its fears that any "studies" would only be used against it. When I asked women attending a regional conference in late 1969 to fill out a lengthy questionnaire on how they first joined the movement—to provide data for my Master's thesis—I experienced little cooperation and much hostility. After much inquiry, I discovered two women from a Left faction were circulating the rumor that my study would be used by the University of Chicago to help them eliminate potential feminists applying for admission. This abortion of my M.A. thesis taught me to be much more cautious about both my intentions and my procedures. While I have never misled anyone about my research and have guarded the anonymity of my sources, I realized that I would have to rely on the more personal methods of observation and interviewing, rather than the impersonal, "scientific" ones of questionnaires and surveys. With these less threatening methods I received greater cooperation.

Methodology

Consequently, the primary research method in this thesis has been participant observation, supplemented by some library research, interviewing, and historiography. Although it has a long tradition, it is still one of the more controversial social scientific methods. The term itself is somewhat misleading, as it does not refer to any particular method but to a complex blend of data-collecting techniques that vary with time and circumstances. It

> involves some amount of genuine social interaction in the
> field with the subjects of the study, some direct observation of
> relevant events, some formal and a great deal of informal
> interviewing, some systematic counting, some collection of
> documents and artifacts, and open-endedness in the
> directions of the study.[1]

As Becker and Geer have pointed out, the value of participant

---

1. George J. McCall and J. L. Simmons, "The Nature of Participant Observation," *American Journal of Sociology* 67 (1962): 566–67.

observation is that it provides a "rich experiential context" through which one can

> become aware of incongruous or unexplained facts, . . . sensitive to their possible implications and connections with other observed facts and thus [to] continually revise and adapt his [sic] theoretical orientation and specific problems in the direction of greater relevance to the phenomena under study.[2]

I was a participant in the younger branch of the Chicago women's liberation movement from 1967 through 1969 and editor of the first (at that time only) national newsletter. I was able, through extensive correspondence and interviews, to keep a record of how many groups around the country first started and their initial development. I was also a member of Chicago NOW, and used the opportunities derived from publishing several papers on the movement to interview many of NOW's initiators, officials, and participants over a period of time. Between 1970 and 1974 I was not actively involved in any movement organization, but I did follow its activities through friends, traveling, lecturing, and publications. This sequence of active participation followed by indirect observation afforded me a more informed perspective on the movement than would be possible for anyone who was either primarily a participant or primarily an observer.

Between 1972 and 1974 I engaged in more active research for this book by seeking out opportunities to interview feminists in various cities, groups, and activities of the movement, often but not always with their knowledge that I intended to publish the results. Several shorter articles have preceded this book and two of them have been incorporated in it. I was aided in this effort by the many women who put me up in their homes and introduced me to feminists they thought would be of interest to me; by feminists traveling around the country who shared with me their observations and knowledge of areas I could not visit; by those

---

2. Howard Becker and Blanche Geer, "Participant Observation and Interviewing: A Comparison," *Human Organization* 16, no. 3 (1957): 28–32.

researching and writing their own books or dissertations who allowed me to read their manuscripts; by those who had archival material which they allowed me to peruse; and in particular by those many busy activists who shared their time and insights with me.

In 1970, 1973, and 1974 I attended the national conventions of NOW and have gone to several local meetings during that time. I interviewed women in WEAL, FEW, and several other small feminist organizations as well as collected and read their publications. Although my own collection of materials was enough to fill a five-drawer file cabinet, I spent three weeks at the Women's History Research Library in Berkeley, California, going through their voluminous collection.

To investigate the development of public policy on women's rights, I relied primarily on interviews with key people, or in the case of most congressional representatives, with their assistants. I also consulted numerous documents and reports by and about the relevant federal agencies. These were done largely in 1969 and 1973. Since the amount of time spent on this latter investigation does not begin to approach the six years I spent researching the movement, I do not state my conclusions about the policy sphere with the same certainty that I make them about the movement. Nonetheless, I do think that the tentative hypotheses that are developed by this research support the premises which guided the entire study.

In the spring of 1974 a draft of this book was sent to over thirty people in government, academia, and both branches of the movement. Replies were received from the following and I incorporated their comments and criticisms into the final draft: Mary Eastwood, Catherine East, Bunny Sandler, Linda Thurston, Beverly Fisher, Charlotte Bunch, Wilma Scott Heide, Jane Mansbridge, Ira Katznelson, Toni Carabillo, David Copus, Gloria Steinem, Nancy Borman, Brenda Feigen Fasteau.

Acknowledgments

At this point, most authors pause to acknowledge the many supporters without whom the book could not have been written: the institution that gave them released time, the foundation that financed their research, the colleagues and students whose probing questions stimulated their thinking, the librarian who ferreted out obscure references, the secretaries who typed the manuscript, and last (and sometimes least) the wife who put up with it all.

I can make few of these traditional acknowledgments. This book was originally written as my dissertation in the spring of 1973; it was my means of getting employment, not a vacation from it. I did apply to a foundation for research support, but I didn't receive any. Fortunately, the National Institute for Mental Health saw fit to continue my subsistence fellowship, so I had neither to starve nor to work full time while writing. I was grateful for access to The University of Chicago library (made possible by my NIMH tuition payments), but since the dissertation was virtually completed before I was officially admitted to candidacy, I could not get doctoral privileges until after I no longer needed them. I do thank Theodore J. Lowi, my official adviser and committee chairperson, for having stated sometime in my third year, "Of course you're going to do your dissertation on the women's liberation movement!" Prior to that time, believe it or not, it had never occurred to me. Dr. Lowi's resignation from U.C. my dissertation year, however, and the absence of any other faculty members interested in feminism, public policy, or social movements, left me with no one with whom to talk. And, like most women I know, I do not have a wife.

Lest these assertions seem like sour grapes, let me add that I do have major acknowledgments to make, without whom this book couldn't have been written, but they are not of the traditional sort. I wish, first of all, to thank deeply the five political science faculty members who departed for other institutions at the end of the Spring 1972 quarter. Their absence created an excess of office space that a few lucky graduate students, if properly sponsored, could squat in until otherwise needed. I have never found it easy to write at home—and I did not have any file cabinets—so therefore thank the departmental staff for helping me to maintain my tenuous hold on an office with sufficient files and bookshelves to organize my material. I also thank the student Political Science Association for letting me appropriate their battered but faithful (usually) electric typewriter as I cannot read my own handwriting.

I would further like to thank Marie Hauville and the staff of the Student Activities Office for keeping me on their payroll at the munificent salary of $16 a week ($2 an hour) plus totin' privileges (leftovers from the official luncheons) which supplied my travel budget and added protein to my diet. They also gave me moral support and lots of tea. My roommate of that year, who wishes to remain anonymous, worked in a strategic place in the library, from which she was able to oversee my overdue notices and intercede before they became too expensive. (She is not a feminist; she said she did it for her own peace of mind.)

Other individuals and groups to whom I am grateful include: The U.C. Judo Club, on whom I took out my frustrations three times a week; the "Sam Ervin Show" whose PBS reruns relieved my tired mind at the end of a hard day; the many drivers and three pilots who (despite their poor intentions) picked me up as I hitchhiked to varying feminist conferences and professional meetings; the "feminist couch" of Washington, D.C. which quite literally supported me for roughly the month (over a period of several weeks) I did research in that city; women in a major hospital (in Chicago), a national broadcasting company (in New York), a small Catholic women's college (in Massachusetts), and several government agencies (in Washington D.C.) who surreptitiously xeroxed reams of material and copies of the manuscript for me on their institutional budgets and who wish to remain anonymous; the staff of *Ms.* magazine who gave me shelter in their air-conditioning during the hottest of last summer's days while I revised and updated this manuscript; and last (but not least) the three typists who pounded out the final draft: Toni Cerutti, Evelyn Dershewitz, and me.

Contents

The Politics of
Women's Liberation

Introduction

T HE DECADE OF THE 1960s WAS A TUMULTUOUS one, giving rise to many challenges to our political system to maintain itself while living up to its traditional values. Fundamental to these challenges was the question of to what extent the political system was capable of responding to, incorporating, and even instigating social change. If, as Lowi has said, "Our system is uniquely designed for maintenance" [1] we still have to ask maintenance of what: the basic values upon which it was structured or the distribution of power and resources as it appears at the moment? When maintenance of one comes into conflict with maintenance of the other, what happens? What process of accommodation takes place or does one inevitably dominate the other? Just as important: Under what circumstances does one come into conflict with the other and thus necessitate a national

---

1. Theodore J. Lowi, *The Politics of Disorder* (New York: Basic Books, 1971), p. 54.

soul-searching of our priorities? Under what circumstances can the political system bring about social change?

The last question at least can be answered heuristically. If one could postulate the necessary political means of social change they would encompass the following conditions: (1) statutory law and judicial interpretation that represent a public commitment to change and specify the means and directions of changes as thoroughly as possible; (2) energetic administrative enforcement and implementation coupled with a sympathetic understanding of the ramifications of the beneficiary's problems; (3) active, organized effort by the beneficiaries to encourage and facilitate their members taking advantage of special programs as well as make demands on the system to improve these programs. These three conditions in turn must take place within a context of crisis to impart the sense of urgency necessary to their execution.

Although these conditions reflect a purely ideal state, they can be used as a standard by which to measure efforts for change. They point out what should have been obvious: that political change does not involve isolated efforts either within or without the system, regardless of the intentions or resources of those making such efforts. Rather it involves a dynamic system of reciprocal influences whose effects are determined by their mutual relationships.

This in turn implies that it is shortsighted to view the whole political system as limited to established institutions and governmental channels. Such a traditional view ignores the process by which new influences, new groups, new institutions, and even new channels are created, seeing these new elements instead as pathological symptoms of an incapacitated system. One can say that change happens only outside the political system, only if one limits one's conception of that political system. Thus, one can examine the political means of social change only by first changing one's definition of the political system.

This thesis starts from the following perspectives: (1) the American political system encompasses the potential for new elements as well as the reality of established ones; (2) these new elements, while they form in varying ways, usually involve what is commonly labeled as "disorderly" behavior; (3) such behavior, rather than taking place outside the normal limits of political action, is part and parcel of the American political process; (4) the existence of such "disorderly behavior" is not a sign of systemic dysfunction but is necessary to keep it effectual; (5) such behavior is as rational and instrumental for its participants, within the context in which they must operate, as most other forms of more traditional political behavior. Thus we would agree with Skolnick that "mass protest is an essentially political phenomenon engaged in by normal people" [2] and expand on Lowi's assertation that "in a very profound sense, new or nascent groups, without necessarily intending to, tend to hold a democratic system to its own pretensions," [3] by adding that that is a basic function of such groups in a democratic system, not merely a by-product.

Such new elements often enter the political arena via a social movement. The latter term is a rubric for a wide variety of related but not identical social phenomena. Because it has such wide application, I will not presume to define it at this time although some elements of a working description will be elucidated in a later chapter.[4] Suffice it to say here that "a successful movement is the point of intersection between personal and social change" [5] and as such often makes use of but is not exclusively restricted to the political institutions of our society. Although the element of personal change is often the most significant, this book will be primarily concerned with social change of a concrete and tangible nature. This is partially because personal change is very hard to measure, and partially because I want to look at change as it has

---

2. Jerome Skolnick, *The Politics of Protest* (New York: Simon & Shuster, 1969), p. xix. See also Michael Lipsky, "Protest as a Political Resource," *American Political Science Review* 62 (December 1968); 1144–58.

3. Lowi, *The Politics of Disorder*, p. 56.

4. One whole book has been written describing the various ways in which a social movement has been defined. None of the many authors writing on social movements at this time really agree with one another. See Paul Wilkenson, *Social Movement* (New York: Praeger, 1971).

5. Luther P. Gerlach and Virginia H. Hine, *People, Power, Change: Movements of Social Transformation* (Indianapolis: Bobbs-Merrill, 1970), p. xvi.

been manifested in public policy on the federal level. It is via such policy and its implementation that conditions 1 and 2 of our earlier heuristic delineation of the political means of social change are or are not met.

The study of social movements and that of public policy are two fields that have heretofore been treated primarily as distinct and unrelated areas in the scholarly literature. While some writers have envisioned social movements as incipient interest groups and/or political parties[6] and thus as having a potential effect on policy, no one has tried to trace out the exact relationships between the two and the way in which each affects the other.[7] The examination of such a mutual relationship is both the hypothesis and purpose of this thesis. Nonetheless, it will be impossible to convey the degree of complexity of the relationship as many of the intervening and contributory variables will be dealt with cursorily. In particular, the effects of the general atmospheric changes caused by the movement will be more assumed than delineated. Instead the focus will be on the specific relationship. It is understood that while the same social conditions which create a social movement may have a direct effect on policy, it is when the people most strongly affected by changes in social conditions are not already part of the policy making process that they must organize themselves for political action. Thus a social movement becomes the vehicle by which policy makers are influenced directly, as well as indirectly through general social change.

---

6. E.g., Rudolph Heberle, *Social Movements* (New York: Appleton-Century-Crofts, 1951); Lowi, *The Politics of Disorder*; Harmon Zeigler, *Interest Groups in American Society* (Englewood Cliffs, N.J.: Prentice-Hall, 1964).

7. Juliet Z. Saltman, *Open Housing as a Social Movement* (Lexington, Mass.: D. C. Heath, 1971), presents data which could be used to develop such an analysis, but it is not a major theme of her book. Paul Schumaker, in "Protest Groups, Environmental Characteristics and Policy-Responsiveness" (Paper given at the 1974 convention of the Midwest Political Science Association), argues that "the policy-responsiveness of urban communities to protest group demands is enhanced, either directly or indirectly, by . . . : (1) private-regarding political cultures, (2) economic development, (3) unreformed governmental institutions and (4) dispersed structures of influence." However, his measures of these variables are crude, their relationships weak, and the specific means by which they effect policy are ignored.

Concomitantly, while policy has an indirect effect on social movements by altering the conditions which gave rise to them, it has a more immediate and direct effect as well. As Schattschneider has pointed out, the outcome of a conflict is determined by its scope, and "the socialization of conflict is the essential democratic process." [8] Social movements are one of the primary means of socializing conflict; of taking private disputes and making them political ones.[9] This is why a successful movement provides an *intersection* between personal and social change. Personal changes can be a *vehicle* to more concrete social changes, and are also often a result; but if a movement restricts itself to change purely on the personal level, its impact on society remains minimal. It is only when private disputes that result from personal changes are translated into public demands that a movement enters the political arena and can make use of political institutions to reach its goals of social change.

Once a social movement enters the political realm, however, it is usually constrained by the limitations of that realm. There already exist many concrete, accepted "rules of the game" which newcomers are expected to abide by.[10] These rules are manifested

8. E. E. Schattschneider, *The Semi-Sovereign People* (New York: Holt, Rinehart & Winston, 1960), p. 142.

9. McWilliams argues that "previously nonpolitical issues will almost inevitably become political whenever two conditions apply: (a) when reality comes to be perceptibly discordant with social myths . . . and (b) when there is the opportunity to compare notes on personal unhappiness." Nancy McWilliams, "Contemporary Feminism, Consciousness-Raising, and Changing Views of the Political," in *Women in Politics*, ed. Jane Jaquette (New York: Wiley, 1974), p. 160.

10. Needless to say, not all social movements play by the rules because those rules do not fit their needs and their resources. The civil rights movement would have died an early death if it had done so, as would the labor movement and many others. Those movements which opt out of playing the game inevitably subject themselves to the criticism that "I agree with your goals but not with your methods." Fortunately, such movements usually have the sense to ignore this criticism, occasionally to the benefit of everyone. Many new tactics created by dissident movements that violated the rules of their day have since become enshrined into the accepted pantheon of political activities. The illegal device of political pamphleteering developed in seventeenth- and eighteenth-century England is now the stalwart democratic concept of freedom of press. The labor movement gave us the strike and boycott, formerly seditious activities now protected by law. The civil rights movement has developed the sit-in, which has not yet become as respectable as many of its predecessors, but might very well through time and use.

not only in norms of behavior but in the very institutions which govern the system and manage the conflicts within it.

> The function of institutions is to channel conflict; institutions do not treat all forms of conflict impartially, just as football rules do not treat all forms of violence with indiscriminate equality.[11]

These institutions in turn, by their ability to "reward" or "punish" efforts for change with "success" or "defeat," often reshape the structure, the activities, and even the goals of social movements.[12]

It is here that we encounter a paradox. Movements that conform themselves to the norms of behavior in order to participate successfully in political institutions often find themselves forsaking their major goals for social change. Long-range ideals are warped for the sake of short-range gains. But movements that hold steadfast to their radical goals and disdain political participation of any kind in an "evil" system often find themselves isolated in a splendid ideological purity which gains nothing for any one. They are paralyzed by their own fear of cooptation; and such paralysis is in turn the ultimate cooptation as inactive revolutionaries are a good deal more innocuous than active "reformists." Thus a successful movement must not only maintain a balance between personal and political change, but also a creative tension between its "politics" and its "vision." [13] It must keep well in mind where it wants to go while accepting the necessity of often following a twisted and tortured road in order to get there.

Ironically, a successful political system must do the same—though its vision if not its politics do not always coincide with those of the groups conflicting within it. It must manage its

---

11. Schattschneider, *The Semi-Sovereign People*, p. 72.

12. This is merely using the language of operant conditioning to express an institutional perspective on the Weber-Michels hypothesis of goal transformation of social movements. The latter will be explained and utilized more fully in a later chapter.

13. My thanks to Sheldon Wolin for this unintended use of his terminology.

conflicts in such a way that it maintains its basic values while not necessarily maintaining the given positions of power of the partisans within it. To do this it must provide for the emergence and growth to power of new elements which are compatible with its basic values while guarding itself against being totally overwhelmed by them. Concomitantly it must maintain its old supporters without allowing itself to be totally controlled by them. It must provide for both continuity and change.[14]

No political system to date has been completely successful in this effort. With the exception of one major schism, the American system has managed more or less so far; though not always with much ease or grace. But it is young yet and will still have many opportunities to stagnate in its own complacency—provided new political elements cease in their constant efforts to keep it from doing so.

Throughout the rest of this book, I want to take a closer look at one of those new elements—the women's liberation movement as it has emerged in the mid-1960s and is still in the process of developing. While there have been many case studies of political and social movements, it is unusual to study one that is yet so new. Most authoritative studies have all taken place long after the movement was over and it was possible to assess more than its immediate impact on American society. Unfortunately, this advantage was offset by the inevitable bias of stressing the end rather than the beginning of the movement. Thus there are several excellent analyses of the institutionalization and/or decline of social movements and virtually none of their origins and early development.[15]

---

14. For an extensive analysis of the relationship between what he labels the "influence" and "social control" perspectives, see William A. Gamson, *Power and Discontent* (Homewood, Ill.: Dorsey Press, 1968). A different approach to this problem is taken by Lipset who asserts that: "A principal problem for a theory of democratic systems is: Under what conditions can a society have 'sufficient' participation to maintain the democratic system without introducing sources of cleavage which will undermine the cohesion?" Seymour Martin Lipset, *Political Man: The Social Bases of Politics* (New York: Doubleday, 1960), p. 14.

15. E.g. Mayer N. Zald and Roberta Ash, "Social Movement Organizations: Growth, Decay and Change," *Social Forces* 44 (March 1966): 327–40; Sheldon

There is value in an early analysis that compensates for the inevitable prematurity of its assessments. Primary among these are the opportunity to collect data on origins and early growth which would otherwise be lost with time and fading memories. Already many significant developments in the feminist movement which affected its subsequent history have become so obscured that few can remember the intensity of their original impact. Ideas and tactics that were once hotly contested are today accepted as dogma. Secondly, the early collection of such data allows us to place it in its contemporary environmental context uncontaminated by hindsight and to make some early assessments on its problems, impact, and potential, which, when compared later with subsequent developments, can provide some standard for judging those assessments.

Although the bulk of the following pages concerns itself with the women's liberation *movement,* it should not be forgotten that the primary concern is the relationship between movement and policy. Policy gets shorter shrift than movement—in part because its development is more recent and thus there is less to talk about, and in part because the movement is an extraordinarily complex phenomenon which simply requires more pages for even a cursory appraisal. Although connections between the two are alluded to throughout, they are not specifically made until the conclusion. Even here, it is understood that their dynamic interrelationship is still in process. The women's liberation movement is just beginning to have an impact on policy and on society.

In the following pages each chapter centers itself around one or more questions, although not all the data presented are directly concerned with those questions. The first consideration inevitably must be why and how the women's liberation movement emerged

---

Messinger, "Organizational Transformation: A Case Study of a Declining Social Movement," *American Sociological Review* 20 (February 1955): 3–10; Mayer N. Zald and Patricia Denton, "From Evangelism to General Service: The Transformation of the YMCA," *Administrative Science Quarterly* 8 (September 1963): 214–34; Abraham Holtzman, *The Townsend Movement: A Political Study* (New York: Bookman, 1963); Joseph Gusfield, "Organizational Change: A Study of the Women's Christian Temperance Union" (Ph.D. dissertation, Department of Sociology, University of Chicago, 1954).

when it did. By the early 1960s the suffrage movement was a vague, historical memory; most everyone assumed that women had equality, at least as much as they wanted; and the very term "feminist" had become an epithet. Within less than a decade feminism was a respectable political position and "women's liberation" had become a household word.

The first chapter analyzes the general social and economic conditions as they have changed over the last fifty years which created the potential for a new social movement. In doing so it uses a modified version of the theory of relative deprivation to explain one other key aspect of the new movement: why all but a few of its originators and early adherents were white, middle-class, college-educated, professionally employed women.

The second chapter deals with the more specific question of what precipitated the movement at precisely the time it occurred. The sociological literature provides no assistance here as it implicitly assumes a "spontaneous generation" theory of social-movement formation. Instead a more original and less mystical theory is proposed based upon an earlier study I did of the origins of six relatively contemporary social movements. While the hypothesis is based on more data than the women's liberation movement by itself supports, that movement does illustrate the major aspects of the hypothesis.

Since the movement had two distinct origins from two different strata of society, with the result of two different styles of organization and orientation, it becomes necessary to separate the analysis. Unfortunately, this presents a problem of ordering the data not created by the more chronological scheme of the earlier chapters. Both branches of the movement and all their progeny have been growing and changing at the same time. The linear presentation of data to which the written word restricts us does not permit a multidimensional view of what was a multidimensioned reality. Therefore a little imagination from the reader is necessary to appreciate the explosive and multifaceted nature of the movement.

With this proviso, the process of growth is looked at in terms of: (1) the inherited values and norms of the originators and the ways

in which these cast the mold of the movement's future development, (2) the internal dynamics of the different groups, and (3)
the environmental influences as they effect the movement's
activities. These parameters are used to illustrate why the two
branches developed in such different ways, with different problems, different strategies of action and different emphases, even
though they have been concerned with much the same issues. The
movement began without an ideology, and has as yet only the
rudiments of one. Thus feminist ideology has played an insignif-
icant role in the development of its structures and strategies,
although nonfeminist ideas have been adapted from the political
context in which each branch grew which have affected its
organizational style. The different strategies of each branch have
not been governed by different ideologies, but by different
structures; it is structure that has determined what kinds of
activities are feasible and which more accurately explains how
various groups have directed their energies.

A comparison of these two branches raises interesting questions
about the Weber/Michels model of goal transformation, oligarchization, and conservatization as social-change organizations
bureaucratize and institutionalize. Contrary to the model's pre-
dictions, in this movement it is the more organized, bureaucratic
older branch that has so far shown less transformation in a
conservative direction over time, and the lesser organized one that
shows more. This process is examined with an eye to the
particular resources of a social-movement organization and the
strains that they create.

Chapter 5 begins with a short description of a major event that
does not fit comfortably under the heading of either branch of the
movement—the grand press blitz of 1969–70—because it equally
affected both. A minor hypothesis on why this occurred when it
occurred is tested but not conclusively proved. The rest of the
chapter is a theater bill of some of the major players in the
ongoing drama. The movement has penetrated most spheres of
life leaving many organizational offspring. While none of these is
significant enough to warrant a chapter by itself, they do deserve
an honorable mention. Some appear on stage elsewhere and thus

require an introduction, while others serve to illustrate the immense scope of the movement.

Chapter 6 gives a cursory review of the major federal policies on women regulating activities in the private sphere through the Ninety-second Congress. For so young a movement, there has been an immense amount of policy made; and the momentum has not yet stopped. The primary concern of this chapter is to analyze the reasons for that initial success. Nevertheless, this analysis is done with the realization that most of the policy is too new for the quality of its implementation to be tested and it is implementation that determines the ultimate success of any policy sphere. Further, of those laws and regulations that have been on the books for several years, the major battles of the movement have been to get sex discrimination placed on the same level as race discrimination—let alone adequately implemented. As is clear by reports of the U.S. Civil Rights Commission, viable implementation of the policies on race discrimination has a long way to go. While the women's liberation movement has been comparatively successful in achieving parity with blacks and the reasons for that success are worth analyzing, it is not something to get overly excited about. The best that can be said at this point is that women can now join with blacks in learning exactly what road is paved with good intentions.

The final chapter attempts to tie the themes of the first six together. It analyzes the symbiotic relationship that has developed between feminists (and some nonfeminists) in government, the private sphere, and even those opposed to the American political system to show the resources that each brings to the common aims of all. The development of policy, in turn, effects movement activities by influencing the structure of available opportunities for action—but only insofar as such opportunities are congruent with movement values and resources. To illustrate these factors the effects of the Equal Rights Amendment and Executive Order 11375 are specifically examined.

I
The Roots
of Revolt

Feminist protest has been with us since this country was founded. As early as 1787 Abigail Adams wrote to husband John, then sitting in the Constitutional Convention, admonishing him not to "put such unlimited power in the hands of the husbands. Remember, all men would be tyrants if they could." She went on to threaten that "if particular care and attention is not paid to the ladies, we are determined to foment a rebellion, and will not hold ourselves bound by any laws in which we have no voice and representation!" [1]

This concern exemplifies one of the two major contributing factors to feminist sentiment in the Western world—the change in social values which justified an attempt to change social relations. The other was a change in social structures which made such a change in relationships possible and even necessary. As William Goode expressed it:

---

1. Quoted in Eleanor Flexner, *Century of Struggle* (New York: Atheneum, 1959), p. 15.

. . . the crucial crystallizing variable—i.e. the necessary but not sufficient cause of the betterment of the Western woman's position—was *ideological:* the gradual, logical, philosophical extension to women of originally Protestant notions about the rights and responsibilities of the *individual* undermined the traditional idea of "woman's proper place."

It appears . . . however, that the social *implementation* of this change in values . . . was the development of a free labor market, in which the individual was hired for his own skill, with little or decreasing regard for his family position.[2]

More specifically, the development of equalitarian values and the legitimization of rebellion that resulted from the French and American revolutions were used by Western women as the philosophical basis for their own insurrections. Mary Wollstonecraft wrote the first major feminist tract, *The Vindication of the Rights of Women*, in 1792 as her British reaction to the events in France. The American Declaration of Independence was the model for the *Declaration of Sentiments* drawn up by the first feminist convention in Seneca Falls, New York, in 1848. Giving a "history of repeated injuries and usurpations on the part of men toward woman," it concluded that "he has endeavored, in every way that he could, to destroy her confidence in her own powers, to lessen her self-respect, and to make her willing to lead a dependent and abject life."

Although the position of American women relative to men actually declined after the Revolution, the concern with equality was heightened. When middle-class women began to work in the Abolitionist movement they found that their effectiveness was hampered by the social stigma against women speaking in public. American women attending a World Anti-Slavery Convention in 1840 were prohibited from participating and made to sit in the balcony. Lucretia Mott and Elizabeth Cady Stanton were among them. Eight years later they organized the first Women's Rights

---

2. William J. Goode, *World Revolution and Family Patterns* (Glencoe, Ill.: Free Press, 1963), p. 56.

Convention. American women discovered they could not work to free the slaves without working to free themselves.[3]

The other major cause was industrialization. This phenomenon is much too complex to be adequately treated here, but it did sufficiently disrupt the components of the traditional sex roles to force many changes and provide maneuvering room for others.[4] Two effects in particular are directly relevant to the development of the women's movement. One was the displacement of major female functions outside the home. The making of textiles was the first to go and was soon followed by primary education. This process has continued until today virtually no production goes on in the home. The other effect was the increasing monetization of the economy. Among other things, this meant that the displaced female functions had to be paid for in cash. A large part of the rise in our national GNP was accomplished by the monetization of those activities which were never before counted in its computation because money did not change hands for their performance. The cash had to be obtained by employment. If the social values prevented women from working outside the home—for that cash—this meant that men had to supply, indirectly, what women had once produced directly.

This monopolistic access to the necessary resources for survival logically gave men more power over women, made women more dependent, and contributed to the feeling of many women that they were useless parasites. In effect women had to enter the labor market in order to get the wherewithal to buy what they had once produced in their own homes. The effects of women moving into paid employment—on women, the economy, the family, and a host of other social institutions—have been the major sources of strain to which the feminist movements of the nineteenth and twentieth centuries have been one response.

The idea of "strain" is the most general formulation of a variety

---

3. Flexner, *Century of Struggle*, p. 71.
4. E.g., Jeanne Clare Ridley, "Demographic Change and the Roles and Status of Women," *Annals of the American Academy of Political and Social Science* 375 (January 1968): 15–25.

of terms used to describe problems in the social environment. As Smelser has commented, "The literature on strain has produced an abundance of words and a poverty of consistent meanings." [5] He adds to both these aspects of the literature with his concept of "structural strain" which he defines as "an impairment of the relations among and consequently inadequate functioning of the components of action." [6] Much more useful in analyzing strain is the idea of "relative deprivation."

This was defined by Gurr as "a perceived discrepancy between men's [sic] value expectations and their value capabilities. Value expectations are the goods and conditions of life to which people believe they are rightfully entitled. Value capabilities are the goods and conditions they think they are capable of attaining or maintaining, given the social means available to them." [7] While this is a good general definition, it subsumes within it several ideas necessary to understand how relative deprivation works in practice.

The most important of these is the concept of a reference group.[8] A reference group actually may not be a group at all; it may be a single person, an abstract idea, or an unrealized standard. Nevertheless, it is something to which people relate their attitudes and judge their rewards. Reference groups serve two functions. The first is a normative one. "A group functions as a normative reference group for a person to the extent that its evaluations of him are based upon the degree of his conformity to certain standards of behavior or attitude and to the extent that the delivery of rewards or punishments is conditional upon these

5. Neil J. Smelser, *Theory of Collective Behavior* (Glencoe, Ill.: Free Press, 1963), p. 47.

6. Ibid.

7. Ted Robert Gurr, *Why Men Rebel* (Princeton, N.J.: Princeton University Press, 1970), p. 13.

8. This term was first used in 1942 by H. H. Hyman, "The Psychology of Status," *Archives of Psychology*, no. 269 (New York: 1942) but the idea goes back much farther. "Relative deprivation" was first used in Samuel A. Stouffer et al., *The American Soldier*, vol. 1, *Adjustment During Army Life* (Princeton, N.J.: Princeton University Press, 1949), p. 125. The concept was first implied by Alexis de Tocqueville, *The Old Regime and the French Revolution*, trans. John Bonner (New York: Harper Bros., 1856).

evaluations." [9] The comparative function operates "to the extent that the behavior, attitudes, circumstances, or other characteristics of [a group's] members represent standards or comparison points which [an individual] uses in making judgements and evaluations." [10] The same reference group can fulfill these functions jointly or independently of each other.

The second concept is that of the "justifying myth." It is quite possible for people to compare themselves to others, feel relatively deprived in an abstract sense, but accept the discrepancy in the real world because they accept the normative belief that the difference is justifiable. Justification can take many forms. If aspirations for change are to be legitimate ones, the justification of the status quo must be destroyed. This is often the role of a new ideology, though it can operate more subtly than as an explicit ideology.

The third necessary ingredient in relative deprivation is aggravation. It has often been noted that people are inherently conservative. They will accept what they are used to rather than undergo the pains of change unless the familiar becomes itself painful. Aggravation may be in the form of a catastrophe, such as a flood, a war, or a panic, or it may be the slow accumulation of many small grievances, which day by day wear down one's inertia. Continual exposure to new possibilities is a form of aggravation as well as a comparison to a potential reference group. Thus Lipset concluded from various evidence that those whose experiences are primarily with persons at their own socioeconomic level tend to be "more conservative than people who may be better off but who have been exposed to the possibilities of securing a better way of life. The dynamic in the situation would seem to be exposure to the possibility of a better way of life rather than poverty as such." [11]

From all this it should be clear that relative deprivation is a complex concept, involving psychological as well as objective

---

9. Harold Proshansky and Bernard Seidenberg, eds., *Basic Studies in Social Psychology* (New York: Holt, Rinehart & Winston, 1965), p. 212.

10. Ibid., p. 213.

11. Seymour M. Lipset, *Political Man: The Social Bases of Politics* (Garden City, N.Y.: Doubleday, 1960), p. 63.

conditions, which do not always interact with one another in precisely the same fashion. While objective conditions can and often are used [12] to measure relative deprivation, it should still "always be understood to mean a *sense* of deprivation; a person who is 'relatively deprived' need not be 'objectively' deprived in the more usual sense that he is demonstrably lacking something." [13] The relationship between these different elements was summed up by Runciman:

> We can roughly say that A is relatively deprived of X when (1) he does not have X, (2) he sees some other person or persons, which may include himself at some previous or expected time, as having X (whether or not this is or will be in fact the case), (3) he wants X, and (4) he sees it as feasible that he should have X. [14]

It is relative deprivation that explains why both the first and second waves of the feminist movement were largely led by and based in the white middle class, and in particular by women in the professions. Thus in analyzing the increase in strain that led up to the current movement, we will pay particular attention to the changing circumstances of middle-class women in order to show that while their absolute deprivation may have been lower than that of other women, relative deprivation increased significantly—and did so in a time when the justifying myth of male precedence was being slowly eroded.

Since the social forces involved in the new feminist movement —industrialization, urbanization, displacement of female functions out of the home, education, changing values—are much the same as those of its predecessor, we need first to look at why that earlier movement disintegrated so thoroughly. Although originally a broad and diverse movement concerned with all aspects of

---

12. Ted Robert Gurr, "A Causal Model of Civil Strife: A Comparative Analysis Using New Indices," *American Political Science Review* 42 (December 1968): 1104–24, is just one example.

13. W. G. Runciman, *Relative Deprivation and Social Justice* (Berkeley: University of California Press, 1966), p. 10.

14. Ibid.

a woman's life, toward the end it attracted primarily two kinds of feminists—the suffragist and the reformist.

To the suffragist the vote was a symbol of a whole intellectual reorientation. Throughout the nineteenth century she had seen her sisters gain the right to education, work, their own identity in marriage, and many other rights and opportunities. The right to vote alone was denied her and without it it seemed impossible to turn women's attention from home and family out into the affairs of the world. However, the vote became not only the symbol of this basic change of attitude, but also was infused with the myth that achieving the symbol would achieve the reality. What was a means to an end became an end in itself. Thus none were quite so surprised as the suffragists when women proceeded to take their newfound political equality in stride rather than use it to revolutionize their lives.[15]

What the suffragists suffered from was a failure of imagination. They failed to foresee women's organizational needs after suffrage and to provide an ongoing program which the vote could be used as a tool to institute. Instead, the movement "divided into warring factions on the question of how best to continue women's progress after winning the vote." [16] The whole momentum of the suffrage movement had been built upon a very flimsy alliance of widely differing women who toiled together through the years from setback to setback toward this common goal. They never faltered until the end. No defeat was as devastating as victory.[17]

The reformist women sought the vote not to free themselves but to reform society. They thought that with it working people could clean up their sweatshops, the traffic in liquor could be stopped, child labor eliminated, and society generally bettered. They were so concerned with fighting other people's battles that they could not conceive of themselves fighting solely their own.[18] By the time

---

15. For example see Anne O'Hagan, "The Serious-minded Young—If Any," *Woman's Journal* 13 (April 1928): 7.

16. J. Stanley Lemons, *The Woman Citizen: Social Feminism in the 1920s* (Urbana, Ill.: University of Illinois Press, 1973), p. 204.

17. See especially William O'Neill, *Everyone Was Brave: The Rise and Fall of Feminism in America* (Chicago: Quadrangle, 1969), chap. 8.

18. Aileen Kraditor has argued that women turned to an "expedience" argument for suffrage after years of appeals for it on the ground of justice alone

the vote was won, unions were already working on sweatshops, Prohibition had been passed, and the reform impulse of the Progressive movement was dying. Although the social feminists did not succumb to the final blows for another decade, essentially they won their weapon after their war was over.[19]

The single-minded pursuit of the vote had its own destructive effect on the woman's movement. In order to meet their opposition's arguments that female suffrage would destroy home and family, the feminists accepted their frame of reference and elaborated an ideological position that political equality could only help women better perform their domestic functions. With the exception of a few rigorous theorists such as the immortal Charlotte Perkins Gilman,[20] the feminists never seriously attacked women's given social role. They urged that she be given the opportunity to compete in the world of men if she so chose, but never challenged the fact that it was a man's world she would compete in and that women's sphere was in the home. "The end of feminism came when people of advanced views conceded that women were unique after all, and thus needed to work out their special destiny." [21]

When the 1920s roared around, the young women inherited a legacy of female independence, but without the political context in which it had been born.[22] So instead of social problems they attacked social conventions. They drank, smoked, cut their hair, and engaged in the real sexual revolution of the twentieth century. Using the shortage of cloth after the war as an excuse, they also shed their heavy, confining dresses and crippling

---

proved ineffective. It was only when women argued that they needed it as a social good, to help "clean up" society, that the idea of suffrage became widely acceptable. *Ideas of the Woman Suffrage Movement* (New York: Columbia University Press, 1965).

19. For a thorough history of this segment of the woman's movement, see Lemons, *The Woman Citizen*, 1973.

20. See especially her *Woman and Economics* (Boston: Small, Maynard, 1898; reprint ed., New York: Harper & Row, 1966) for a good synthesis of her major theories.

21. O'Neill, *Everyone Was Brave*, p. 315.

22. Ibid., p. 307.

foundation garments in a dress-reform movement that many thought did women far more good than the vote.[23]

Egged on by a developing consumption economy, an increased emphasis on sexual gratification, a glorified cult of domesticity, and advertising propaganda that "scientific" homemaking could be a truly challenging and creative experience, they began to seek their personal emancipation in the very home that traditional feminists had always regarded as little more than a jail. Women didn't stop working. They continued to join the labor force in a steady trend that brought the percentage of women from one-fifth in 1920 to one-third in 1960. But they did lower their sights. One Ph.D. in seven went to a woman in 1920, but only one in ten in 1960. The proportion of M.A.s given to women peaked in 1930 and of B.A.s in 1940. It was not until 1950 that the percentage began to increase again. Now that women had the right to work, it no longer seemed worth fighting for.

As a symbol of freedom and equality, the vote had exactly the opposite effect it was intended to have. Ambitious women still used their new freedom to expand their opportunities in the business and professional worlds, but for most, the psychological trend toward the home had already started before the New Victorianism, as Andrew Sinclair called it[24] solidified into the Feminine Mystique.

The 1930s Depression briefly reversed this trend, and at the same time set another in motion that would eventually come into conflict with it. On the one hand, women were told they should not work, or be promoted, in order not to deprive a male breadwinner from a necessary job. The magazine stories of the day depicted the unhappy career woman neglecting her family, and the myth that women worked only for "pin-money" was propagated widely. Many laws were passed that prohibited married women from working at all, and most school systems forced a female teacher to give up her job when she married. On the other hand, sending the women home deprived some house-

---

23. Ibid., p. 270.
24. Andrew Sinclair, *The Better Half* (New York: Harper & Row, 1965).

holds of their only means of support and others of the difference between starvation and survival. Consequently,

> although the percentage of females seeking employment reached a new high as a result of the need to supplement meager family incomes, most of the jobs that women took were part-time, seasonal and marginal. . . . Women experienced special difficulty in finding work which paid a living wage. In Philadelphia there were three times as many applications as jobs in 1934. . . . Over 175,000 women sought clerical positions in 1937, but only 5,300 were placed.[25]

The expanding clerical field provided middle- and upper-class women with an opportunity to do work that was socially acceptable, where factory and domestic work had not been. Thus necessity and opportunity coincided. Women *had* to work who had never worked before, and economic necessity became an acceptable reason for heretofore leisured women of the middle class to bring home a paycheck.

World War II disrupted traditional patterns of behavior, and with them most of the myths about what work women could do. The U.S. Employment Service reported that women could fill 80 percent of the war-related jobs with only brief training. The proportion of women receiving government-sponsored vocational training went from 1 to 4 percent within four months after Pearl Harbor. Within seven months, the number of jobs for which employers were willing to consider female applicants had gone from 29 to 55 percent.[26]

With this change in employment came a change in attitudes. Prior to the war, it was considered improper for married women to work. These attitudes were made irrelevant by the war as women's participation in the labor force became an act of patriotism. The Lanham Act was interpreted to allow funds for the construction of day-care centers as a war-related expense, and

25. William Henry Chafe, *The American Woman: Her Changing Social, Economic and Political Roles, 1920–1970* (New York: Oxford University Press, 1972), p. 58.

26. Ibid., p. 137.

married women were generally encouraged to join the work force. As a result, almost 7 million women were employed for the first time, 75 percent of them married. The change in attitudes was reflected in the polls. During the Great Depression, over 80 percent of the American people strongly opposed work by married women. By 1942 only 13 percent were opposed. In contrast, 60 percent said wives should be employed in war industries and 71 percent that there was a greater need for female labor.[27]

A similar change occurred in the employment of middle-aged women as the supply of young women was quickly exhausted.

> In January 1941 many firms refused to consider hiring any female over thirty-five years of age. At the beginning of the war, the majority of women workers were thirty-two or under. Within the next four years, however, 60 percent of all the women added to the labor force were over thirty-five. Mary Anderson persuaded government arsenals to begin hiring women over forty in early 1942, and private business quickly followed suit. By the end of the war, the proportion of women thirty-five to forty-four in the labor force had jumped from 27 percent to 38 percent, and the number over forty-five had grown from 16 to 24 percent. Almost all the older workers were also married. For the first time in their lives, they played an important part in the economic processes of the country. And four out of five indicated in a Women's Bureau survey that they wished to stay in the labor force after the war.[28]

These wishes were doomed to partial frustration. Both men and women had heeded their country's call to duty to bring the war to a successful conclusion. Yet men were rewarded for their efforts and women punished for theirs. The returning soldiers were given the GI Bill and other veterans benefits, as well as their jobs back. Women, on the other hand, saw their child-care centers disman-

27. Hadley Cantril, *Public Opinion, 1935–1946* (Princeton, N.J.: Princeton University Press, 1951), p. 1045.

28. Chafe, *The American Woman*, p. 146.

tled and their training programs cease. They were fired or demoted in droves[29] and often found it difficult to enter colleges flooded with ex-GIs matriculating on government money. Labor unions insisted on contracts with separate job categories, seniority lists, and pay scales for men and women.

Despite these obstacles, women's participation in the labor force remained above the prewar levels. It was not their numbers but their position in the work force that dropped drastically. The low-paid, low-prestige jobs were flooded with women seeking a "second income" while their percentage of professional and technical positions went down by a third.

The wartime need for female employment was continued after the peace by the precarious state of the economy.

> In the years immediately following the war, inflation racked the nation. Meat prices rose by 122 percent between 1945 and 1947, and repeated strikes in major industries sent the cost of basic purchases sky-rocketing. The inflationary spiral created a severe economic pinch for almost everyone, but it especially affected those families which had postponed their desire for consumer products during the war. At just the moment when husbands and wives were planning to build new homes, buy new cars, and purchase improved appliances, a series of arbitrary price hikes stood in the way. Many couples found it impossible to fulfill their quest for a higher standard of living on one income alone.[30]

---

29. Often, state protective legislation, waived during the war years, was used to remove women from their jobs. According to Jean T. McKelvey, "Sex and the Single Arbitrator," *Industrial and Labor Relations Review* 24 (April 1971): 337–38, "arbitrators were faced with numerous cases involving alleged sex discrimination in the reconversion period following World War II. These arose for the most part when employers sought to replace the female employees they had hired during the war with male employees who traditionally had performed certain jobs in the prewar period. . . . Most of the published decisions of this period indicate that arbitrators would not uphold a woman's right to a job if the consequences would entail a violation of state protective legislation by the employer." Some of these cases were *Ford Motor Co.*, 1 LA 462 (1945, Harry Shulman, arbitrator); *Republic Steel Corp.*, 1 LA 244 (1945, Harry H. Platt, arbitrator); *Manion Steel Barrell Co.*, 6 LA 164 (1947, Robert J. Wagner arbitrator); *Pittsburgh Corning Corp.*, 3 LA 364, 366 (1946, C. W. Lillibridge, arbitrator); *U.S. Rubber Co.*, 3 LA 555 (1946, George Cheney, arbitrator).

30. Chafe, *The American Woman*, p. 190.

During the 1950s the pattern of the female labor force changed drastically. Prior to the war it had been composed largely of young (median age 25), single women who quit permanently when they got married and had children. Even if they had wanted to return later, the policies of most employers against hiring married women prevented them. Now these prejudices had been softened and industry discovered that it needed married women if it was to find the workers necessary for the now-booming economy. The low birthrates of the 1930s meant that the traditional female labor force, then coming of age, was quite small. Further, women were marrying earlier and having more children. At the same time, the female sector of the job market was expanding rapidly and there was a high need for well-educated low-paid clerical and service workers. There simply weren't enough young single women to fill the need. As Oppenheimer has shown,[31] it was this increase in demand for specifically female labor coupled with a demographic alteration in the supply that changed the composition of the labor force. Although the demographic factors did change over time, the new pattern has become a permanent one. Today the median age of working women is forty, 60 percent are married, and two-thirds of these have children under eighteen.

The consequences of these changes was that during the 1950s, when women were supposedly returning to home and motherhood, work for married women

> became an integral element in the lives of many middle-class families. Sociologists observed that more and more wives were seeking jobs even though their husbands earned enough to support them, and the National Manpower Council reported in 1954 that in 40 percent of all families receiving a total income of $6,000–$10,000 a year both the husband and wife worked. Indeed, a plausible argument could be made that female employment was the crucial means by which

---

31. Valerie K. Oppenheimer, "The Interaction of Demand and Supply and its Effect on the Female Labour Force in the United States," *Population Studies* 21 (November 1967): 239–59.

some families achieved middle-class status.[32]

While many women were enlarging their role to incorporate part of what had been traditionally thought of as man's—paid employment—many others were suffering an attack on their traditional role. The 1940s and 1950s witnessed the phenomenon of "momism." [33] Everything was all mom's fault—she was trying to run her husband and was ruining her children. Only a few noticed that this happened at the same time women were being encouraged to return home and devote their lives to husband and family. As Rossi pointed out, even for large families, childbearing occupied a far shorter portion of a woman's life span than ever before, at precisely "the first time in the history of any known society [when] motherhood has become a full-time occupation for adult women." [34]

Torn between myth and reality, a damned-if-they-did-and-damned-if-they-didn't attack, American women were plagued by a deepening sense of bewilderment about how to define their identity. In

the decade following World War II . . . a century of growing discontent with a limited domestic role burst into open rebellion. . . . In the immediate post-war years educated women sensed as never before that they had capabilities far greater than were being entirely used in the traditional feminine role. The result during the 1950s was a decade of literature expressing futility. The American woman did not always understand why she felt so suddenly rebellious, and

---

32. Chafe, *The American Women*, p. 183.
33. See Philip Wylie, *Generation of Vipers* (New York: Rinehart, 1942), chap. 11. Wylie, who created and popularized the term, almost gave his "sub-species" a feminist interpretation in his commentary on the 10th edition (1955) of his infamous book. He said, "When we and our culture and our religions agreed to hold women the inferior sex, cursed, unclean and sinful—we made her mom. And when we agreed upon the American Ideal Woman, the Dream Girl of National Adolescence, the Queen of Bedpan Week, the Pin-Up, the Glamour Puss—we insulted women and . . . thus made mom. The hen-harpy is but the Cinderella chick come home to roost; the taloned crackling residue of burnt-out puberty in a land that has no use for mature men or women" (p. 197).
34. Alice S. Rossi, "Equality Between the Sexes: An Immodest Proposal," in *The Woman in America*, ed. Robert J. Lifton (Boston: Beacon Press, 1964), p. 106.

many who voiced the feminine protest were afflicted with a
sense of guilt that home, husband, and children did not
satisfy their longings for more complete self-realization.[35]

These feelings of guilt were exacerbated by "the pervasive
permeation of psychoanalytic thinking throughout American
society," [36] which emphasized that a woman's fulfillment came
solely through her exclusive devotion to marriage and motherhood. Women who sought other outlets or interests were made to
feel inadequate.[37] The psychoanalytic approach also stressed the
solution of problems on an individual basis. This fit well into the
general American stress on individualism, and the result was that
more and more middle-class American women turned to "psychi-
atric involvement" to resolve their identity conflicts.[38]

Middle-class employed women were especially susceptible to
the psychological definition of femininity as passive, nurturant,
dependent, etc., because it provided a concrete anchor of identity.
Because of the immense changes of previous years, their "place"
in society, and hence their social identity, was no longer sharply
defined. It would appear that because their structural roles were
no longer so clear, they made an extra effort to fit their
psychological roles. The more women operated in what was
defined as the male sphere, the more rigidly they fell back on the
old stereotypes, dressed up in the language of social science, in
order to manifest their femaleness. The major impetus of the
postwar feminine mystique was to urge women to overcompensate
psychologically for what they no longer were structurally. But all
it really did was create an even more painful double bind.

Women found themselves having to work, while having to

---

35. Gladys E. Harbeson, *Choice and Challenge for the American Woman* (Cambridge,
Mass.: Schenkman, 1965), p. 8.

36. Rossi, "Equality," p. 103.

37. See especially Ferdinand Lundberg and Marynia Farnham, *Modern Woman:
The Lost Sex* (New York: Harper & Bros., 1947); Helene Deutsch, *The Psychology of
Women* (New York: Grune & Stratton, 1944).

38. See Phyllis Chesler, *Women and Madness* (Garden City, N.Y.: Doubleday,
1972), for an examination of how psychology is used as a means of social control to
keep women in their traditional roles. She views psychotherapy and marriage as
the two major institutions for "socially controlling and oppressing women."

express a preference for being full-time wives and mothers, or be thought abnormal. This conflict adversely affected both their jobs and their homes. On the one hand, women said they worked only because they had to, but kept finding reasons why they had to. They accepted part-time jobs, lower pay, inferior positions, and denied any desire for career achievement as a compromise between their own needs and desires and the social expectations they judged their actions by. On the home front, women became obsessed with doing their domestic duty to the point of physical exhaustion, but felt guilty when they asked their husband for help. They worried about their children "as though they were hot-house plants psychologically, on whose personalities any pressure might leave an indelible bruise." [39]

The increasing frustration women felt with unreconcilable demands and expectations went by many names. Sociologists called it role conflict, psychologists refrred to identity crises. Some wrote about the "great reservoir of rage in women," [40] and Friedan labeled it "the problem that has no name." [41] Whatever it was called, it was clear that something was wrong.

Into these muddy waters came a new idea—or perhaps one should say the resurrection of an old one. It was the newly activated sentiments of freedom and equality that prompted Abigail Adams to make her statement of defiance in 1787 and it was their reemergence into the public consciousness that caused women to take a new look at their situation in the 1960s. The black civil rights movement had a very profound effect on many segments of our society. Even though it cannot be measured, its influence on American women—on white, middle-class, often racist American women—should not be underestimated. Just as the status of women had been "the nearest and most natural analogy" [42] for those seeking a legal status for slaves in the seventeenth century and for those justifying slavery in the

---

39. Rossi, "Equality," p. 113.
40. Richard Farson, "The Rage of Women," *Look*, 16 December 1969, p. 2123.
41. Betty Friedan, *The Feminine Mystique* (New York: Dell, 1963).
42. Gunnar Myrdal, *An American Dilemma* (New York: Harper & Row, 1944), vol. 2, appendix 5; "A Parallel to the Negro Problem," p. 1073.

nineteenth,[43] so was it similarly easy for women in the twentieth century to identify with and respond to efforts by blacks to change their position in society. There is no easy way to document this identification beyond pointing out that the analogy was often made very early in the women's liberation movement. For a while, "woman as nigger" was one of the most popular short ways of describing how women's position in society was perceived. What was most potent to the most people, however, was not this analogy, but the idea of equality, and equality *now,* that accompanied it.

The 1960s was a very political decade. Not only civil rights, but also the student revolt, antiwar protest, and a renewed interest in regular party battles created a general consciousness of the political means of attacking social problems. This politicization of the population was a potent antidote to the style of personal solution that dominated the 1950s. It provided a real alternative for action. Of course individual women, with some exceptions, did not automatically interpret their personal problems in a political framework. But the renewed legitimation of political activity made them susceptible to such a reinterpretation. As will be shown in the following chapter, it took women who were deeply enmeshed in the "insystem" and "outsystem" politics of our country to make that interpretation a public one and organize around it. But a political form of acting on women's problems would not have been received so quickly if women had not been well sensitized to a political perspective by the events of the preceding years.

While frustration, conflict, and strain are usually experienced on the personal level, their basis is more easily seen with aggregate statistics. The following are the most salient:

> 1. The birthrate has been declining since 1957. This cannot be attributed to the pill as it was not introduced until 1960. The change does not mean that fewer women are deciding to have children, but that they are deciding to have

---

43. George Fitzhugh, *Sociology for the South* (Richmond, Virginia: A. Morris, 1854).

fewer children. The rate for first births has declined only moderately but that for second and especially third children has gone down significantly. The illegitimate birth rate has been rising steadily, however.[44]

2. The latter phenomena is in part due to the fact that younger women are increasingly remaining single. "The proportion of women living alone or with roommates rose 50 percent during the 1960s, and the increase was 109 percent for those in the crucial marrying range of 20 to 34 years old." [45] Between 1959 and 1969 the percent of both white and nonwhite women aged 18 to 29 who are single increased by 2 to 12 points, while the percent of those married declined accordingly. Concomitantly, the number of sole female heads of families increased by two-fifths to 5.4 million, or roughly 10 percent of all families.[46] Thirty-five percent of all women of marriageable age are not married.

3. From its nadir of 24 percent in 1950, women's percentage of bachelor's and first professional degrees rose to 43.5 percent in 1968. Most of this increase occurred between 1960 and 1965, when the number of degrees earned by women went up 57 percent compared to only a 25 percent increase for men. From 1966 to 1968 the rate of increase was only slightly greater (24 percent) for women than for men (19 percent). In absolute terms the number of women earning degrees went from 49,000 in 1930 to 139,000 in 1960 to 279,000 in 1968. The ratio of female college graduates to the total population 21 years of age went from 4 per 100 in 1930, to 12 per 100 in 1960, to 19 per 100 in 1968. The corresponding ratios for men were 7 per 100 in 1930, 23 per 100 in 1960, and 26 per 100 in 1968.[47] There was a similar increase in both the percentage and absolute numbers of master's and doctor's degrees. As of 1968 women were receiving roughly 36 percent of all M.A.s and 13 percent of all Ph.D.s.

---

44. Abbott L. Ferriss, *Indicators of Trends in the Status of American Woman* (New York: Russell Sage Foundation, 1971), pp. 63–78.

45. Chafe, *The American Woman*, p. 243.

46. Ferriss, *Indicators*, pp. 49–61.

47. U.S. Department of Labor, *Trends in Educational Attainment of Women* (Washington, D.C.: Government Printing Office, 1969), p. 5.

4. Participation of women in the total civilian labor force increased from 28 percent in 1947 to 37 percent in 1968. Forty-two percent of all women aged 16 and over work, and 42 percent of these work full-time. The number of women in the labor force is expanding at five times the rate of men.[48] This expansion is largely among married women. In 1940, 15 percent of all married women were employed, in 1967 it was 37 percent.[49] The strongest predictor of employment status is educational attainment. In 1968, 71 percent of all women with five years of higher education were employed, 54 percent of those with college degrees, 48 percent of those with at least high school diplomas, and only 24 percent of those with 8 years of schooling. Although this pattern holds even when controlled for age, the participation rate for women with at least a high school education is greater now than it was in 1952 by several percentage points.[50] Married women were most likely to work in 1966 if their husbands earned between $5,000 and $10,000 a year. There is a similar curvilinear relationship between husband's income and the percent of family income accounted for by wives' earnings. Wives contributed the most—a median 28.1 percent—to families earning between $10,000 and $15,000 a year.[51] This clearly indicates that it is largely middle-class families who have two income earners and that the wives' earnings are what make possible a middle-class standard of living.

5. In 1966, 61 percent of all women over age 14 and 92 percent of the men had some income of their own. Median income for these women was $1,638 and for men was $5,306. Of all full-time workers, women earned 58.2 percent of the median income of men. This varied from 40 percent for sales workers to 66 percent for professionals.[52] Although women do better compared to men when they have more education, they do not do much better. The median income of full-time working women with college degrees is still lower than that of

---

48. Women's Bureau, U.S. Department of Labor, *Handbook on Women Workers* (Washington, D.C.: Government Printing Office, 1969), p. 15.

49. Ibid., p. 26.

50. U.S. Department of Labor, *Educational Attainment*, p. 10.

51. Women's Bureau, *Handbook*, pp. 33–35.

52. Ibid., p. 133.

male high school dropouts, and this relationship has shown little indication of changing over time.[53]

6. The distribution of women across the range of major occupations has shifted moderately from blue collar to white collar but not to the highest prestige categories. In 1968, one-third of all employed women were clerical workers, as compared to one-fifth in 1940. Roughly 15 percent were each working as professional or technical workers, operatives, and service workers. Between 1940 and 1968 women's share of the professional and technical jobs went from 45.4 percent down to 38.6 percent while their proportion of clerical jobs went up from 52.6 percent to 72.6 percent. In these 28 years, the percentage of women employed in *all* major occupational categories *except* that of professional and technical workers, rose.[54]

From these statistics several things should be clear:

1. The role of provider has become at least partially legitimated as a female function. This is evident from the declining birthrate, the decrease in women supported solely by husbands and the fact that a wife's contribution to family income is crucial to maintaining a middle-class standard of living.

2. The educational preparation of women for middle-class-type jobs approximates that of men more closely each year.

3. Women's share of both quantitative and qualitative occupational rewards decreases each year.

If we take these conclusions and plug them back into our concept of relative deprivation, it is clear that it is middle-class, college-educated women who are subject to the greatest strain. This group of women is more likely to compare themselves to people of similar educational attainment than to those of the same sex status. In particular, their comparative reference group is more likely to be their husbands and their former classmates.

53. Women's Bureau, U.S. Department of Labor, "Fact Sheet on the Earning Gap" (Washington, D.C.: Government Printing Office, 1966, 1968, 1969, 1970).
54. Women's Bureau, *Handbook*, p. 92.

Secondly, the occupational achievements of this reference group are more likely to appear both desirable and feasible to such women than those of the equivalent group of men to either lower- or upper-class women.

Feelings of anger that middle-class employed women might have at these discrepancies could be kept socially controlled so long as marriage and serious employment were seen to be incompatible, male dominance as a social value prevailed, and women saw no alternative courses of action to individually "making it." The war and the postwar period made severe dents in the practice, and to a lesser extent the attitude, that a married woman should stay at home. Male dominance is still a social value, but as Goode and others have noted, this has decreased with time, and varies inversely both with education and class level.

> Lower-class men concede fewer rights *ideologically* than their women in fact *obtain,* and the more educated men are likely to concede *more* ideologically than they in fact grant. One partial resolution of the latter tension is to be found in the frequent assertion from families of professional men that they should not make demands which would interfere with his *work.* He takes precedence as *professional, not* as family head or as male; nevertheless, the precedence is his. By contrast, lower-class men demand deference as *men,* as heads of families.[55]

While, on the one hand, taking precedence as *professional* is just a more subtle form of male dominance, on the other hand it creates the potential for greater relative deprivation for professionally trained women. It is a little difficult for a woman readily to perceive herself as a man; it is not difficult for her to perceive herself as a professional, and consequently to feel entitled to the rights of professionals. There is little distance between the rights a

---

55. Goode, *Family Patterns,* pp. 21–22. (Italics author's.)

lower-class woman has and the rights she feels entitled to. There is a great deal of difference between what a professional woman married to or simply associating with professional men has and can feel she is legitimately entitled to. The right of male dominance per se no longer carries weight as a justifying myth of inequity.

As is clear from the statistics, in the postwar period there has been a squeeze in the job market. There are proportionally fewer and fewer jobs for more and more educated women. For several reasons, women have been steadily driven out of the traditional "female" professions such as social work and teaching, but because of the highly segregated nature of the job market[56] they have not been successful in integrating the "male" professions. Thus, women as a group are grossly underemployed. Nineteen percent of all female college graduates and 7 percent of those with some graduate education work as clerical, sales, factory, or service workers. Sixty-nine percent of all women with at least one year of college are employed in these occupations.[57] With the value of work increasing in salience and the quality of job decreasing in availability, the number of individual experiences of thwarted occupational expectations most likely increased significantly in this period. This was no doubt especially true for young women, themselves part of the baby boom, who have been coming of age in the 1960s. They were raised with different expectations from their mothers. In 1962 Gallup reported that only 10 percent of all women wanted their daughters to have the same kind of lives they did.[58] These expectations manifested themselves in an increasing similarity in the ways that at least middle-class parents raised their children.[59] By 1958, sociologists were reporting that a

---

56. Edward Gross, "Plus Ça Change . . . ? The Sexual Structure of Occupations Over Time," *Social Problems* 16 (1968): 198–208.

57. Women's Bureau, U.S. Department of Labor, *Underutilization of Women Workers* (Washington, D.C.: Government Printing Office, 1971), pp. 16–17.

58. George Gallup and Evan Hill, "The American Woman," *Saturday Evening Post*, 22 December 1962.

59. Urie Bronfenbrenner, "Socialization and Social Class Through Time and Space," in *Readings in Social Psychology*, ed. E. Maccoby, T. M. Newcomb, and E. L. Hartley (3rd ed.; New York: Holt, Rinehart & Winston, 1958).

gradual convergence of sex roles was taking place in our society.[60]

The two most significant factors affecting the expectations of young women were the employment of their mothers and the college experience. As marriage and family expert Robert Blood has commented:

> Employment emancipates women from domination by their husbands and, secondarily, raises their daughters from inferiority to their brothers (echoing the rising status of their mothers). The employment of women affects the power structure of the family by equalizing the resources of husband and wife. A working wife's husband listens to her more, and she listens to herself more. She expresses herself and has more opinions. Instead of looking up into her husband's eyes and worshipping him, she levels with him, compromising in the issues at hand. Thus her power increases, and relatively speaking, the husband's falls.
>
> This shift in the balance of power is echoed in the children. . . . Daughters of working mothers are more independent, more self-reliant, more aggressive, more dominant, and more disobedient. Such girls are no longer meek, mild, submissive, and feminine like "little ladies" ought to be. They are rough and tough, actively express their ideas, and refuse to take anything from anybody else. . . . Because their mothers have set an example, the daughters get up the courage and the desire to earn money as well. They take more part-time jobs after school and more jobs during summer vacation. . . .
>
> In such ways, the shape of the American family is being altered by the exodus of women into the labor market. The roles of men and women are converging for both adults and children. As a result the family will be far less segregated internally, far less stratified into different age generations and different sexes. The old asymmetry of male-dominated, female-serviced family life is being replaced by a new symmetry.[61]

---

60. Daniel Brown, "Sex-Role Development in a Changing Culture," *Psychological Bulletin* 54 (July 1958): 232–42.

61. Robert O. Blood, "Long-Range Causes and Consequences of the Employment of Married Women," *Journal of Marriage and the Family* 27 (February 1965): 43–47.

Not all young women went to college, but a very significant proportion of them did. There, in most schools, they were exposed to a less rigidly segregated education and set of expectations than was available to young women in other places and other times. Many grew used to thinking of themselves as the intellectual equals of their male colleagues and they certainly acquired much the same training and "qualifications."

The campus also provided a testing area for new interpersonal relationships, which subsequently led many women to question their roles within the traditional family structure. Women no longer go from the house of their father to that of their husband. They go to college first. There the experience of college room-mates, particularly outside the dormitories, provides a model of living with someone else in an egalitarian relationship which is easily transferred by both men and women into marriage. The growing practice of living with someone of the opposite sex as a test of compatibility before marriage is still another transitional stage. This new "gradualism" of family formation, which incorporates at least some egalitarian experiences, can provide the time necessary to work out new living arrangements which was not possible under the rigid, traditional system.

In general, college women have greater expectations and lesser opportunity for realizing them. If they are professionally trained, particularly in one of the male-dominated professions, their relative deprivation is as tangible as their comparatively lower paychecks.[62] Their comparative reference group consists largely of their male and female classmates and colleagues, and even their husbands. They accept to a significantly lesser extent the justifying myth of the male "breadwinner" who has a right to a

---

62. See especially David H. Roethel, "Chemists' Salaries See Record Gains," *Chemical and Engineering News*, 21 October 1968, which showed that, with seniority held constant, women chemists with Ph.D.s made little more than men with only B.A.s. A more thorough study by James J. White of every woman graduate from a law school from 1956 to 1965 compared to a male cohort showed that, with every variable he could think of controlled for, a year after graduation the average man earned 20 percent more than the woman lawyer, and ten years later he earned 200 percent more. James J. White, "Women in the Law," *Michigan Law Review* 65 (April 1967): 1057.

job while a woman ought to stay home even if she has no young children. And they are likely to experience continual aggravation as they try for the kinds of jobs and income they expected to get with their degrees and find themselves asked to take the inevitable typing test. The sense of anger this can generate is analogous to that felt by the numerous underemployed university graduates in underdeveloped countries, where educational opportunities have expanded faster than concomitant occupational opportunities. They too find that they cannot attain the good positions and high status they expected their education to make available.[63]

As there is no accurate way of measuring the population of feminists in this country, there is no definitive means of testing the hypothesis of relative deprivation. Nevertheless, some general measures, beyond observational evidence, can be used to support the hypothesis. *Ms.* magazine is a slick, popular, mass publication that is generally perceived as being a feminist periodical. A *Ms.* subscriber—especially the initial ones—could be defined as at least a supporting feminist.[64] In September 1972 *Ms.* conducted a small pilot survey of their 144,000 subscribers and in April 1973 a larger one was made of by then 196,000 subscribers. While cross tabulations are not available, the gross statistics, compared to those of the general female population, give a good idea of what the general social base of the women's liberation movement was at that time, even though 82 percent of the first respondents and 76.6 percent of the second said they were not members of a movement group. Statistics from the second survey will be given in parentheses when comparable questions were asked.[65]

---

63. Hugh H. Smythe and Mabel M. Smythe, *The New Nigerian Elite* (Stanford, Calif.: Stanford University Press, 1960), chap. 10. Robert C. Williamson, "University Students in a World of Change: A Columbian Sample," *Sociology and Social Research* 48 (July 1964): 397–413.

64. This analysis is contaminated by the fact that both political participation in general and reading of national slick magazines tends to occur more frequently among people of higher social, educational, and economic status. See Sidney Verba and Norman H. Nie, *Participation in America: Political Democracy and Social Equality* (New York: Harper & Row, 1972).

65. Although the responses to the two surveys are quite similar, there are three major discrepancies between them which require a note of explanation. (1). Responses to the question on job position or title were categorized according to

A significant 84 (89.8) percent of *Ms.* subscribers have some college education, compared to roughly 20 percent of the total female population. Seventy-one (74.6) percent work full or part time, and 47 percent of those who do not work are in school (compared to 43 percent of all women over 16 who are in the labor force). Of those who do work, 91 (66.5) percent are in professional, technical, managerial, or official occupations (no accurate comparison possible due to different categorizations). Eighty-nine (91.2) percent are between the ages of 18 and 49, but only 60 percent of the total population is between these ages. Sixty-two (72) percent are under 35—largely the generation to come of age during the political turmoil of the 1960s. Fifty (50.2) percent are married, which indicates a slight bias in the single direction. But if education and employment status could be held constant it is likely that marital status would not emerge as a significant variable, as both education and employment tend to correlate inversely with marriage for women. More significant than marital status is income. The median personal income of the *Ms.* respondents—54 (53.7) percent of whom work full time—is $6,013 ($9,880) per year. But the median household income is $14,520 ($17,740) per year. Without cross-tabulations it is hard to generalize, but supporting feminists, at least those that subscribe to *Ms.*, appear to be highly educated, employed, and earning considerably less than their husbands.

The salience of relative deprivation can also be seen by comparing the initial joiners of the movement with those who were not. In particular, it was often commented on that black

different criteria. Also, the response rate to that question on the pilot survey was only 20 percent while on the second survey it was 45.5 percent. (2). The figure for median personal income in the pilot survey was computed from those who had any income at all. In the second, the median income was figured only for those respondents who were employed full time. (3). The highest category for median household income which could be indicated in the pilot survey was $20,000 and above, while that in the second survey was $50,000 and above. Thus, in the second survey both personal and household median incomes are considerably higher. None of these figures are controlled for sex and in the pilot survey respondent's sex was not asked. However, in the second survey only 1.4 percent of those answering were men, so the statistics on respondents can be assumed to reflect a female population of subscribers.

women were noticeably absent from feminist activities. Indeed, many black women referred to the movement as the *white* women's liberation movement. Black women have held several leadership positions within the movement, and there are separate black women's liberation groups. But prior to 1973 these dealt largely with problems within the black community and at any large feminist conference or convention, one would see a mere sprinkling of black women—usually involved in persuading the meeting to support antiracist activity.

This lack of participation was, obviously, due in part to the years of mutual antagonism between black and white women and the reluctance of blacks to participate in any white-dominated organization. But it was not due to a lack of support for the issues that concern the women's liberation movement.

The 1972 Louis Harris Virginia Slims poll showed that 62 percent of black women favored "efforts to strengthen or change women's status in society" compared with only 45 percent of white women. Sixty-seven percent of black women expressed "sympathy with efforts of women's liberation groups" compared with only 35 percent of white women. The answer to why there was so little initial participation obviously lies elsewhere. It requires a much higher degree of commitment than mere sympathy to participate actively in a movement for change. People make priorities on how to spend their time, and a problem must be felt as acute in order to divert people's interest from their more immediate day-to-day concerns. Despite the fact that black women have the highest unemployment rates and the lowest median income of any race/sex group in the population, they have not placed women's liberation very high on their priorities. To understand why we have to look both at aggregate deprivation and the nature of the justifying myths which operate as barriers.

Black women are likely to have two comparative reference groups: black men and white women—the first because they live with them intimately, and the latter because the nature of our racist society has used such a comparison as a way of internalizing in black women a sense of inferiority. Thus they are less likely than white women to compare themselves to the dominant and most successful group in society—white men. When the material status of black women is compared with that of these two underclasses, steady progress is shown for at least the last twenty years. Between 1952 and 1972 the gap in median educational attainment for white and nonwhite women went from 4.0 years to 1.2 years. During the same period black women increased their lead over black men from .9 to 1.2 years. In 1939 the median income for full-time working black women was only 38 percent that of white women and 51 percent that of black men. In 1966 it was 71 and 66 percent respectively.[66] Of all race/sex groups of full-time workers, nonwhite women have had the greatest percentage increase in their median income since 1939, and white women have had the lowest.

Although there are now more black men in college than black women, this has not always been the case. Consequently, of the black population over twenty-five, there are more female than male college graduates. This partially accounts for the greater access of black women to the professions. Of all employed black women, 7 percent are professionals, compared to 3 percent of all employed black men. While the picture is more traditional in the higher professions, i.e., excluding teaching, black women still have roughly twice the proportion of black professional jobs than white women have of white professional jobs. Similarly, in most professions black women have a larger proportion of women than black men do of men in these groups; and in many, black women have a higher median income than white women professionals. Nonetheless, there are still very few black women in the higher professions.[67]

If, as hypothesized earlier, professional women, especially women in the male-dominated professions, are likely to experience more relative deprivation than other women, the scarcity of

---

66. Women's Bureau, U.S. Department of Labor, *Negro Women in the Population and the Labor Force* (Washington, D.C.: Government Printing Office, 1967), pp. 8, 11.

67. Cynthia Fuchs Epstein, "Positive Effects of the Multiple Negative: Explaining the Success of Black Professional Women," *American Journal of Sociology* 78 (January 1973): 916–17.

black professional women in part explains their absence from feminist activity. The social base for such participation is simply too small. There are still quite a few employed, college-educated black women, however, and their absence cannot be explained by scarcity alone. Here, it is evident that their relative material deprivation, in relation to their likely comparative reference groups, is not as great as that of white women, and is decreasing over time. This too, however, is inadequate as a complete explanation.

More relevant are the kinds of ideological barriers black women, especially middle-class black women, have to participating in a movement protesting women's status. While the justifying myth that "a woman's place is in the home" was being whittled away for white women, the black movement was adopting a more overt version of the same myth to the tune of "a woman's place is behind her man." This was in part a reaction to the myth of the Negro matriarchy created by white sociologists[68] and in part a continuance of the traditional black pattern of imitating white society. Commented one black writer who was simultaneously trying to "prevent any unintelligent alliance of black people with white women in this new liberation movement" and urging black women against seeking "a warmed-over throne of women's inferiority":

> The black woman has been made to feel ashamed of her
> strength, and so to redeem herself she has adopted from
> whites the belief that superiority and dominance of the male
> are the most "natural" and "normal" relationship. She
> consequently believes that black women ought to be
> suppressed in order to attain that "natural balance." . . .
>   Because the white woman's role has been held up as an

---

68. Especially by Daniel P. Moynihan, *The Negro Family: A Case for National Action* (Washington, D.C.: Government Printing Office, 1965). Contrary to popular belief, Moynihan does not denigrate matriarchical family organization per se—he argues that it is dysfunctional for a subgroup to have a matriarchical family in an otherwise patriarchical society. However, the fact that he assumes the black family is basically matriarchical, based on the greater number of sole female heads of families and larger female participation in the labor force than in white families, reflects his own bias of taking the white family as the norm.

example to all black women, many black women feel inadequate and so ardently compete in "femininity" with white females for black male's attention. . . .

Finally, the black woman emphasizes the traditional role of women, such as housekeeping, children, supportive roles and self-maintenance, but she politicizes these roles by calling them the role of black women. She then adopts the attitude that her job and her life is to have more children who can be used in the vanguard of the black struggle.[69]

That this attitude is not at all restricted to militants is clear from a statement made by Dorothy Heights, president of the National Council of Negro Women:

If the Negro woman has a major underlying concern, it is the status of the Negro man and his position in the community and his need for feeling himself an important person, free and able to make his contribution in the whole society in order that he may strengthen his home.[70]

Thus, not only are "black and white women in a race to change places," as black lawyer and feminist Eleanor Holmes Norton[71] described it, but women's liberation has often been perceived as inimical to the interests of blacks, and hence the ultimate interests of black women.

One reason that women's liberation doesn't or won't attract black women is that blacks are suspicious of whites who might coopt their support, energy and drive. Feminists are perceived as whites before they are seen to be oppressed. Secondly, black lower-class women are presently emphasizing their independence of, and prideful difference from, white women. Thirdly, poor black women are too occupied struggling for essentials: shelter, food and clothing to organize themselves around the issue of women's rights.

---

69. Linda J. M. LaRue, "Black Liberation and Women's Lib," *Trans-Action* 8 (November, December 1970): 61–63. (Notice the contrast between the derogatory abbreviation "women's *lib*" and the more respectable "black *liberation*.")

70. Quoted in Cellestine Ware, *Woman Power: The Movement for Women's Liberation* (New York: Tower Publications, 1970), p. 81.

71. Personal communication, Fall 1970.

Fourthly, lower-class black women have deliberately submerged their identities in the struggle for racial equality. . . . In this context it is possible to view an autonomous women's drive for rights as an obstacle to radical changes. Black feminism would thus be another attempt by the power structure to divide black men and women. Feminist goals, like abortion on demand and easily obtainable birth control, are viewed with paranoid suspicion by some black militants.[72]

Despite much early hostility, there eventually developed a still suspicious but more ambivalent attitude toward women's liberation among black women,[73] as many began to see the inherent "sexual colonialism" in the "black women step back" argument.[74] Hernandez summed up both the impetus and the constraints to participation by black women:

They have been asked to step to the back of the civil rights movement by some who believe it is the black man's time. They have been largely absent from the feminist movement because some black sisters are not sure that the feminist revolution will meet their current needs—and the wounds of racism do not heal easily.[75]

As Pinard et al.[76] have pointed out, the "most deprived" (in an absolute sense) tend to be absent from the early phases of a movement, but as "late joiners" are often the most active. If they are right, then the potential is great that black women will eventually be among the most committed to the women's liberation movement as some individual black women have been in the past. Some moves in this direction occurred in 1973 with

---

72. Ware, *Woman Power*, p. 78.
73. "Women's Lib Has No Soul," *Encore*, March 1973, p. 41.
74. For example, see "Black Women Organizing," *Monthly Review*, October 1972.
75. Aileen Hernandez, "Money: Small Change for Black Women," *Ms.*, August 1974, p. 18. Hernandez was a founding member of NOW and its second president (1970–71).
76. Maurice Pinard, Jerome Kirk, and Donald Von Eschen, "Processes of Recruitment in the Sit-In Movement," *Public Opinion Quarterly*, 33 (Fall 1969): 355–69.

the formation of Black Women Organized for Action in San Francisco and the National Black Feminist Organization in New York.

Similarly, the fact that the white women's liberation movement began as a largely middle-class, college-educated movement does not preclude the entry of other white women into it who at least share some of the same goals (as trade-union women have begun to do). Nonetheless, the initial direction and tone of the movement, as determined by its originators, will guide its course for some time to come.

2
The Origins of the Women's Liberation Movement

SOCIAL STRAIN DOES NOT CREATE SOCIAL MOVEMENTS; it only creates the potential for movements. This strain often occurs, or is perceived, as a sharp break with the past; and a movement's psychological, if not necessarily organizational, origin is pinpointed from that time. Thus the 1954 Supreme Court decision on school desegregation is usually marked as the beginning of the civil rights movement.

Without such a signpost, a movement's origins are far less clear, and the women's liberation movement was not the only such movement to catch most thoughtful observers by surprise. Most attempts to explain why feminism emerged precisely when it did in the mid-1960s had to conclude with Ferriss[1] that "from the close perspective of 1970, events of the past decade provide evidence of no compelling cause of the rise of the new feminist

---

1. Abbott L. Ferriss, *Indicators of Trends in the Status of American Women* (New York: Russell Sage Foundation, 1971), p. 1.

movement." His examination of time-series data over the previous twenty years did not reveal any significant changes in socioeconomic variables which could account for the emergence of a women's movement at the time it was created. From such strain indicators one could surmise that any time in the last twenty years was as conducive to movement formation as any other.

Given the appropriate conditions for a movement, what then is the "spark of life" by which the "mass is to cross the threshold of organizational life"? [2] From the literature one would be forced to assume a "spontaneous generation" theory of movement formation. No one has really dealt with exactly *how* a movement starts[3] and only Blumer has acknowledged that "a movement has to be constructed" and "cannot be explained merely in terms of the psychological disposition or motivation of people, or in terms of a diffusion of an ideology." [4]

This gap occurs largely because the study of social movements "has been a neglected area of sociology" [5] and within that field virtually no theorists have dealt with movement origins. As Dahrendorf commented: "the sociologist is generally interested not so much in the origin of social phenomena as in their spread and rise to wider significance." [6] This interest is derived from an emphasis on cultural processes rather than people as the major dynamic of social change.[7] Consequently, even the "natural history" theorists have delineated the stages of development in a way that is too vague to tell us much about how movements

---

2. Theodore J. Lowi, *The Politics of Disorder* (New York: Basic Books, 1971), p. 40.

3. Anthony Oberschall, in *Social Conflict and Social Movements* (Englewood Cliffs, N.J.: Prentice-Hall, 1973), published after this chapter first appeared in the *American Journal of Sociology* (January 1973), postulated a mobilization theory of value to this question. However, it assumes "that a collectivity . . . already exists [whose] members are dissatisfied and have grievances" (pp. 118–19).

4. Herbert Blumer, "Collective Behavior," *Review of Sociology: Analysis of a Decade*, ed. Joseph B. Gittler (New York: John Wiley, 1957), p. 147.

5. Lewis M. Killian, "Social Movements," *Handbook of Modern Sociology*, ed. R. E. L. Faris (Chicago: Rand McNally, 1964), p. 426.

6. Ralf Dahrendorf, *Class and Class Conflict in Industrial Society* (Palo Alto, Calif.: Stanford University Press, 1959), p. 64.

7. Killian, "Social Movements," p. 426.

actually start,[8] and a theory as comprehensive as Smelser's[9] is postulated on too abstract a level to be of microsociological value. (For a good critique see Currie and Skolnick.)[10]

Part of the problem results from extreme confusion about what a social movement really is. Movements are rarely studied as distinct social phenomena but are usually subsumed under one of two theoretical traditions—that of collective behavior or that of interest group and party formation. The first of these traditions views social movements as a slightly more organized aspect of collective behavior, of the same genre as fads, riots, crowds, and panics.[11] From this perspective a social movement is a form of "elementary collective behavior on a large scale."[12] The other approach sees social movements as merely one way in which interest groups or political parties are formed, and thus interesting only in what they lead to rather than what they are.[13] It is primarily concerned with the organized aspects of a movement, its public program, and its institutional impact, often to the neglect of the personal changes it might instigate, its effect on public attitudes, and implicit ideology.

While the former approach emphasized the spontaneous aspects of a movement, the latter stresses the structured ones. Yet movements are neither fully collective behavior nor incipient interest groups except in the broadest conception of these terms.

---

8. C. A. Dawson and W. E. Gettys, *An Introduction to Sociology* (New York: Ronald Press, 1929), pp. 787–803; Lowi, *The Politics of Disorder*, p. 39; Herbert Blumer, "Social Movements," *New Outline of the Principles of Sociology*, ed. A. M. Lee (New York: Barnes & Noble, 1951); C. Wendell King, *Social Movements in the U.S.* (New York: Random House, 1956).

9. Neil J. Smelser, *Theory of Collective Behavior* (Glencoe, Ill.: Free Press, 1963).

10. Elliott Currie and Jerome H. Skolnick, "A Critical Note on Conceptions of Collective Behavior," *Annals of the American Academy of Political and Social Science* 391 (September 1970): 34–45.

11. Smelser, *Theory of Collective Behavior*; Kurt Lang and Gladys E. Lang, *Collective Dynamics* (New York: Crowell, 1961); Ralph H. Turner and Lewis M. Killian, *Collective Behavior* (Englewood Cliffs, N.J.: Prentice-Hall, 1957).

12. Lang and Lang, *Collective Dynamics*, p. 496.

13. Rudolph Heberle, *Social Movements* (New York: Appleton-Century-Crofts, 1951); C. Wendell King, *Social Movements in the U.S.*; Lowi, *The Politics of Disorder*; William Bruce Cameron, *Modern Social Movements* (New York: Random House, 1966).

Rather they contain essential elements of both, being purposive in direction, involving a critical amount of group consciousness,[14] and resulting in both personal and institutional changes. It is "the dual imperative of spontaneity and organization"[15] that sets social movements apart from collective behavior on the one hand and pressure groups on the other.

Recognizing with Heberle[16] that "movements *as such* are not organized groups" it is still the structured aspects which are more amenable to study, if not always the most salient. Turner and Killian[17] have argued that it is when "members of a public who share a common position concerning the issue at hand supplement their informal person-to-person discussion with some organization to promote their convictions more effectively and insure more sustained activity, a social movement is incipient."[18] Such organization(s) and other core groups of a movement not only determine much of its conscious policy but also serve as foci for its values and activities. Just as it has been argued that society as a whole has a cultural and structural "center" about which most members of the society are more or less "peripheral,"[19] so too can a social movement be conceived of as having a center and a periphery. An investigation into a movement's origins must be concerned with the microsociological preconditions for the emergence of such a movement center. From where do the people come who make up the initial, organizing cadre of a movement? How do they come together and how do they come to share a similar view of the world in circumstances which compel them to political action? In what ways does the nature of the original center affect the future development of the movement?

14. See especially Karl Marx, *The Eighteenth Brumaire of Louis Bonaparte* (1852), (New York: International Publishers, 1964).

15. Lang and Lang, *Collective Dynamics*, p. 497.

16. Heberle, *Social Movements*, p. 8.

17. Turner and Killian, *Collective Behavior*, p. 307.

18. Killian, "Social Movements," p. 426.

19. Edward Shils, "Center and Periphery," *Selected Essays* (Chicago: Center for Social Organization Studies, Department of Sociology, University of Chicago, 1970). I'd like to thank Richard Albares of Northwestern University for alerting me to this idea. He and Florence Levinshon read and criticized earlier versions of this chapter written in 1971 and 1972.

Most movements have very inconspicuous beginnings. The significant elements of their origins are usually confused or forgotten by the time a trained observer seeks to trace them out, making retroactive analyses difficult. Consequently, it is not only difficult to generalize on the basis of a detailed examination of one social movement, but difficult also to find the data of enough movements adequately to support a generalization. Nonetheless, while such theorizing is imperfect, it can aptly illustrate both weaknesses in the theoretical literature and new directions for research. To this end, an analysis of the origins of the women's liberation movement, supplemented by five other origin studies made by the author, would support the following three propositions:

Proposition 1. The need for a preexisting communications network or infrastructure within the social base of a movement is a primary prerequisite for "spontaneous" activity. Masses alone do not form movements, however discontented they may be. Groups of previously unorganized individuals may spontaneously form into small local associations—usually along the lines of informal social networks—in response to a specific strain or crisis, but if they are not linked in some manner the protest does not become generalized and remains a local irritant or dissolves completely. If a movement is to spread rapidly, the linking communications network must already exist. If only the rudiments of one exist, movement formation requires a high input of "organizing" activity.

Proposition 2. Not any communications network will do. It must be a network that is cooptable to the new ideas of the incipient movement. It is unlikely that any communications network is cooptable for any movement. Instead it must be composed of like-minded people predisposed to be receptive to the particular ideas of a new movement through their own backgrounds, experiences, or location in the social structure.

Proposition 3. Given the existence of a cooptable communications network, or at least the rudimentary development of a potential one, and a situation of strain, one or more precipitants are required. Here, two distinct patterns emerge that often overlap.

In one, a crisis—usually one or more events that symbolically embody the underlying discontent—galvanizes the network into spontaneous action in a new direction. In the other, one or more persons begin organizing a new organization or disseminating a new idea. For spontaneous action to occur, the communications network must be well formed or the initial protest will not survive the incipient stage. If it is not well formed, organizing efforts must occur, that is, one or more persons must specifically attempt to construct a movement and, given the extent of strain felt, may or may not succeed. To be successful, organizers must be skilled and have a fertile field in which to work. If no communications network already exists, there must at least be emerging spontaneous groups which are acutely attuned to the new ideas, albeit uncoordinated. To sum up, if a cooptable communications network is already established, a crisis is all that is necessary to galvanize it. If it is rudimentary, an organizing cadre of one or more persons is necessary. Such a cadre is superfluous if the former conditions fully exist, but it is essential if they do not.

Before examining these propositions in detail, let us look at the origins of the women's liberation movement, with particular emphasis on the salient factors that will later be teased out. The movement manifests itself in an almost infinite variety of groups, styles, and organizations. Yet this diversity has sprung from only two distinct origins, representing two different strata of society, with two different styles, orientations, values, and forms of organization. In many ways there were two different movements which only in the last two years have begun to merge.

The first of these I call the older branch of the movement, partially because the median age of its original activists was older and partially because it began first. Its most prominent organization is the National Organization for Women (NOW) but it also contains such groups as the National Women's Political Caucus (NWPC), Federally Employed Women (FEW), and the self-defined "right-wing" of the movement, the Women's Equity Action League (WEAL). While the programs and aims of the older branch span a wide spectrum, their activities have tended to be concentrated on legal and economic problems. These groups are primarily made up of women—and men—who work, and they are substantially concerned with the problems of working women. The style of organization of the older branch groups tends to be traditionally formal, with elected officers, boards of directors, bylaws, and the other trappings of democratic structure and procedure. All started as top-down national organizations lacking a mass base. Some have subsequently developed that base, some have not yet done so, and others do not want to.

The younger branch of the movement is all mass base and no national organization. It consists of innumerable small groups engaged in a variety of activities, whose contact with one another is at best tenuous. Its composition, like that of the older branch, tends to be predominantly white, middle class, and college educated, but much more homogeneously so.[20]

It is a common mistake to try to place the various feminist organizations on the traditional left/right spectrum and, concomitantly, to describe the two branches as "women's rights" and "women's liberation." [21] The terms "reformist" and "radical" by which the two branches are so often designated are convenient and fit into our preconceived notions about the nature of political activity, but they tell us little of relevance. In fact, if an ideological typography were possible it would show minimal consistency with any organizational characteristic.[22] Some groups

---

20. This observation was confirmed by Patricia Bayer Richard's 1972 questionnaire study in Syracuse, N.Y., of "The Feminist Movement: Parameters of Participation" (Paper given at the March 1974 convention of the Ohio Association of Economists and Political Scientists).

21. Judith Hole and Ellen Levine, *Rebirth of Feminism* (New York: Quadrangle, 1971); Maren Carden Lockwood, *The New Feminist Movement* (New York: Russell Sage Foundation, 1974). Both make this mistake.

22. I am using ideology in the narrow sense to refer to a specifically feminist belief system rather than a general world view on the nature of politics and society. Participants in younger branch groups would be more likely to call themselves socialists or use revolutionary rhetoric than those in older branch groups. However, if one questions individuals in each branch on their views of the major feminist issues (e.g., abolition of marriage, continuation of the nuclear family, payment for housewives, abolition of the housewife role, child care, abortion, access of women to predominantly male occupations, abolition of sex roles, building a female culture, welfare, lesbianism, etc.), the answers will not correspond with branch membership. See the *Psychology Today* survey showing that respondents claiming membership in NOW compared with those participating in

often called "reformist" have a platform that would so completely change our society it would be unrecognizable. Other groups called "radical" concentrate on the traditional female concerns of love, sex, children, and interpersonal relationships (although with nontraditional views). The ideological complexity of the movement is too great to be categorized so simply.

The activities of the two branches are similarly incongruous. Ironically, the most typical division of labor is that those groups labeled "radical" engage primarily in educational work and service projects, while the so-called reformist groups are the political activists. Structure and style rather than ideology more accurately differentiate the two branches, and even here there has been much borrowing on both sides. In general the older branch has used the traditional forms of political action while the younger branch has been experimental.

As will be seen, the different style and organization of the two branches was largely derived from the different kind of political education and experiences of each originating group of women. Women of the older branch were trained in and had used the traditional forms of political action; while the younger branch inherited the loose, flexible, person-oriented attitude of the youth and student movements. The different structures that have evolved from these two distinctly different kinds of experience have, in turn, largely determined the strategy of the two branches, irrespective of any conscious intentions of their participants. These different structures and strategies have each posed different problems and possibilities. Intramovement differences are often perceived by the participants as conflicting, but it is their essential complementarity that has been one of the strengths of the movement.

Despite the multitude of differences, there are very strong similarities in the way the two branches came into being. These similarities serve to illuminate some of the microsociological factors involved in movement formation. NOW was the first older

---

small groups showed no differences in their positions on various women's issues. Carol Tavris, "Woman and Man," *Psychology Today*, March 1972, p. 57.

branch organization to be formed and is the parent of many of them. The forces that led to its formation were set in motion in 1961 when President Kennedy established the President's Commission on the Status of Women, at the behest of Esther Petersen, then director of the Women's Bureau.[23] Operating under a broad mandate, its 1963 report, *American Women*, and subsequent committee publications documented just how thoroughly women are still denied many rights and opportunities. The most concrete response to the activity of the President's Commission was the eventual establishment of fifty state commissions to do similar research on a state level. These commissions were often urged by politically active women and were composed primarily of women. While many governors saw them as an easy opportunity to pay off political favors, many women saw them as opportunities to turn attention to their concerns. These commissions in turn researched and wrote their own reports, which varied widely in quality and depth.

The activity of the federal and state commissions laid the groundwork for the future movement in three significant ways: (1) it brought together many knowledgeable, politically active women who otherwise would not have worked together around matters of direct concern to women; (2) the investigations unearthed ample evidence of women's unequal status, especially their legal and economic difficulties, in the process convincing many previously uninterested women that something should be done; (3) the reports created a climate of expectations that something would be done. The women of the federal and state

---

23. The Women's Bureau was created in 1920. Although its main concern has been with women workers it has done an excellent job of producing reports and pamphlets on many aspects of women's situation. Its *Handbook on Women Workers* is the movement's main source book on legal and economic discrimination. The existence of an agency such as the Women's Bureau with its cooperative attitude and freely available publications facilitated the development and spread of the movement by, in effect, having done much of the basic fact-gathering and primary research necessary to support the feminist interpretation of women's status. However, it once had a conservative influence by directing (nonfeminist) women's groups away from support of such issues as the Equal Rights Amendment. Nonetheless, it was a latent resource for the spread of feminism, once groups developed that could make use of its material.

commissions who were exposed to these influences exchanged visits, correspondence, and staff and met with each other at an annual commission convention. Thus they were in a position to share and mutually reinforce their growing awareness and concern over women's issues. These commissions created an embryonic communications network among people with similar concerns.

During this time two other events of significance occurred. The first was the publication of Betty Friedan's book *The Feminine Mystique* in 1963. An immediate best seller, it eventually stimulated many women to question the status quo and some to suggest to Friedan that a new organization should be formed to attack their problems. The second was the addition of "sex" to Title VII of the 1964 Civil Rights Act, prohibiting discrimination in employment.

Many men thought the "sex" provision was a joke—that its initiator, Representative Howard W. Smith of Virginia, only wanted to make the employment section of the bill look silly and sufficiently divide the liberals to prevent its passage.[24] However, the provision was taken very seriously by most of the female members of the House, regardless of party or politics. Representative Martha Griffiths of Michigan, the leading feminist of the House, claims she intended to sponsor the amendment but held off when she learned of Smith's intentions as she knew he could bring another 100 votes with him. Most of the House liberals opposed the provision, arguing that it would weaken the bill, and Representative Griffiths knew it needed every vote it could get. Despite their many disagreements, both Smith and the liberal opponents played the provision for all the laughs it was worth and

---

24. Caruthers Gholson Berger, "Equal Pay, Equal Employment Opportunity and Equal Enforcement of the Law for Women," *Valparaiso Law Review* 5 (Spring 1971): 326–73, maintains that hearings the previous year on the Equal Pay Act and pressure by the National Women's Party (infra, p. 63) were primarily responsible for the addition of the sex provision to Title VII. However, Berger has been a member of the National Council of the National Women's Party since 1960, and Rep. Martha Griffiths (D.–Mich. until 1974) told me in 1969 that the NWP did not have a great influence on congress.

the ensuing uproar went down in congressional history as "Ladies Day in the House." [25]

Thanks to determined leadership by the congresswomen and concerted lobbying by the provision's supporters, "sex" joined the bill, only to be aborted by the very agency set up to administer it. The first executive director of the Equal Employment Opportunity Commission (EEOC), Herman Edelsberg, publicly stated that the provision was a "fluke" that was "conceived out of wedlock." He felt "men were entitled to female secretaries." [26] This attitude caused Griffiths to blast the agency in a June 20, 1966, speech on the House floor. She declared that the EEOC had "started out by casting disrespect and ridicule on the law" but that their "wholly negative attitude had changed—for the worse." [27]

Not everyone within the EEOC was opposed to the "sex" provision. There was a "pro-woman" coterie which argued that "sex" would be taken more seriously if there were "some sort of NAACP for women" to put pressure on the government. As government employees they could not organize such a group, but they spoke privately with those whom they thought could do so.

On June 30, 1966, these three strands of incipient feminism were knotted together to form NOW. The occasion was the last day of the Third National Conference of Commissions on the Status of Women, ironically titled "Targets for Action." The participants had all received copies of Representative Griffith's remarks. The opportunity came with a refusal by conference officials to bring to the floor a proposed resolution that urged the EEOC to treat sex discrimination as seriously as race discrimination. Despite the fact that these state commissions were not federal agencies, officials of the Interdepartmental Committee on the Status of Women and

---

25. For a thorough documentation of this event, see Caroline Bird, *Born Female: The High Cost of Keeping Women Down* (New York: David McKay, 1968), chap. 1. For a blow-by-blow account of the floor happenings, see *Congressional Record, House,* 8 February 1964.

26. Herman Edelsberg, at the New York University 18th Conference on Labor, cited in *Labor Relations Reporter* 61 (25 August 1966): 253–55.

27. U.S. Congress, House, speech of Martha Griffiths, 89th Cong., 2nd sess., 20 June 1966, *Congressional Record.*

the Citizen's Advisory Committee on the Status of Women who were running the conference replied that those attending were not elected delegates and thus that resolutions would be inappropriate. The small group of women who had desired the resolution had met the night before in Friedan's hotel room to discuss the possibility of a civil rights organization for women. Not convinced of its need, they chose instead to propose the resolution. When the resolution was vetoed, the women held a whispered conversation over lunch and agreed to form an action organization "to bring women into full participation in the mainstream of American society now, assuming all the privileges and responsibilities thereof in truly equal partnership with men." The time for conferences was over, they felt. Now was the time to fight. The name NOW was coined by Friedan, in town researching her second book. Before the day was over, 28 women paid $5 each to join.[28]

By the time the organizing conference was held the following October 29–30, over 300 men and women had become charter members. It is impossible to do a breakdown on the composition of the charter membership, but one of the first officers and board is possible. Such a breakdown accurately reflected NOW's origins. Friedan was president, two former EEOC commissioners were vice-presidents, a representative of the United Auto Workers Women's Committee was secretary-treasurer, and there were seven past and present members of the State Commissions on the Status of Women on the twenty-member board. Of the charter members, 126 were Wisconsin residents—and Wisconsin had the most active state commission. Occupationally, the board and officers were primarily from the professions, labor, government, and the communications industry.[29] Of these, only those from

---

28. Betty Friedan, "NOW: How It Began," *Women Speaking*, April 1967.

29. The employment background of the national board and officers was as follows: Board—labor, 3; academe, 7; church-related, 1; government, 2; law, 2; communications, 2; miscellaneous, 3. Officers—labor, academe, church, and communications, 1 each; government, 2. Most recent occupation as of the 1966 conference was used as the criterion for classification, and potential cross-filing was arbitrarily eliminated. For example, two academic nuns were counted under "academe" rather than "church." According to observers present at the confer-

labor had any experience in organizing, and they resigned a year later in a dispute over support of the Equal Rights Amendment. Instead of organizational expertise, what the early NOW members had was media experience, and it was here that their early efforts were aimed. They could create an appearance of activity but did not know how to organize the substance of it. As a result, NOW often gave the impression of being larger than it was. It was highly successful in getting publicity, much less so in bringing about concrete changes or organizing itself. It suffered from constant administrative chaos during the first years of its life and was frequently unable to answer the mail from potential members let alone coordinate the activities of current ones. NOW's initiators were very high-powered women who lacked the time or patience for the slow, unglamorous, and tedious work of putting together a mass organization. Chapter development had to wait for the national media to attract women to the organization or the considerable geographical mobility of contemporary women to bring proponents into new territory.

In the meantime, unaware of and unknown to NOW, the EEOC, and the state commissions, younger women began forming their own movement. Contrary to popular myth, it did not begin on the campus, nor was it started by Students for a Democratic Society (SDS). However, its activators were, to be trite, on the other side of the generation gap. While few were students, all were "under 30" and had obtained their political education as participants or concerned observers of the social-action projects of the 1960s. These projects, particularly the civil rights movement, attracted a large number of women. Many were to say later that one of the major appeals of this movement was that the social role if not the economic condition of blacks was similar to that of women. But this observation was a retrospective one. At the time most women would not have expressed these thoughts even if they could have articulated them. The few who did were quickly put down.

---

ence, the participants tended to reflect the occupational background of the board, but to have a lower median age. Participants were primarily between the ages of 25 and 45, while officers tended to be at least 35.

Whether as participants in civil rights groups, the New Left, peace groups, or in the free universities, women found themselves quickly shunted into traditional roles. One early pamphlet described these roles as those of the "workers" and the "wives"; the former serviced the radical organizations with their typing and clerical skills and the latter serviced the radical men with their homemaking and sexual ones. Those few women who refused these roles and insisted on being accepted in the "realm of the mind" found themselves desexed and often isolated by their comrades.[30]

The situation in which these women found themselves unavoidably conflicted with the ideologies of "participatory democracy," "freedom," and "justice" that they were expressing. They were faced with the self-evident contradiction of working in a "freedom movement" but not being very free. Nor did their male colleagues brook any dissent. The men followed the example of Stokeley Carmichael who cut off all debate on the issue at a 1964 Student Non-violent Coordinating Committee conference by saying "the only position for women in SNCC is prone."

The problems for women in the radical movement were raised again and again over the next three years. In Seattle, members of the Socialist Workers Party (SWP) defected and formed the independent Freedom Socialist Club in 1964. The refusal of the SWP to consider "the woman question" was a major cause. Civil rights workers, housewives, and students in New Orleans formed a summer free-school discussion group in 1965. Women on the 1966 Meredith Mississippi march held secret nightly meetings after they were ordered to walk on the inside of the march line and be accompanied by a man at all times.

The idea of women's "liberation" was first raised at an SDS convention in December 1965. It was laughed off the floor by the male radicals. Undaunted, some New Left women circulated papers on the issue[31] and tried to interest SDS women in organizing

---

30. Judi Bernstein, Peggy Morton, Linda Seese, Myrna Woods, "Sisters, Brothers, Lovers . . . Listen . . . ," originally distributed by the Student Union for Peace Action, Toronto, Canada, 1966.

31. "A Kind of Memo" by Casey Hayden and Mary King was circulated in

themselves. Although they largely failed, the workshops on women in SDS regional conferences attracted many women who were later to be instrumental in the formation of feminist groups. At the summer 1967 national conference, SDS women finally succeeded in passing a resolution calling for the full participation of women in SDS. Generalizing from their experiences (and unknowingly paralleling the developing NOW program), they also suggested that SDS work on behalf of all women for communal child care, wide dissemination of contraceptives, easily available abortions, and equal sharing of housework. More specifically, they requested that SDS print relevant literature and that the SDS paper solicit articles on women. These requests were largely ignored. Instead, the SDS organ, *New Left Notes,* decorated the page on which the women's resolution appeared with a freehand drawing of a girl in a baby-doll dress holding a picket sign and petulantly declaring "We want our rights and we want them now!" [32]

No single group or organization among these protest movements directly stimulated the formation of independent women's liberation groups. But together they created a "radical community" in which like-minded women continually interacted or were made aware of each other. This community consisted largely of those who had participated in one or more of the many protest activities of the 1960s and had established its own ethos and its own institutions. Thus the women in it thought of themselves as "movement people" and had incorporated the adjective "radical" into their personal identities. The values of their radical identity and the style to which they had been trained by their movement participation directed them to approach most problems as political ones that could be solved by organizing. What remained was to translate their individual feelings of "unfreedom" into a collective consciousness. Thus the radical community provided

---

mimeograph form for many months prior to the 1965 SDS convention and largely stimulated the discussion there. The essay was later published in *Liberation* 11, no. 2 (April 1966): 35 entitled "Sex and Caste: A Kind of Memo."

32. *New Left Notes,* 10 July 1967.

not only the necessary network of communication; its radical ideas formed the framework of analysis that "explained" the dismal situation in which radical women found themselves.

In this fertile field the younger branch of the women's movement took root in 1967 and 1968. At least five groups in five different cities (Chicago, Toronto, Seattle, Detroit, and Gainsville, Florida) formed spontaneously, independently of each other. They came at a very auspicious moment. 1967 was the year in which the blacks kicked the whites out of the civil rights movement, student power had been discredited by SDS, and the organized New Left was on the wane. Only draft-resistance activities were on the increase, and this movement more than any other exemplified the social inequities of the sexes. Men could resist the draft. Women could only council resistance.[33] What was significant about this point in time was that there was a lack of available opportunities for political work. Some women fit well into the "secondary role" of draft counseling. Many did not. For years, their complaints of unfair treatment had been ignored by movement men with the dictum that those things could wait until after the revolution. Now these movement women found time on their hands, but the men would still not listen.

For months, women met quietly to analyze their perpetual secondary roles in the radical movement, to assimilate the lessons learned in free university study groups, or to reflect on their treatment in the civil rights movement. They were constantly ridiculed by the men they worked with and told that their meetings with other women were "counterrevolutionary" because they would further splinter an already badly factioned movement. In many ways this very ridicule served to increase their growing rage.

A typical example was the August 1967 National Conference on New Politics convention held in Chicago. Although a women's caucus met for days, it was told its resolution was not significant

---

33. Barrie Thorne, "Girls Who Say Yes to Guys Who Say No: Women in the Draft Resistance Movement" (Paper given at the 1972 convention of the American Sociological Association).

enough to merit a floor discussion. By threatening to tie up the convention with procedural motions, the women succeeded in having their statement tacked to the end of the agenda. It was never discussed. The chair refused to recognize any of the women standing by the microphones, their hands straining upward. When instead he called on someone to speak on "the forgotten American, the American Indian," five women rushed the podium to demand an explanation. But the chairman just patted one of the women on the head and told her, "Cool down, little girl, we have more important things to talk about than women's problems."

The "little girl" was Shulamith Firestone, future author of *The Dialectic of Sex* (1971), and she did not cool down. Instead, she joined with another Chicago woman, at the NCNP who had been trying to organize a women's group that summer, to call a meeting of those women who had halfheartedly attended the summer meetings. Telling their stories to those women, they stimulated sufficient rage to carry the group for three months; and by that time it was a permanent institution.

Another somewhat similar event occurred in Seattle the following winter. At the University of Washington, an SDS organizer was explaining to a large meeting how white college youth established rapport with the poor whites with whom they were working. "He noted that sometimes after analyzing societal ills, the men shared leisure time by 'balling a chick together.' He pointed out that such activities did much to enhance the political consciousness of the poor white youth. A woman in the audience asked, 'And what did it do for the consciousness of the chick?' " [34] After the meeting, a handful of enraged women formed Seattle's first group.

This was only the beginning. In January 1968, *Ramparts,* a would-be radical slick magazine, did a cover article on "A History of the Rise of the Unusual Movement for Woman Power in the United States: 1961–1968." It was so patronizing that even

---

34. Hole and Levine, *Rebirth of Feminism,* p. 120.

New Left Notes had to condemn it.[35] *Ramparts* at first accepted a rebuttal article from three Chicago participants in the incipient movement, then refused to print it. The cover had featured a woman's leotard-clad torso, cut off at the neck, with a Jeanette Rankin Brigade button dangling from one breast. "Woman Power" *Ramparts* titled the picture. "Two tits, No head" was the general interpretation. As much as a year later the radical movement's hostility had not changed. At the 1969 demonstrations at Nixon's inauguration women had asked and received time for two short speeches at the rally after many objections from the men organizing it. When they tried to speak they were hooted down with cries of "Take her off the stage and fuck her!"

Despite this friction, women still continued to work within the radical community and to use the underground press and the universities to disseminate women's liberation ideas. Many women traveled widely to Left conferences and demonstrations, using the opportunity to talk with other women about the new movement. Some Left organizations even held special conferences for women. The southern women's liberation movement was launched when the Southern Students Organizing Committee (ssoc) did so in February 1969. In spite of public derision by movement men, or perhaps because of it, young women steadily formed new groups around the country.

Unlike NOW, the women in the first groups of the younger branch had had years of experience as local-level organizers. They did not have the resources, or the desire, to form a national organization, but they knew how to utilize the infrastructure of the radical community, the underground press, and the free universities to spread the movement. In particular Chicago was responsible for the creation of many new groups in that city and elsewhere and started the first national newsletter. As a center of New Left activity, it had the largest number of politically conscious organizers and was thus in a favorable position to use the institutions of the radical community. Similarly, the group in

---

35. Naomi Jaffe and Bernadine Dohrn, *New Left Notes,* 18 March 1968, p. 5.

Washington, D.C. was able to organize the sole national conference in 1968 under the auspices of the Institute for Policy Studies, a radical research organization. Using IPS facilities, this group subsequently became a main literature distribution center. Although New York groups organized early and were often featured in the media, New York was not a source of early organizers. The movement in New York has been more diverse than in other cities and has made many major ideological contributions, but, contrary to popular belief, women's liberation did not begin in New York. In putting together their stories, the news media, concentrated as they are in New York, rarely looked past the Hudson for their information. This eastern bias is exemplified by the fact that, although the younger branch of the movement has no national organization and abjures leadership, all but one of those women designated at one time or another by the press as movement leaders live in New York.

Initially the new movement found it hard to organize on the campus, but, as a major congregating area of women and, in particular, of women with political awareness, campus women's liberation groups eventually became ubiquitous. While the younger branch of the movement never formed any organization larger or more extensive than a city-wide coordinating committee, it would be fair to say that, at least in the first years, it had a larger "participationship" than NOW and the other older branch organizations. While the members of the older branch knew how to use the media and how to form national structures, the women of the younger branch were skilled in local community organizing.

From this description, there appear to be four essential elements contributing to the emergence of the women's liberation movement in the mid-1960s: (1) the growth of a preexisting communications network which was (2) cooptable to the ideas of the new movement; (3) a series of crises that galvanized into action people involved in this network; and/or (4) subsequent organizing effort to weld the spontaneous groups together into a movement. To understand these factors more fully, let us examine them in detail with reference to other relevant studies.

Communications Network

Both the Commissions on the Status of Women and the "radical community" created a communications network through which those women initially interested in creating an organization could easily reach others. Such a network had not previously existed among women. Historically tied to the family and isolated from their own kind, women are perhaps the most organizationally underdeveloped social category in Western civilization. By 1950, the nineteenth-century organizations that had been the basis of the suffrage movement—the Women's Trade Union League, the General Federation of Women's Clubs, the Women's Christian Temperance Union, the National American Women's Suffrage Association—were all either dead or a pale shadow of their former selves.

The closest exception was the National Women's Party (NWP) which has remained dedicated to feminist concerns since its inception in 1916. The daughter of the radical Congressional Union for Women's Suffrage (CUWS), it was organized originally to mobilize women's voting power in suffrage states to compel the adoption of the federal suffrage amendment.[36] Under the leadership of Alice Paul, the NWP was responsible for most of the serious agitation (marches, pickets, jail-ins, fasts) that preceded the passage of the Nineteenth Amendment.[37] Unlike the moderates in the much larger sister organization, NAWSA—which transformed itself into the League for Women Voters in 1920—the more radical NWP decided that the battle was not yet won. From 1923 through 1972 Alice Paul and the NWP lobbied Congress to pass the Equal Rights Amendment (ERA).

---

36. Its founder, Alice Paul, had spent three years in Britain working with the militant suffragists there, and adopted from them the idea of holding the party in power responsible for all governmental policies, and hence for the failure to pass the Anthony Suffrage Amendment. Since the Democrats controlled the White House, the NWP worked against the election of all Democratic congressmen in suffrage states, even though many of them individually supported and voted for suffrage and the Democrats had at least voiced token support in their national convention.

37. Inez Haynes Irwin, *The Story of the Women's Party* (New York: Harcourt, Brace, 1921).

Until a few years ago, the Equal Rights Amendment was the best kept government secret of the century. It is safe to say that as late as 1969 even the majority of avowed feminists in this country had never heard of it nor of the NWP. When the ERA finally passed Congress in 1972 the NWP still was unknown to most women. Although much of this ignorance of the ERA resulted from the general refusal by society to be seriously concerned with women's issues, it also reflected the style of the NWP. From its beginning, the NWP believed that a small group of women concentrating their efforts in the right places was more effective than mass appeal. Ensconced in a large, ancient house near the Senate, it has been harassing Congress for half a century with a small, tightly knit lobbying operation whose members have grown old with the organization. Many people dismissed it as a joke and snidely referred to its indefatigable canvassers as "the tennis shoe ladies," but it did succeed in having the ERA introduced every year since 1923 and be included in every Democratic and Republican platform since 1944. The NWP also provided a core of knowledge-able lobbyists to aid in the addition of "sex" to Title VII of the 1964 Civil Rights Act. Despite its years of political savvy about the intricacies of congressional operation, the NWP was so isolated from any other group of active or interested women that it was incapable of catalyzing a new women's movement. It kept a small flame of feminist feeling burning dimly, but it established no roots in a potential social base.

References to the salience of a preexisting communications network appear frequently in the case studies of social movements, but it has been given little attention in the theoretical literature. It is essentially contrary to the mass-society theory which "for many . . . is . . . the most pertinent and comprehensive statement of the genesis of modern mass movements."[38] This theory hypothesizes that those most likely to join a mass movement are those who are atomized and isolated from "a structure of groups intermediate between the family and the

---

38. Maurice Pinard, "Mass Society and Political Movements: A New Formulation," *American Journal of Sociology* 73 (May 1968): 682.

nation." [39] However, the lack of such intermediate structures among women has proved more of a hindrance than a help in movement formation. Even today, it is those women who are most atomized, the housewives, who are least likely to join a feminist group.

The most serious attack on mass-society theory was made by Pinard in his study of the Social Credit Party of Quebec. He concluded that intermediate structures exerted *mobilizing* as well as restraining effects on individuals' participation in social movements because they formed communications networks that assisted in the rapid spread of new ideas. "When strains are severe and widespread," he contended, "a new movement is more likely to meet its early success among the more strongly integrated citizens." [40]

Other evidence also attests to the role of previously organized networks in the rise and spread of a social movement. According to Buck, [41] the Grange established a degree of organization among American farmers in the nineteenth century which greatly facilitated the spread of future farmers's protests. In Saskatchewan, Lipset has asserted:

> The rapid acceptance of new ideas and movements . . . can be attributed mainly to the high degree of organization. . . . The role of the social structure of the western wheat belt in facilitating the rise of new movements has never been sufficiently appreciated by historians and sociologists. Repeated challenges and crises forced the western farmers to create many more community institutions . . . than are necessary in a more stable area. These groups in turn provided a structural basis for immediate action in critical situations. [Therefore] though it was a new radical party, the

39. William Kornhauser, *The Politics of Mass Society* (Glencoe, Ill.: Free Press, 1959), p. 93.

40. Maurice Pinard, *The Rise of a Third Party: A Study in Crisis Politics* (Englewood Cliffs, N.J.: Prentice-Hall, 1971), p. 192.

41. Solon J. Buck, *The Agrarian Crusade* (New Haven, Conn.: Yale University Press, 1920), pp. 43–44.

C.C.F. did not have to build up an organization from scratch.[42]

More recently, the civil rights movement was built upon the infrastructure of the southern black church[43] and early sds organizers made ready use of the National Student Association.[44]

Indirect evidence of the essential role of formal and informal communications networks is found in diffusion theory, which emphasizes the importance of personal interaction rather than impersonal media communication in the spread of ideas[45] and in Coleman's[46] investigations of the role of prior organizations in the initial development of conflict.

Such preexisting communications networks appear to be not merely valuable but prerequisites, as one study on "The Failure of an Incipient Social Movement" made quite clear.[47] In 1957, a potential tax-protest movement in Los Angeles generated considerable interest and public notice for a little over a month, but was dead within a year. According to the authors, its failure to sustain itself beyond initial spontaneous protest was largely due to "the lack of a preexisting network of communications linking those groups of citizens most likely to support the movement." [48] They said that "if a movement is to grow rapidly, it cannot rely upon its own network of communication, but must capitalize on networks already in existence." [49]

The development of the women's liberation movement high-

---

42. Seymour Martin Lipset, *Agrarian Socialism* (Berkeley: University of California Press, 1959), p. 252.

43. Martin Luther King, Jr., *Stride Toward Freedom* (New York: Harper & Row, 1958).

44. C. Clark Kissinger and Bob Ross, "Starting in '60: Or From slid to Resistance," *New Left Notes,* 10 June 1968, p. 16; Kirkpatrick Sale, sds (New York: Random House, 1973), p. 34.

45. Everett M. Rogers, *Diffusion of Innovations* (New York: Free Press, 1962); Herbert F. Lionberger, *Adoption of New Ideas and Practices* (Ames: Iowa State University Press, 1960).

46. James Coleman, *Community Conflict* (Glencoe, Ill.: Free Press, 1957).

47. Maurice Jackson, Eleanora Petersen, James Bull, Sverre Monsen, and Patricia Richmond, "The Failure of an Incipient Social Movement," *Pacific Sociological Review* 3 (Spring 1960): 40.

48. Ibid., p. 40.

49. Ibid., p. 37.

lights the salience of such a network precisely because the conditions for a movement existed *before* a network came into being, but the movement did not exist until afterward. Socioeconomic strain did not change for women significantly during a twenty-year period. It was as great in 1955 as in 1965. What changed was the organizational situation. It was not until a communications network developed among like-minded people beyond local boundaries that the movement could emerge and develop past the point of occasional, spontaneous uprising.

Cooptability

However, not just any network would do; it had to be one that was cooptable by the incipient movement because it linked like-minded people likely to be predisposed to the new ideas of the movement. The 180,000-member Federation of Business and Professional Women's (BPW) Clubs would appear to be a likely base for a new feminist movement but in fact was unable to assume this role. It had steadily lobbied for legislation of importance to women, yet as late as "1966 BPW rejected a number of suggestions that it redefine . . . goals and tactics and become a kind of 'NAACP for women' . . . out of fear of being labeled 'feminist.' " [50] While its membership has become a recruiting ground for feminism, it could not initially overcome the ideological barrier to a new type of political action.

On the other hand, the women of the President's and State Commissions on the Status of Women and the feminist coterie of the EEOC were cooptable, largely because their immersion into the facts of female status and the details of sex-discrimination cases made them very conscious of the need for change. Likewise, the young women of the "radical community" lived in an atmosphere of questioning, confrontation, and change. They absorbed an ideology of "freedom" and "liberation" far more potent than any latent "antifeminism" might have been. The repeated contradictions between these ideas and the actions of their male colleagues created a compulsion for action which only required an opportu-

---

50. Hole and Levine, *Rebirth of Feminism*, p. 81.

nity to erupt. This was provided by the "vacuum of political activity" of 1967–68.

The nature of cooptability is much more difficult to elucidate. Heretofore, it has been dealt with only tangentially. Pinard noted the necessity for groups to "*possess* or *develop* an ideology or simply subjective interests congruent with that of a new movement" for them to "act as mobilizing rather than restraining agents toward that movement" but did not further explore what affected the "primary group climate." [51] More illumination is provided by the diffusion of innovation studies which point out the necessity for new ideas to fit in with already-established norms for changes to happen easily. Furthermore, a social system which has as a value "innovativeness" itself (as the radical community did) will more rapidly adopt ideas than one which looks upon the habitual performance of traditional practices as the ideal (as most organized women's groups did in the fifties). Usually, as Lionberger points out, "people act in terms of past experiences and knowledge." [52] People who have had similar experiences are likely to share similar perceptions of a situation and mutually to reinforce those perceptions as well as their subsequent interpretation.

A cooptable network, therefore, is one whose members have had common experiences which predispose them to be receptive to the particular new ideas of the incipient movement and who are not faced with structural or ideological barriers to action. If the new movement as an "innovation" can interpret these experiences and perceptions in ways that point out channels for social action, then participation in a social movement becomes the logical thing to do.

The Role of "Crisis"

As our examples have illustrated, these similar perceptions must be translated into action. This is the role of the "crisis." For

---

51. Pinard, *The Rise of a Third Party: A Study in Crisis Politics*, p. 186.
52. Lionberger, *Adoption of New Ideas and Practices*, p. 91.

women of the older branch of the movement, the impetus to organize was the refusal of the EEOC to enforce the sex provision of Title VII, precipitated by the concomitant refusal of federal officials at the conference to allow a supportive resolution. For younger women, there were a series of minor crises. Such precipitating events are common to most movements. They serve to crystallize and focus discontent. From their own experiences, directly and concretely, people feel the need for change in a situation that allows for an exchange of feelings with others, mutual validation, and a subsequent reinforcement of innovative interpretation. Perception of an immediate need for change is a major factor in predisposing people to accept new ideas.[53] Nothing makes desire for change more acute than a crisis. If the strain is great enough, such a crisis need not be a major one; it need only symbolically embody collective discontent.

Role of the Organizer

A crisis will only catalyze a well-formed communications network. If such networks are no more than embryonically developed or only partially cooptable, the potentially active individuals in them must be linked together by someone. As Jackson et al. stated, "Some protest may persist where the source of trouble is constantly present. But interest ordinarily cannot be maintained unless there is a welding of spontaneous groups into some stable organization." [54] In other words, people must be organized. Social movements do not simply occur.

The role of the organizer in movement formation is another neglected aspect of the theoretical literature. There has been great concern with leadership, but the two roles are distinct and not always performed by the same individual. In the early stages of a movement, it is the organizer much more than any "leader" who is important, and such an individual or cadre must often operate behind the scenes.[55] Certainly, the "organizing cadre" that young

---

53. Rogers, *Diffusion of Innovations,* p. 280.
54. Jackson et al., "Failure," p. 37.
55. The nature and function of these two roles was most clearly evident in the Townsend old-age movement of the 1930s. Townsend was the "charismatic"

women in the radical community came to be was key to the growth of that branch of the women's liberation movement, despite the fact that no "leaders" were produced (and were actively discouraged). The existence of many leaders but no organizers in the older branch of the women's liberation movement and its subsequent slow development would tend to substantiate this hypothesis.

The crucial function of the organizer has been explored indirectly in other areas of sociology. Rogers devotes many pages to the "change agent" who, while he does not necessarily weld a group together or "construct" a movement, does many of the same things for agricultural innovation that an organizer does for political change. Mass-society theory makes reference to the "agitator" but fails to do so in any kind of truly informative way. A study of farmers' movements indicates that many core organizations were organized by a single individual before the spontaneous aspects of the movement predominated. Further, many other core groups were subsidized by older organizations, federal and state governments, and even by local businessmen.[56] These organizations often served as training centers for organizers and sources of material support to aid in the formation of new interest groups and movements.

Similarly, the civil rights movement provided the training for many another movement's organizers, including the young women of the women's liberation movement. It would appear that the art of "constructing" a social movement is something that requires considerable skill and experience. Even in the supposedly spontaneous social movement, the professional is more valuable than the amateur.

---

leader but the movement was organized by his partner, real estate promoter Robert Clements. Townsend himself acknowledges that, without Clements' help, the movement would never have gone beyond the idea stage. See Abraham Holtzman, *The Townsend Movement: A Political Study* (New York: Bookman Associates, 1963).

56. Robert H. Salisbury, "An Exchange Theory of Interest Groups," *Midwest Journal of Political Science* 13 (February 1969): 13. John D. McCarthy and Mayer N. Zald also discuss sources of outside support in *The Trend of Social Movements in America: Professionalization and Resource Mobilization* (Morristown, N.J.: General Learning Press, 1973).

3

The National Organization for Women

IN MUCH OF THE SOCIOLOGICAL LITERATURE A SOCIAL-movement organization is often confused as being the social movement itself. Thus, the orientation, goals, and even the success of the movement are judged by those of the organization. This usually leads to mistaken assessments. While there is certainly a relationship between the two, it is an imperfect one, changing over time, and the inevitable concentration of a study on a movement organization should not be mistaken as a thorough analysis of the movement itself.[1]

The study of a movement's organizations is not necessarily the study of its structure. Every collectivity has a structure; not all have organizations. Social movements usually have both informal structures and formal organizations.

> The defining criterion of a formal organization . . . is the existence of procedures for mobilizing and co-ordinating the

---

1. Rudolph Heberle, *Social Movements* (New York: Appleton-Century-Crofts, 1951), p. 269.

efforts of various, usually specialized, subgroups in the pursuit of joint objectives.[2]

Because social-movement organizations are usually the focus of important movement decisions and activities, they are deserving of study regardless of the accuracy of their reflection of the movement itself. Nonetheless, they cannot be studied like ordinary organizations. First, they are often operating to change the society in which they originate, not adapt to its needs. Thus their environment is often a hostile one and creates organizational pressures unknown to less threatening groups. Second, the resource base of social-movement organizations is different. The numbers, kinds, and commitment of its supporters are all it ultimately has to rely on. Other organizations, especially voluntary ones, rely on these factors also, but rarely totally.

A social-movement organization's lack of legitimacy and its dependence on the kind of commitment of its social base inevitably make it much more a creature of its environment than a traditional organization. This environment is a dual one, consisting of both society at large and the movement's supporters in particular, and is often inconsistent in its demands.[3] Yet a social-movement organization is not solely a creature of its environment; it has its own internal dynamics, its own values, and its own structures. And, like most organizations, it is not ahistorical. The way an organization is structured in the beginning "loads the dice" not only for its goals, but also its strategy of how to attain them. Thus one must look at the process of growth and change of a social-movement organization as the result of three major influences: (1) the inherited values and norms of the

---

2. *International Encyclopedia of the Social Sciences* (1968), s.v. "Theories of Organization" by Peter Blau, 11: 298. See also Heberle, *Social Movements*, pp. 269–74.

3. For an analysis of the effect of the political environment on political parties, see Maurice Duverger, *Political Parties: Their Organization and Activity in the Modern State*, trans. Barbara and Robert North (3rd rev. ed.; New York: Barnes & Noble, 1959). For a more thorough examination of the role of the dual environment on a social movement, see Mayer N. Zald and Roberta Ash, "Social Movement Organizations: Growth, Decay, and Change," *Social Forces* 44 (March 1966): 327–41. See also John Hammond, "The Organization of Political Movements" (Manuscript, Chicago, 1969).

originators and the ways in which these cast the mold of the movement's future development; (2) the internal dynamics of the organization and the different subgroups within it; and (3) the environmental effects and structure of available opportunities for action.

Within the women's liberation movement, the National Organization for Women is the largest and most prominent organization. As such it is deserving of special study. When NOW was created in 1966 there appeared to be minimal foresight about its future direction. It was conceived of as a national, action organization, yet it was little more than a superstructure concentrated on the East Coast whose members contained few activists and fewer organizers. At the organizing meeting in Washington a statement of purpose and a national structure were hammered out. But these told less about its future than the nature of its roots. The women and men who formed NOW were knowledgeable about the legal, political, and media institutions of our country; they were not oriented toward constructing a social-movement organization.

Despite much talk about forming chapters and a realization that local organization would increase national influence, NOW lacked the resources, the knowledge, and in reality the interest to aim its efforts in this direction. It did not think of itself as a traditional organization, but, at least initially, it could function only within the limits of traditional pressure-group activity.

It is instructive to contrast NOW's founders with those of another social-movement organization begun about the same time—the National Welfare Rights Organization. Most of NWRO's initiators had been active in the civil rights movement; they were experienced movement people. They felt the organizational style of that movement had been a mistake that they did not want to repeat. Commented one welfare organizer:

> The civil rights movement was let down because it didn't have a grass-roots membership base and because it had to depend on liberal fundraisers. The movement had no real membership base, just small, scattered activist cadres. The

ghetto was never really involved in CORE and groups like
that. The philosophy of these groups was total action. They
had no grass-roots, no participation by the people
themselves.[4]

Consequently, the NWRO concentrated its energies on building
local membership groups and quickly developed a program of
local as well as national activity.[5] Even though the material
resources of its participants were considerably lower than those of
NOW, it was initially much more effective. Its organizers understood the nature of what they were working with—a social
movement—and how to mobilize its most valuable resource—
people.

Nonetheless, NOW's conceptualization created the potential for
development in a variety of directions, and only time and
circumstances could dictate in which of these it would go. The
founding statement of purpose articulated a general philosophy of
equality and justice under law, rather than specific areas for
action.

> . . . it is no longer either necessary or possible for women to
> devote the greater part of their lives to child-rearing; yet
> childbearing and rearing which continues to be a most
> important part of most women's lives—still is used to justify
> barring women from equal professional and economic
> participation and advance. . . . We believe that a true
> partnership between the sexes demands a different concept of
> marriage, an equitable sharing of the responsibilities of home
> and children and of the economic burdens of their support.
> . . . We are . . . opposed to all policies and practices—in
> church, state, college, factory, or office—which, in the guise
> of protectiveness, not only deny opportunities but also foster
> in women self-denigration, dependence, and evasion of
> responsibility, undermine their confidence in their own
> abilities and foster contempt for women.

---

4. Quoted in George T. Martin, "The Emergence and Development of a Social
Movement Organization Among the Underclass: A Case Study of the National
Welfare Rights Organization" (Ph.D. dissertation, Department of Sociology,
University of Chicago, 1972), p. 87.
   5. Ibid.

The statement also emphasized that "women's problems are linked to many broader questions of social justice; their solution will require concerted action by many groups." To research the need for specific actions, seven task forces were set up on: (1) discrimination against women in employment, (2) discrimination against women in education, and (3) discrimination against women in religion, (4) the family, (5) women's image in the mass media, (6) women's political rights and responsibilities, and (7) the problems of poor women. To handle NOW's administrative needs the office was moved from its temporary location in the Center for Continuing Education at the University of Wisconsin to Detroit, where it was run by Caroline Davis out of the United Auto Workers' Women's Committee.

NOW's activities for the next year reflected its limited origins more than its broad goals. Its main target was the executive branch where it sought to bend the might of federal power to the benefit of women. In its three main thrusts it scored an even 50–50: success in one, failure in another, and partial success in a third.

NOW's first action was to induce President Johnson to amend Executive Order 11246 which prohibited discrimination on the basis of race, color, religion, or national origin by all holders of federal contracts. In response to this and other pressures he signed Executive Order 11375, on October 13, 1967, amending the previous one by the addition of "sex" and also prohibiting sex discrimination in the federal government. This stroke of the pen began a battle between the Office of Federal Contract Compliance, set up to enforce the Order, and feminist groups to make the ruling a viable weapon against sex discrimination. It was not until January 14, 1969, that the OFCC published *proposed* guidelines to combat sex discrimination and not until eight months later that public hearings were held—in which the proposals were largely supported by women's groups. Nonetheless, the guidelines promulgated on June 9, 1970, were so seriously watered down that they seemed more harmful than helpful. Only six months before, the OFCC had issued Order 4, which outlined the requirements for affirmative action programs for contractors with goals and timetables to eradicate discrimination by race only. A secret memo had been prepared by the OFCC staff on administration of a sex discrimination program under the Order, but it was never issued. It was not until December 4, 1971, that Order 4 was properly revised and issued. Although NOW succeeded in having the original Executive Order amended to include sex, it took it much longer to teach the compliance agency how to read that amendment.[6]

Despite this "second-class" interpretation, on June 25, 1970, NOW filed a blanket complaint of sex discrimination against over 1,300 corporations receiving federal funds. The organization has also joined with the Women's Equity Action League in its effort to file complaints against all colleges and universities holding federal contracts.

NOW's initial success with the promulgation of the Executive Order was not matched in its continuing war with the Equal Employment Opportunity Commission (EEOC). Even before the organizing conference the temporary steering committee had fired off telegrams to the EEOC urging it to change its ruling that help-wanted advertisements listed under separate male and female columns was not a violation of Title VII. In the following months NOW added two more demands: (1) that the *bona fide occupational qualification (bfoq)* exemption of the EEOC not be interpreted so as to permit employers in states with "protective legislation" [7] to use those laws as rationales for denying equal job

---

6. Ann Scott and Lucy Komisar, *And Justice for All* (Chicago: National Organization for Women, 1971).

7. So-called "protective legislation" had been passed at the turn of the century in an attempt to curb sweatshop conditions. Originally intended to apply to both sexes, the Supreme Court declared a violation of the right to contract those laws which applied to both sexes, but allowed those that applied only to women on the grounds that women's "physical structure and a proper discharge of her maternal functions—having in view not merely her own health, but the well-being of the race—justify legislation to protect her" (*Mueller* v. *Oregon*, 208 U.S. 422 [1908]). Though the extent and kind of the protective laws differed by state, the bulk of them limited the hours a woman could work, usually to 48 per week, and the amount of weight she could lift on the job, generally to 35 pounds. Over the years the major use of "protective legislation" was to prevent women from earning overtime pay, promotion to jobs in which overtime might be required, and access to jobs which occasionally require lifting more weight than the limit. For an

opportunity, and (2) that the *bfoq* specifically not be interpreted to allow airline requirements that stewardesses must retire upon marriage or reaching age thirty-two. Hearings on these issues were held in May 1967 after much lobbying by NOW and eventually favorable rulings were obtained on the latter two demands.

The fight over the help-wanted advertisements has not yet been settled. Title VII does not specifically prohibit newspapers from having separate columns by sex or race. It prohibits employers from advertising in them. To facilitate this intention the EEOC early prohibited separate columns by race but allowed "male" and "female" headings to "indicate that some occupations are considered more attractive to persons of one sex than the other." [8] From the first angry telegram NOW actively pressured the EEOC to change its ruling in order to avoid an employer by employer legal battle to prove that each used separate columns in their advertising out of intent to discriminate. NOW had conferences with commissioners, wrote letters, and testified at the EEOC hearings. In December 1967, NOW organized perhaps the first contemporary feminist demonstration with a national day of picketing against the EEOC in New York, San Francisco, Pittsburgh, Washington, D.C., and Chicago. It also filed a formal complaint against the *New York Times*, and a mandamus suit against the EEOC to force it to comply with Title VII on February 15, 1968. Finally, on August 14, 1968, the EEOC ruled that separate want ads were a violation of Title VII and ordered newspapers to desegregate their want ads by December 1. The American Newspaper Publishers Association and the *Washington Star* promptly filed suit.[9] ANPA claimed that compliance would hurt job seekers, employers and newspapers, and the "newspapers

---

excellent analysis of the past and present role of these laws see Susan Deller Ross, "Sex Discrimination and 'Protective' Labor Legislation," in *The "Equal Rights" Amendment*, Hearings before the Subcommittee on Constitutional Amendments of the Committee on the Judiciary, U.S. Senate, 5–7 May 1970, p. 408.

8. EEOC guidelines, 22 April 1966.

9. *American Newspaper Publishers Association* v. *Alexander*, 294 F. Supp. 1100 (D.D.C. 1968).

and their advertisers are unwilling to depart so radically from a successful system." The newspaper publishers lost the first round but the district court did order the new EEOC guidelines suspended until an appeal could be decided. On October 22, 1970, ANPA asked the court to dismiss the case without prejudice. Although the guidelines remained intact, they were without force of law as the question of whether Title VII applies to newspaper columns was undecided.[10]

In the meantime, Pennsylvania adopted a Human Relations statute, and Pittsburgh a Human Relations ordinance, both of which specifically prohibited sex-segregated want ads. When the *Pittsburgh Press* failed to desegregate its advertisements, NOW filed a complaint in October 1969. On July 24, 1970, the Pittsburgh Human Relations Commission ordered the *Pittsburgh Press* to remove all sex labels from its help-wanted advertisements. With legal support provided by ANPA, the *Press* appealed all the way to the Supreme Court, losing each step of the way. In a 5–4 decision, the Court on June 21, 1973 rejected the *Press*'s argument that its right to establish its own help-wanted format was protected by Constitutional guarantees of freedom of the press. The Court made a distinction between free speech, which was protected by the Constitution, and commercial speech, which was not. Sex-segregated job advertising was not only commercial activity, but where prohibited, illegal commercial activity.[11]

However, this ruling applies only to newspapers in the close to thirty states that have state or local laws specifically prohibiting sex-segregated advertising. Several attempts have been made to broaden federal regulations to cover this area and all have failed. In *Brush* v. *San Francisco Newspaper Printing Co.*[12] it was argued that newspapers act as employment agencies within the definition used in Title VII via their help-wanted advertisements. The circuit

---

10. Elizabeth Boyer, "Help-Wanted Advertising—Every Woman's Barrier," *Hastings Law Journal* 23 (November 1971): 221.
11. *Pittsburgh Press Co.* v. *Pittsburgh Commission on Human Relations,* 93 S. Ct. 515 (1973).
12. 315 F Supp. 577 (N.D. Cal. 1970), affirmed 469 F.2d. 89 (9th Circuit, 1972).

court ruled otherwise. Attempts have been made to get the Federal Trade Commission to judge the segregated want ads as a deceptive trade practice, and to persuade the Internal Revenue Service to deny such advertising as a legitimate business expense. These were unsuccessful. Thus, despite EEOC and Court rulings, the legality of sex-segregated want ads remains unresolved.[13]

NOW's third initial target was much more recalcitrant than either of the other two. At that time Title VII permitted the Justice Department to enter suits where it felt there was a "pattern and practice" of discrimination, and many women's groups strongly urged it to file one on sex discrimination. But Justice was deaf to their pleas. It was not until July 1970 that it filed its first sex-discrimination case[14] and that one was settled out of court in what many feminists and EEOC staff members felt was a "sell out." [15]

Justice claimed its disinterest was because the EEOC referred only one case to them, but since they had an informal arrangement with the agency to decide jointly which cases they would file on before the EEOC referred them, it appears they did not want one. As late as the fall of 1969 their lack of political sensitivity to this issue was apparent in an interview the President's Task Force on the Status of Women had with one official of the Civil Rights Division. "We respond to social turmoil," he told them. "The fact that women have not gone into the streets is indicative that they do not take employment discrimination too seriously." [16] In 1972

---

13. Despite this confusion, many newspapers desegregated, partially because of local regulations prohibiting separate listing of want ads and partially because of feminist pressure. For example, in November 1968 New York City Consumer Affairs Commissioner Gerard M. Weisberg mailed letters to 956 New York City employment agencies saying that their licenses would be revoked if they violated the new ordinance. In part, however, the newspaper's compliance was due to NOW's consistent picketing of the venerable *Times*. To celebrate, NOW held a "thank-you" picket of the *Times* the day it desegregated. Jo Freeman, "The New Feminists," *Nation*, 24 February 1969, p. 243.

14. *U.S.* v. *Libbey-Owens, United Glass and Ceramic Workers of North America, AFL—CIO, Local No. 9.*

15. Judith Hole and Ellen Levine, *Rebirth of Feminism* (New York: Quadrangle, 1971), pp. 32–33.

16. Interview with Benjamin Mintz, Office of Civil Rights, Justice Department, October 1969.

Title VII was amended to give the EEOC power to go to court except in cases involving a government agency, and Justice's irresponsibility became irrelevant.

By NOW's Second Conference in November 1967, the organization had grown to 1,200 members and lines of tension were already apparent. As the only action organization concerned with women's rights, it had attracted many different kinds of people with many different views on what and how to proceed. With only a national structure and at this point no base, it was difficult for individuals to pursue their particular concerns on a local level; they had to persuade the whole organization to support them. Given NOW's top-down structure and limited resources, this placed severe limits on diversity, and in turn severe strains on the organization.

Diverse concerns came to a head when the 1967 conference proposed a Bill of Rights for women to be presented to candidates and parties in the 1968 elections. Six points called for enforcement of laws banning sex discrimination in employment; maternity-leave rights in employment and in social security benefits; tax deduction for home and child-care expenses for working parents; child-care centers; equal and unsegregated education; and equal opportunities for job training, housing, and family allowances for women in poverty. These presented no problem to the organization, but when women also proposed that support for the Equal Rights Amendment and repeal of all abortion laws be added, several members threatened to walk out.

Women from the United Auto Workers opposed inclusion of the ERA not because they were against it but because their union was. They said they would be forced out of NOW if the organization took a stand on the issue. Another group said they would walk out if NOW did not take a stand. When the ERA was added to the Bill of Rights, the UAW women did not resign, but did withdraw from active participation. This action cost NOW the use of the UAW office and clerical services, compelling relocation of the national office to Washington, D.C., and creating administrative chaos in the process. Two years later the UAW reversed their stand on the ERA, and the members of their Women's Committee resumed active participation in NOW.

The second major disagreement was over the inclusion of "reproductive issues." Several women had viewed NOW as an "NAACP type organization" and thought it should shun noneconomic or nonlegal issues. At this time abortion repeal was not a national issue, and its public discussion was considered controversial. Some NOW members thought abortion was not a woman's rights issue and support would only scare off potential financial contributors. Nonetheless, NOW supported abortion-law repeal, making it the first time "control of one's body" was stated as a woman's right. This action cost it its "conservative" wing a year later.

In the fall of 1968 the many disagreements erupted and NOW fissioned off several new organizations. The "conservatives" announced the formation of the Women's Equity Action League, which would concentrate on legal and economic issues, especially in the area of employment and education. Initially it was concentrated in Ohio and consisted primarily of friends of its founder, Dr. Elizabeth Boyer, who had also organized the Ohio NOW chapters.

The "radicals" left because of disagreements on structure, not program. By now the younger branch of the movement was becoming publicly known as was its disavowal of traditional structure. The "radicals," essentially from New York, wanted to replace what they felt was NOW's "elitist" structure with decision-making positions chosen by lot and rotated frequently. The rejection of this proposal represented not only preference for traditional forms of structure, but also a certain amount of fear of the New York chapter. It held over half the national membership, and was the most active and best known of all the chapters. To many, the New York chapter was NOW. To keep it from totally swamping the organization, there has never been a national conference in New York (such a conference was urged by the radicals at the time they proposed their structure changes). NOW chapters in other cities had gone through many false starts, forming, then collapsing in confusion and inactivity. Unlike New York, which had easy access to the national media and many people skilled at using it, the other chapters had difficulty developing programs not dependent on the media. As the national program was almost exclusively devoted to the support of legal cases or federal lobbying, the regional chapters could not fit easily into that either. By the fall of 1968, two years after NOW's founding, the chapters were beginning to get on their feet with local programs. They did not want to see the national organization taken over by New York.

As it turned out, New York did not like the proposed structure changes either, and a month later rejected a move to use them in the New York chapter. At this time the three strongest proponents of these changes walked out and formed the October 17 Movement (commemorating the day they left), a group eventually known as The Feminists. Although The Feminists started as a splitoff from NOW, most of their new members came from the younger branch of the movement, and the group became one of the more prolific sources of radical feminist ideas.

If the conservatives walked out over program and the radicals over structure, the third group to leave that fall departed from impatience. Since 1966 NOW had been trying to form a tax-exempt sister organization to handle legal cases modeled on the NAACP Legal Defense and Education Fund. In 1968 it was running into numerous problems, and two of the younger lawyers walked out in disgust. With them they took two of NOW's most important legal cases on which they had been doing the legal work under NOW's sponsorship.[17] Eventually these lawyers formed Human Rights for Women, a nonprofit, tax-exempt corporation to support sex-discrimination cases.

With the lawyers' departure also went the Washington office as

---

17. These were *Bowe* v. *Colgate-Palmolive Co.* 416 F.2d 711 (7th Cir. 1969) and *Mengelkoch* v. *Industrial Welfare Commission* 442 F.2d 1119 (9th Cir. 1971). Both were settled favorably. The Legal Defense Fund did not incorporate until 1971 and did not finally begin operation until June 1973. However, due to lack of funds it has not been able to initiate and support litigation on its own. Instead it has provided amicus briefs and minor financial support to some 40 cases on invitation.

they had been its prime volunteers. In an attempt to avoid a repetition of this problem the NOW office moved to New York and hired its first (poorly) paid staff member who serviced the organization out of her home. This was not the end of office problems, and in 1970 the membership service functions were contracted out to a newly created small business owned by two NOW members in Chicago so that mail could be answered, referrals made to chapters, and material distributed. As NOW's needs grew three national offices were added in 1973 with a total of 12–15 paid staff members: a legislative office in Washington in February, a public information office in New York in May, and an administrative office in Chicago in November. Since NOW's officers were usually spread around the country, this wide geographic distribution of functions made NOW very decentralized and often chaotic.

The next few years were spent putting together a grass-roots organization. Regional divisions were created and several regional directors, as well as many local chapter officials, spent countless hours recruiting people into NOW and encouraging the formation of new chapters. NOW also attempted to form liaisons with the younger branch of the movement. In November 1969, the first Congress to Unite Women was held in New York, and several others were held elsewhere during the next year. They were largely unsuccessful. Fraught with dissension, back-biting, and name-calling, they did not result in any umbrella organization to speak for the interests of all feminists. But this very failure portended some success as feminists from both branches—particularly NOW—began to realize that a diverse movement might be more valuable than a united one. The multitude of different groups reached out to different kinds of women, served different functions within the movement, and presented a wide variety of feminist ideas. Although they made coordinated action difficult, they allowed an individual woman to relate to the movement in the way most appropriate to her life. Fission began to seem creative as it broadened the scope of the movement without weakening its impact. The groups agreed to disagree and to work together where possible. As the various feminist groups became more tolerant of one another they also became more cooperative, and today most of the bitter enmity of the early years has long since been forgotten. Ties between the groups have increased and strengthened and those women who are members of both NOW and younger branch groups are no longer viewed with suspicion by either.

The first serious attempt at cooperation occurred when NOW initiated and largely organized the August 26 strike in 1970 to commemorate the fiftieth anniversary of the Nineteenth Amendment. Virtually every feminist group supported the strike in some manner or other. In some major cities, especially New York, younger branch groups were actively involved in its planning. This strike marked a turning point for the whole women's liberation movement. It was the first time that the potential power of the movement became publicly apparent; and with this the movement came of age. It was also the first time the press gave a feminist demonstration purely straight coverage. Weeks before they had been giving it a good deal of publicity but mostly because it was a slow summer for news and this appeared to be the most entertaining event of the season. Whether encouraged by the amount of publicity or angered by its tone of wry amusement, women turned out by the thousands in cities all over the country. The sheer numbers shocked everyone—including the organizers —and made it clear that the movement would now have to be taken seriously.

The idea for the strike had originally been a shock to NOW— and not a pleasant one. Betty Friedan announced it unilaterally in her farewell speech at the March 1970 convention. It got instant attention from the press and instant groans from NOW members who despaired of how ridiculous they would look when the majority of American women failed to strike.

Spurred by Friedan's announcement to do something, they first redefined the word "strike" from its usual sense to a "do-your-own-thing" strike. This made it possible for women to participate privately, in their own homes and offices, without having to take to the streets. It made many women conscious that something was happening of which they were a part.

The strike swelled the ranks of NOW tremendously—chapters often expanded as much as 50 to 70 percent. The new members tended to be younger than the original ones but did not come from the same strata as the younger branch of the movement. The latter, though young, had the same university education and professional background as the older branch. The new young women often did not have degrees and were embedded in the massive white-collar and clerical labor force. This influx of young NOW members helped relieve the tension between the two branches of the movement.

The newer members were also less likely to be career-oriented or even working women than the original NOW participants. Many were housewives, concerned with the emptiness in their own lives and worried lest the same fate befall their daughters. Such women preferred joining NOW to a women's liberation group partially because NOW was easier to find than the amorphous small groups and partially because it seemed more respectable. Many had previously formed their own suburban discussion groups and were looking for a way to make connection with the national movement. The publicity NOW received from the 1970 "strike" made it the most obvious place to go.

These new members brought with them different interests and different problems for the organization. They were less interested in working on job discrimination and more concerned with such projects as the media image of women and the portrayal of sex-role stereotypes in children's books. Several local groups eventually engaged in major analyses of stereotyping—though they have been less successful in pressuring for changes in sexist images than in pointing out their existence. They also brought new needs. Most had little more than a perfunctory acquaintance with feminism. They had been able to identify with it, but had not really understood it. Because many were not employed and did not have the tangible experience of job discrimination to direct their interest, they wanted to explore the meaning of feminism to their personal lives and personal relationships. They wanted to start "rap groups."

The function and operation of these groups is discussed in the next chapter. Suffice it to say here that as a phenomenon closely associated with the younger branch of the movement NOW's early members had viewed them with disdain. Many had thought them a "crutch" that young women who did not know their own minds needed before they "progressed" to political action. Thus it was with great reluctance that many NOW chapters set them up to "cater" to the needs of their newest members. The idea of "consciousness raising" as a significant activity was contrary to NOW's image of itself as an *action* organization. There was a great deal of fear that people's energies would be diverted to solving personal problems rather than attacking political ones.

Although set up primarily in response to members' demands, NOW chapters soon became convinced of the value of rap groups. They saw they helped women put their personal conflicts into political perspective and thus increase their awareness and understanding of feminism. They also alleviated the growing problem of having to educate new members who did not have a clear feminist perspective to the rationale of many NOW actions while simultaneously trying to plan and execute these actions. Older members had frequently complained of how time consuming it was to have to go over old ground with new members every time they wanted to do something. Rap groups served the function of feminist education as a prelude to feminist activity. Eventually many chapters institutionalized "C-R" into ten- and fifteen-week courses with specific discussion topics.[18]

Most of these new members had no previous experience in either political or voluntary organizations. Thus as NOW's expansion swelled its ranks, it proportionately decreased its share of trained personnel—in particular people who had any knowledge of the problems of running large organizations. As a general rule, the core of activists in a NOW chapter never gets much beyond 50, regardless of the size of the membership; and this point is usually reached when chapter membership reaches 200 to 300. Subsequently, the bigger a chapter gets, the greater proportion of its

18. The Los Angeles NOW Consciousness Raising Committee has even published a 60-page *Consciousness Raising Handbook* (May 1974).

time, energy, and finances goes into administration, and the less is left for action. Problems of communications, finance, and cohesion have been evident on both the local and national level.

Between 1967 and 1974 NOW went from 14 chapters to over 700; from 1,000 to 40,000 members. As it grew larger, the individual chapters began to feel more and more isolated. The national newsletter came out only quarterly, and occasionally not at all. Letters to the national office often did not get referred to the right official or even answered. Requests for material were backlogged for months and occasionally lost. Chapter presidents did not get the National Task Force Reports and thus were often unable to connect local task force projects with the national efforts. Chapters would find themselves duplicating one another's work, unaware of common efforts. A couple of times two separate chapters were started in the same city, each thinking it was the only one. Potential members could not find the local chapter and were not referred by the national office. Other people wanted to start NOW chapters, but could not find out how to. In general, the communications problem has increased geometrically with the membership. But it is only in part a natural result of size, as testified to by the more smooth functioning of many larger organizations. Much of the problem is due to

> the members' lack of experience: they have not been familiar with techniques for keeping themselves and others informed about what is going on. In addition, however, several other conditions have contributed: members' impatience to get involved in social action and their consequent failure to keep in touch with other parts of the organization; the chronic shortage of funds for mailings, telephone calls, or travel; the general acceptance of local autonomy; and, again, the near-absence of that small army of secretarial staff which, in many other organizations, keeps communication channels operating smoothly.[19]

NOW began as a national structure and in many ways remains

---

19. Maren Lockwood Carden, "The New Feminist Movement," 1972. Typewritten, p. 303.

one. Local chapters have sprung up almost incidentally, usually through the efforts of local people, not national organizers. They continue to function very autonomously from one another. What has not been developed adequately is a set of middle-level structures to connect national efforts with local ones. This is not due to lack of trying, however. In 1970 four regional directors were elected to coordinate activities in their own area and organize chapters. They had no staff, no budget, no expense allowance, too much territory, and too much work. Close to thirty national task forces have been created to attempt to coordinate local efforts so that individual projects can combine a national thrust with instrumentation on the local level. In 1972 state organizations began to develop, initially as a result of ERA ratification efforts. They now exist in roughly half the states, but with widely varying structures, power, and acceptance.

Despite these problems, NOW manages to function rather well because its members make up for its organizational deficiencies. Because the quarterly newsletter was inadequate, a board member personally began a second one to suggest specific activities for chapters and report on how individuals could make waves locally. Other members have developed extensive "kits" on how to form chapters, file discrimination complaints, pressure the media and advertisers to change their sexist images of women, how to lobby, and even how to write letters. Local newsletters report on national activities by setting up exchanges with similar publications. And many local and national officials put a great deal of their own time and money into NOW activities. Individual enthusiasm substitutes for organizational efficiency.

Nevertheless, there is still a good deal of conflict and misunderstanding between local and national NOW. As in the younger branch of the movement, these conflicts are rarely expressed in political terms. More frequently they are manifested in personal attacks. National board members are accused of drawing up national programs without adequate participation of local chapters or to the disregard of local interests. Chapters are especially aggravated when national officials make demands on them for information about local activities without reciprocating. Criticisms that national officials are "self-seeking," "cliquish," and do not draw upon the talents of the whole membership are common. There is a certain degree of truth in these complaints. Officers do not see themselves as NOW's "staff" whose job is to service the chapters, but as political activists. They feel they are representatives of the NOW membership specifically and feminists generally, and ought to be able to rely on that membership's support of their activities in the movement's behalf. Both the national's and the chapters' expectations of the other are out of line with reality.

> The causes of this intergroup conflict . . . lie with . . . each side's misunderstanding of the other's situation. Neither side has thoroughly appreciated the other's role in the organization. Local chapters, preoccupied with their own activities, see national's function as one of providing information, advice and support. For their part, the national board members have seen themselves primarily as activists and only secondarily as people who facilitate the operation of the whole organization. The problem is aggravated by a general failure to appreciate each other's urgent need for money. Local groups do not understand why national complains that dues of $10.00 per person is a hopelessly inadequate sum when their own groups are managing on proportionally far smaller budgets. The national board members, preoccupied with their own activities tend to overlook the great expenses incurred at a local level. . . .[20]

These conflicting perspectives are especially evident in the feelings by many chapters that they do not get adequate "services" from the national office for their $10 per member annual dues. They complain that the Chicago office is inefficient, there is a lack of national direction, and that national board members are "elitists" with no conception of grass-roots activities. The past president of one 600-member chapter even declared that because "the national dues are too high, there is no incentive to increase membership." She explained that, regardless of chapter growth, the activist core stayed the same. The $5 local dues they

---

20. Carden, "The New Feminist Movement," pp. 321–22.

charged (for a total of $15 per year per member) barely paid the cost of mailings to local members; it did not leave enough for other chapter expenses. Beyond a certain point the declining margin of utility of new members was sharp. Recruitment generated more money for the national NOW but only more work, not more workers, for the local chapter. Given the feelings of estrangement from national NOW, this chapter felt, they saw no reason to help it at their expense.[21]

The view of many national officials is that this interpretation is self-seeking and short-sighted. In the "Report of the Finance Vice-President to the NOW National Conference" of May 1974, Gene Boyer deplored

> attitudes toward the national organization which view it as a super Jewish mama from whom all goodies and chicken soup supposedly flow. "What have you done for me lately?" is the question I hear directed at Super-Mama from members, chapters, states and regions. Yet, I believe that the greater the self-reliance, independence and autonomy of the local units, the stronger and healthier the organization will be . . . and this is the reverse of the child-like posture of seeking national mother-love.[22]

The report asserted that 1973 per capita income from membership dues was only $8.50—down $.50 from 1972—and that the cost of membership services had gone up to close to $6 per person, leaving very little for action programs.[23] In fact, although income went up significantly between 1972 and 1973, the percentage of the budget spent on action programs decreased from over 25 percent to less than 18 percent, while the percentage allocated for membership services and administrative expenses increased concomitantly.

Nonetheless, Boyer characterized 1973 as the year in which

---

21. Interview with Roberta Benjamin, Boston NOW, 7 February 1973.
22. p. 17.
23. Ibid., p. 2. The fact that per capita income from dues is lower than the national dues charged "may reflect an increase in low-income members electing the 'special' dues of $5 each, or of chapters' failing to transmit full national dues for each member."

NOW "graduated from a seat-of-your-pants operation to 'big business.' " [24] NOW's budget has grown astronomically in its short life; from $6,888.38 in 1967, its first full fiscal year, to $99,505.93 in 1972 and $293,499 in 1973. In 1974, $430,000 was budgeted for general expenses in addition to two special funds for ratification of the ERA ($140,750) and work on reproductive issues ($34,900).

The obvious solution to the squeeze between member resources and organizational needs is to find other means of raising money—which NOW has only begun to do. For the first three years, all of NOW's budget came from dues. In 1970 it began some fund-raising activities, and there were some independent contributions; but in 1972 these totaled less than $20,000, and in 1973 only $34,000. NOW also began to seek foundation financing for special projects through its Legal Defense and Education Fund, and has received or been promised several small and moderate grants totaling $237,550 for general LDEF operating expenses, an ad campaign to combat sexism, and a Washington office to monitor the enforcement of federal laws prohibiting sex discrimination in education.

During 1973 and 1974 NOW launched five direct-mail campaigns to solicit additional funds. Two appeals for special funds for the support of ERA ratification effort and reproductive issues were quite successful. Two other mailings to selected feminist lists to recruit members provided adequate returns for the expense. The one failure was a membership solicitation to 30,000 subscribers of *Redbook* and *McCalls*, magazines geared to homemakers. Despite the influx of housewives into NOW over the last few years, it appears that feminism still has its greatest appeal to the employed woman.

This pattern could be seen in a sample survey of 500 NOW members made in early 1974. Of the 383 replies, only 17 percent listed homemaker as their primary occupation, even though 55 percent were married. Sixty-three percent were employed full-time and another 15 percent part-time, but only 36 percent made

24. Ibid., p. 1.

over $10,000 a year. Students made up 14 percent of the membership, teachers 11 percent, and 25 percent were professionally employed. Despite the fact that clerical workers make up 35 percent of the employed female population, they were only 8 percent of the NOW membership.

As would be expected, the NOW membership was highly educated. Sixty-six percent had bachelor's degrees, and 30 percent also had advanced degrees. Nonetheless, almost half were under age thirty and over two-fifths were between the ages of thirty and fifty. Racially, 5 percent were black, and 5 percent fell into other nonwhite categories.

If one could generalize from these figures, the NOW member of 1974 resembles very closely that population described in Chapter 1 as experiencing the greatest amount of relative deprivation—highly educated and professionally employed. The NOW membership has diversified in its short history, but the only significant departure from its original profile is its increasing youth.

This increasing youth has accompanied a change in style. While still relying on bylaws and Robert, Rules of Order to conduct organizational business, NOW has consciously sought to incorporate the person-centered attitude of the younger branch of the movement into its activities. NOW has never been autonomous from the rest of the movement. Over time it has become even less so. Its membership has always had a liberal orientation—62 percent of the NOW survey said their political philosophy was liberal and 9 percent said it was radical left—and it has been very susceptible to the influence of the younger branch of the movement. In the last two years many feminists from the younger branch have overcome their initial prejudice against NOW and have themselves become members. Twelve percent of those replying to the NOW survey were still members of other specifically feminist organizations. This is in part due to problems within that branch of the movement, discussed below, which made political action within it difficult. NOW was often the only feminist *action* organization available, even if its image was somewhat conservative. Too, as is often the case in other situations, greater contact between the two branches increased familiarity, and in turn decreased prejudice. Radical feminists began to view NOW as "pragmatic" rather than "reformist" and thus acceptable as a concomitant arena of activity along with their other, "radical" activities. NOW was OK in its place. Consequently, NOW has moved over time from being the main older branch organization to being the main feminist organization. It has become very much an umbrella group for all kinds of feminists, even those whose primary loyalty lies elsewhere. The resultant overlapping membership has brought into NOW new ideas and new conflicts.

Local chapters have always been fairly autonomous, despite the central control implied by the national bylaws. Thus they have been free to initiate organizational experiments and very free to develop local projects. This kind of flexibility has been felt necessary because NOW is purely a voluntary organization and finds it can encourage more participation if members can work in the ways they find most comfortable. For several reasons, later recruits to NOW have objected to its hierarchical organization and the authoritarian sound of the bylaws which dictated officers, elections, etc. Many new chapters just disregarded the national-proposed structure and created their own. The Berkeley chapter, for example, has three convenors, which divide up among themselves the usual duties of chapter officers. Several chapters have co-presidents. Even those chapters that have not restructured themselves have absorbed the basic ethic of participatory democracy from the younger branch and in turn have made demands on chapter leadership that are not always compatible with greatest organizational efficiency.

The creation of rap groups was one such demand—though it is not yet apparent whether their formation did siphon off energy from action as feared by older NOW members or saved time by separating those who were ready for actions from those who were not. Another such demand, though rarely explicitly stated, is that leaders spend a lot of energy on maintaining good personal relations, and that members' behavior in meetings have a wider range of tolerance than that common to formal business meetings. "Loose" chairing of meetings, unstructured and occasionally irrelevant discussion, expression of personal feelings and enthusiasm, avoidance of authoritarian or domineering styles, and decision making by consensus as much as possible have become more and more characteristic of NOW over time under the label of feminist-humanism.

> Such activities take up a great deal of time, emotional energy, and individual forbearance. Thus, boards of officers, committees and task forces must all accept as necessary long, tiring decision-making sessions. . . . More than in other organizations, the NOW leader is seen as someone who facilitates decision making and who can *legitimately* be sanctioned if she tries to force her ideas on the group. Similarly, while NOW may make as many decisions by vote as does any normal committee or board of directors, in principle it rejects the assumption that "one side must win" for the assumption that, with sufficient effort invested, a compromise acceptable to all can be found.[25]

These changes mean that an increasing proportion of the organization's energy goes to maintaining the organization—to creating a comfortable environment for its members to work, to grow personally, to develop individual skills and talents; often to the sacrifice of at least short-run efficiency. This sacrifice is justified on the grounds that as much as possible NOW should practice the humanistic principles that it preaches. Feeling that women have too long been "kept down" by domineering men and oppressive structures, they do not want to repeat the phenomenon in their own organization. This viewpoint is adopted directly from the younger branch of the movement, but it found ready acceptance among the new recruits to NOW as they were unfamiliar and uncomfortable with organization and power. A more personal and more personable environment made them feel more at home. This style is not entirely uncontested,[26] but a debate over organizational approach has not yet become a major one.

---

25. Maren Lockwood Carden, *The New Feminist Movement* (New York: Russell Sage Foundation, 1974), pp. 130–31.

26. Beverly Jones, "Toward A Strong and Effective Women's Movement (The Chambersburg Paper)," Hershey, Pa., January 1973. Mimeographed.

Nevertheless, differences in approach underlay the frustrating, conflict-ridden convention of 1974. It was the first time NOW faced a contest for president of the organization, and members got an experience very different from what they expected. People came to NOW conventions to celebrate, not politic; they wanted to go to issue workshops, talk to feminists from around the country, exchange ideas, and gather material. Instead they found themselves tied up in endless plenary sessions enduring parliamentary maneuvers and repeated balloting for officers.

Two radically different interpretations of those events were expressed in the New York State and Chicago chapter newsletters—home bases of the two major presidential candidates. From the New York group:

> Upon arrival in Houston New York State NOW members, who had not endorsed any officer or Board candidates, discovered that the Illinois candidate for President had running with her a slate of persons for various offices and the Board. Position papers which violated the spirit (and very likely the letter) of the campaign rules reflected these candidates' positions, although in many instances the position papers were trite reiterations of NOW policy. Additionally, a special NOW button was given only to supporters of this slate, making those persons easily identifiable. Campaign strategies, including queuing up at the microphones, were carefully planned.[27]

And from Chicago:

> At many points during the conference, appreciation of skill—whether in leadership, organizing, successful action, or even knowledge of the organization—was rejected in favor of glorification of amateurism and anti-leadership rhetoric. The Chicago chapter, known for its skill, accomplishments, leaders, and real dedication to NOW, was viciously attacked for working hard and openly for candidates who campaigned on issues. In fact, it was also an attack on positive programs,

---

27. Eileen Kelly, "Coming of Age in Houston," *New York State* NOW (newsletter), July/August 1974, p. 2.

on leadership, and on the vital position of strong chapters in the organization and their rights. Clearly, when this kind of irresponsible attack takes place, fear, distrust, and manipulation win out and NOW suffers. . . . Throughout the weekend, guilt politics and abstract discussion about "changing the mainstream" got more conference attention than how we go about winning rights for women.[28]

These contrasting views are symptomatic of two problems characteristic of a changing organization composed of inexperienced people. First, the Chicago group made the serious tactical error of failing to understand their constituency. Although led by some of the most organizationally experienced NOW members, it was not adequately sensitive to the individualistic value structure of the current NOW population, and thus violated many people's ideas of legitimate campaign behavior.

Social movements by their very nature are amateurish, precisely because they depend upon the commitment of volunteers to get their work done. Many NOW members, influenced by the participatory ethic of the younger branch, found the existence of an organized, relatively efficient (by NOW standards) subgroup, knowledgable about traditional political and parliamentary tactics, to be a threat. They felt the potential was there for control, whether it was intended or not.

This fear was exacerbated by the second problem: Since NOW had never faced a situation like this before, and since most of its members had had little experience in other political organizations, it had no basis for making rational assessments of others' behavior. Every organization develops a set of informal ground rules about the limits of permissible activity which are rarely spelled out in the bylaws. With time and a sense of continuity appropriate expectations are defined and passed on to new members. NOW had not had an opportunity to develop such rules and expectations. Consequently, people tended to overreact and read the most ominous intentions into the Chicago group's activities.

---

28. Anne Ladky, "From the President," *Act* NOW, June 1974, pp. 8–9.

Because NOW is issue-conscious, different groups tried to read ideological differences into the conflict. There was no consistency among these interpretations, however; they were superimposed upon what was essentially a conflict of styles. Despite the discord, it was fortunate that NOW's political coming of age occurred in this manner. The fact that it was a conflict of style and not of ideology precluded serious issue polarization and thus the possibility of a split. While most attendees were dismayed by the 1974 convention, it was a necessary and valuable experience for the organization.

NOW has not had severe conflict over issues since 1968. Nonetheless, it has consistently moved in a more radical direction. The August 26 strike compelled the movement to define its goals narrowly for the first time. Until then, the whole history of the movement had been one of broadening its scope and narrowing its immediate goals—a very necessary process for any social movement. The strike was centered around three central demands—abortion on demand, twenty-four-hour child-care centers, and equal opportunity in employment and education. These were not viewed as the sole ends of the movement, merely the first steps that must be taken on the road to liberation. At the same time, as NOW task forces and members explored the ramifications of women's situation, they gained a broader conception of just how integrated are all social phenomena. By its fifth convention in the fall of 1971, NOW was ready for a major expansion of concerns and numerous resolutions were passed giving a feminist position on a multitude of subjects—such as the war—not directly related to women. This move was anticipated by the original Statement of Purpose, NOW's early support of the guaranteed annual income, and its concern with women in poverty. Nonetheless, it was a major break with the past. Task force activities similarly increased their scope. In its 1973 convention, NOW was even following the lead of the younger branch of the movement in taking positions favoring the decriminalization of prostitution; the investigation of "fundamental questions concerning the structure of society premised on profit and competition"; and setting up further task forces on such topics as older women, women in sports, and rape. It also resolved "that a major organizational effort be mounted immediately within NOW on behalf of the needs of *all* minority persons, and that . . . actions be undertaken toward elimination of structures, policies, and practices that contribute to racism within NOW."

The increasing broadening and "radicalization" of NOW's objectives has not met with serious dissent within the organization since the splits over abortion and the Equal Rights Amendment that marked its first two years. There are several reasons for this:

1. There is an inherent logic to feminism. Once one adopts the feminist perspective on the world, it is very easy to apply it to an ever-widening circle of issues; one can analyze all aspects of society, and easily come to the conclusion that all of society must be changed. The relevant questions then become where to begin and what to do first—and these are strategic, not ideological, questions.

2. NOW has always been a liberal organization.[29] Its members, and especially its leaders, have thought of themselves as being in the forefront of social change. Many of the older women in it have thought of themselves as "radicals" even if they did not actually use the word. They often complained bitterly about being called "reformists" by the younger feminists because such an appellation was contrary to their self-image. NOW was very open to moving "left" because it represented an extension of its basic liberal humanitarian values. As old issues, such as the ERA and abortion, became socially acceptable, it deliberately looked for new ground to break.

3. Although there is no sharp ideological distinction between the older and younger branches of the movement, the latter does operate as an ideological vanguard. Here, new issues and new interpretations are first raised and legiti-

---

29. Patricia Bayer Richard, in her 1972 Syracuse, New York, study of "The Feminist Movement: Parameters of Participation" (Paper given at the 1974 meeting of the Ohio Association of Economists and Political Scientists), found that members of NOW and other feminist organizations shared the same liberal values, lack of religious commitment, general nonconventionality, and openness to change.

mated. With the domination of the feminist media by the younger branch, and the increasing overlap of membership between the small groups and NOW, these newer concerns are easily transferred; what began as a debate within the radical underground feminist media eventually emerges as a NOW resolution. This transference is facilitated in part because of the common middle-class composition of both branches of the movement, and the many personal and friendship relationships that link participants on both sides. Like it or not, their members share a common culture, a common background, a common education, and consequently, a common interpretation of the meaning of feminism.

A good example of this radicalization is the NOW position on lesbianism. In 1969 and 1970 Betty Friedan was using McCarthy scare tactics to "purge" NOW of what she called the "lavender menace." Through a series of almost accidental events she had concluded that lesbians were trying to take over the organization. Although she succeeded in driving many lesbians out of the organization and others back into the closet, NOW's 1971 convention passed a resolution declaring that "a woman's right to her own person includes the right to define and express her own sexuality and to choose her own lifestyle; therefore we acknowledge the oppression of lesbians as a legitimate concern of feminism." By 1973 NOW had held a workshop on lesbianism at its convention, established a Task Force on Sexuality and Lesbianism, and passed a resolution declaring that as "women have the basic right to develop to the maximum their full human sexual potential," NOW should therefore "actively introduce and support civil rights legislation to end discrimination based on sexual orientation . . . in areas such as . . . housing, employment, credit, finance, child custody, and public accommodations." This did not happen because NOW had been taken over by lesbians, or even because there was any overwhelming interest within the organization in lesbianism. Only 8 percent of the NOW survey claimed they were homosexual and 9 percent said they were bisexual. The 1973 convention workshop on marriage, family, and divorce, presumably of greater interest to heterosexuals, had

had the largest attendance of any, 600. The NOW resolution was the aftermath of a three-year discussion of the relation between feminism and lesbianism in the feminist media, the small groups, and many NOW chapters. Although many NOW members still felt that lesbianism was not a feminist issue and that NOW's support would only tarnish its image, the resolution was adopted because lesbianism had been defined as a civil rights issue and a women's issue, and because support was the liberal, humanistic thing to do.

NOW's major problems have not been ideological but structural; how to develop grass-roots activity with national coordination, how to have national policy without alienating the membership, how to allocate limited resources, how to get money, how to operate efficiently, etc. These problems reflect the classic dilemma of social-movement organizations: the fact that the tightly organized, hierarchical structures necessary to change social institutions conflict directly with the participatory style necessary to maintain membership support and the democratic nature of the movement's goals.

The major analysis of this dilemma stems from the work of Weber and Michels.[30] This model claims that as an organization obtains a base in society, a bureaucratic structure emerges and a general accommodation to the society occurs.[31] The bureaucrats acquire a vested interest in maintaining their position within the organization and consequently the organization's place within society. This concern with organizational maintenance inevitably leads to conservatization and oligarchization. Yet, as Zald and Ash point out,[32] this does not necessarily have to be the only outcome. NOW's radicalization does reflect an accommodation, but so far it is an accommodation to its feminist environment, not to its social one. This is largely due to the ideological pull of the younger branch. Without this influence NOW might not be able to resist conservatization.

---

30. *From Max Weber: Essays in Sociology*, ed. H. J. Gerth and C. W. Mills (New York: Oxford University Press, 1946). Robert Michels, *Political Parties* (Glencoe, Ill.: Free Press, 1949).

31. F. Stuart Chapin and John Tsouderos, "The Formalization Process in Voluntary Organizations," *Social Forces* 34 (May 1956): 342–44.

32. Zald and Ash, "Social Movement Organizations," p. 330.

The fact that a social movement is a curious protean medley of structure and spontaneity creates a set of unique problems for any social-movement organization. The drive toward pure rationality, with its concomitant hierarchy, specialization of function and routinization, which characterizes the ideal bureaucratic organization, is often counterproductive for a social-movement organization. Lacking material resources with which to reward its participants, it must rely on other kinds. Clark and Wilson outline three major types of incentives available to organizations, and classify organizations according to whether the ones they use are primarily material (money and goods), solidary (prestige, respect, friendship), or purposive (value fulfillment).[33] Most social movements use a combination of purposive and solidary incentives—although material ones are not necessarily excluded. Its major incentive is purposive—the promise that a desired social goal will someday, somehow, be reached. Because these goals are often remote and delayed gratification usually insufficient, the ongoing incentives are solidary ones. Yet they are a peculiar kind of solidary incentive. Contrary to Hoffer,[34] it is not merely the opportunity to "belong" that is valued, but the opportunity to be part of a group that shares one's values and will validate one's often deviant perspective on the world. One can "belong" to most any social group by appropriate adaptive behavior; it is the reinforcement of self that is valued.[35]

A social movement's primary resource is the commitment of its members. It must rely on their own enthusiasm and dedication to its goals to get work done. Participants in a social movement do not do things because they have to, they do them because they want to. This is why NOW can function quite well despite its rampant insufficiencies. The dependency on membership commitment means that maintaining morale and motivation is a

33. Peter B. Clark and James Q. Wilson, "Incentive System: A Theory of Organization" *Administrative Science Quarterly* 6 (June 1961): 129–66.
34. Eric Hoffer, *The True Believer* (New York: Harper & Bros. 1951).
35. Ada Finifter, "The Friendship Group as a Protective Environment for Political Deviants" (Paper given at the convention of the American Political Science Association, Washington, D.C., September 1972).

prime need of any social-movement organization. It takes a lot of its energy and determines a lot of its activities. Hammond[36] draws the distinction between "instrumental" action and "consummatory" action; the former is strictly goal oriented, the latter is determined by group-maintenance needs. A social movement must necessarily use both; in fact, the more it relies on solidary incentives, the more consummatory its activities will be as the pleasure of participation is all it has to offer. A corollary to this is that the more remote are its goals, the greater the role of solidary incentives and the more consummatory its actions. Thus consummatory activities, though superficially unrelated to a movement's goals, may be indirectly instrumental. The major problem a movement organization faces is to keep from degenerating into solely consummatory activities on the one hand, or rationalizing itself into too rigid a structure on the other and in so doing alienating its membership. Its major task is manipulating the incentive structure to recruit and mobilize its members for instrumental action. It is the tension between the needs of goal achievement and those of group maintenance which are at the root of the conflict between the oligarchic and democratic tendencies discussed by Michels.

---

36. "Organization of Political Movements," p. 3.

4
The Small Groups

THE YOUNGER BRANCH OF THE MOVEMENT DOES not have any prominent organizations, but it is organized. Like many other similar movements, it has an infrastructure which "can be characterized as a network—decentralized, segmentary, and reticulate." [1] Its basic unit is the small group of from five to thirty women held together by an often tenuous network of personal contacts and feminist publications. These groups have a variety of functions but a very consistent style. Their common characteristics are a conscious lack of formal structure, an emphasis on participation by everyone, sharing of tasks, and the exclusion of men. The thousands of sister chapters around the country are virtually independent of one another, linked only by numerous publications, personal correspondence, and cross-country travelers. They form and dissolve at such a rate that no one

---

1. Luther P. Gerlach and Virginia H. Hine, *People, Power, Change: Movements of Social Transformation* (Indianapolis: Bobbs-Merrill, 1970), p. 33.

can keep track of them. With time and growth the informal communications networks have partially stratified along functional lines, so that within a single city participants of, say, a feminist health clinic, will know less of different groups in their own area than other health clinics in different cities.

A few cities have a coordinating committee which attempts to maintain communication between the local groups and channel newcomers into appropriate ones. Many more cities have women's centers which also provide places for meetings, classes, informal gatherings, and emergency assistance to individual women. Neither centers nor coordinating committees have any real power over group activities, let alone group ideas, and most small groups are not associated with them anyway.

This conscious lack of hierarchy means that the groups share a common culture but are politically autonomous. Even within the groups the lines of authority and the process of decision making are often diffuse and hard to discern. The groups are not purely democratic, and there is usually a power structure, but only occasionally is it an overt one with elections, voting, and designated authoritative positions.

Membership in the movement is purely subjective—the participants are those who consider themselves participants—and not always accompanied by membership in a small group. Some of these groups require dues or, more often, regular attendance at meetings and participation in the common tasks. These requirements are not determinant of movement participation, however, as it is easy to quit one group and join another or even start one's own. Thus there is no mechanism of regulation over a participant's behavior other than peer-group pressure. The movement can neither be directed, controlled, nor even counted. Given its decentralized, segmentary, reticulate nature, the younger branch of the movement can best be described as a social system rather than a political organization.

The creation of a diffuse social system rather than a political movement was not consciously in the minds of its originators, but it was an inevitable consequence of the values, assumptions, and experiences that they brought with them. The values came largely from the radical movement's interpretation of basic American concerns.[2] Their concepts of participatory democracy, equality, liberty, and community emphasized that everyone should participate in the decisions that affected their lives, and that everyone's contribution was equally valid.[3] The values led very easily to the idea that all hierarchy was bad because it gives some people power over others and does not allow everyone's talents to develop. The belief was that all people should be able to share, criticize, and learn from one another's ideas—equally. Any kind of structure, or any kind of leader who might influence this equal sharing, was automatically bad.[4] The logical conclusion of this train of thought—that all structure and all forms of leadership are intrinsically wrong—was not initially articulated. But the potential was clearly there and it did not take long for the idea of leaderless, structureless groups to emerge and eventually dominate this branch of the movement.

The adherence to these values was premised on the assumption that all women were equally capable of making decisions, carrying out actions, performing tasks, and forming policy.[5] These assumptions could be made because the women involved had little experience in democratic organizations other than those of the New Left where they saw dominance for its own sake, competition for positions in the leadership hierarchy, and "male ego-tripping" rule the day.[6] They had felt similar domination and control for its own sake in the social structures—primarily school and family—they had been part of. The idea that there was some relationship between authority and responsibility, between organ-

2. Daniel C. Kramer, *Participatory Democracy: Developing Ideals of the Political Left* (Cambridge, Mass.: Schenkman, 1972).

3. Linda Lewis and Sally Baideme, "The Women's Liberation Movement," in *New Left Thought: An Introduction*, ed. Lyman T. Sargent (Homewood, Ill.: Dorsey Press, 1972), p. 83.

4. Martha Shelley, "Subversion in the Women's Movement, What Is to be Done," *off our backs*, 8 November 1970, p. 7.

5. Lewis and Baideme, "The Women's Liberation Movement," p. 87.

6. Marge Piercy, "The Grand Coolie Dam," in *Sisterhood Is Powerful*, ed. Robin Morgan (New York: Random House, 1970). Robin Morgan, "Goodbye to All That," *Voices from Women's Liberation*, ed. Leslie Tanner (New York: New American Library, 1970).

ization and equal participation, and between leadership and self-government was not within their realm of experience. This is evident in the following argument:

> All women have the ability to make decisions, be creative, and to recognize that each woman's personal experience must be taken into account in every decision. Further, since the ultimate goal is a completely cooperative and equal society, our organizations must reflect that now. Direct participation is not as smooth running or as "efficient" as a structured hierarchical process, because it requires flexibility and a willingness to struggle to understand the many positions on particular issues or problems. Only in this way can the policy decided upon be the fairest and most inclusive. To say that this has been and is still difficult is an understatement. Women's Liberation groups often find themselves in a state of disarray and factionalism because there is no one leader to guide the way. However, in the larger society where the few control and determine decisions, the outcome is seldom beneficial to those directly concerned, even though the process may be more efficient. Our "efficient" system has gotten us gross inequality of the races and sexes, an alien, inhuman, technological society, destruction of the environment, and never-ending war.[7]

Early Growth and Conflicts

These conclusions were more assumed than discussed in the first national gatherings of the embryonic movement in 1968. It was never decided that there would be no structure or leaders, but none was ever set up. The first meeting in Sandy Springs, Maryland, was attended by twenty-two women primarily from the six cities then known to have women's liberation groups (New York, Boston, Chicago, Washington, D.C., Baltimore, and Gainesville, Fla.) in August of that year. It was intended to be a clarification of the main issue of the moment: should the movement remain a branch of the radical left or be an

---

7. Lewis and Baideme, "The Women's Liberation Movement," p. 93.

independent women's movement? There tended to be a rough correlation between people's political background and their initial stand on this split. Those from the New Left favored remaining within the radical fold and those from civil rights and related pasts favored independence. Proponents became known as "politicos" or "feminists" respectively and traded arguments about whether "capitalism was the enemy," or the male-dominated social institutions and values. They also traded a few epithets with politicos calling feminists politically unsophisticated and elitist, while in turn being accused of subservience to the interests of left-wing men.

The only major agreement to come out of the Sandy Springs meeting was to hold an open national conference in Chicago the coming Thanksgiving. Four women from different cities volunteered their time to arrange it.[8] Working from a borrowed office and mimeograph supplied by Washington's Institute for Policy Studies, a nonprofit foundation which supported many radical projects, they sent out notice of the convention less than a month before it was to begin. Nevertheless, over 200 women attended from 20 states and Canada, most of whom had not previously been involved in women's liberation. There the growing diversity of the movement became apparent as well as its exponential growth. Discussions were intense, disagreements sharp, and debates often discouraging, but the women returned to their cities turned on by the *idea* of women's liberation, to organize more and more groups.

The burgeoning influx of large numbers of previously apolitical women eventually settled the question as an independent, autonomous women's liberation movement developed irrespective of the efforts of politicos or feminists. The unremitting hostility of radical men also convinced many politicos that that was not where their true interests lay, and others left women's liberation for radical organizations. Though the spectrum shifted to the feminist direction, the basic difference in orientation still remained.

---

8. They were Marilyn Salzman Webb, Washington D.C.; Charlotte Bunch, Cleveland, Ohio; Laya Firestone, Chicago; Helen Kritzler, New York.

Politicos also called themselves feminists, and many left the Left; but most saw women's issues within a broader political context[9] while the original feminists continued to focus almost exclusively on women's concerns. Although much of the bitterness of the original dispute eventually subsided, politicos generated such distrust about their motives that they prejudiced many women against all concerns of leftist ideology. This led some feminists to the very narrow outlook that the politicos most feared they would adopt.

Another early disagreement—which did not overlap with the politico-feminist split—was over what to call the new women's groups. These discussions occurred primarily in New York and Chicago and centered around the preferability of "radical women" or "women's liberation." The former was favored by most politicos as they were women radicals whose identity was tied up with the idea of "radicalism" and who wanted to develop the concept of being radical as a woman, not just a woman who was a radical. Since many feminists in New York also thought that the term "women's liberation" was too much an imitation of politico jargon, the factions there agreed jointly to call themselves New York Radical Women. Women in Seattle likewise adopted the name Seattle Radical Women as did several developing groups elsewhere. In Chicago most favored "radical women" but the opposition was staunch enough to lead to a compromise on Cadres of Women—which no one liked because of the acronym (COW).[10]

The advocates of "women's liberation" liked the term not so much because of its implied identification with Third World and

---

9. After several years, the politico viewpoint metamorphized into the socialist-feminist faction in the movement. However, only in Chicago did this faction predominate. From its formation in December 1969, the primary younger branch organization, the Chicago Women's Liberation Union, required all members to agree with a statement that they would "struggle against racism, imperialism, and capitalism and dedicate ourselves to developing consciousness of their effect on women."

10. In December 1972 a group in New York adopted the name *Community of Women* precisely because they liked the acronym. Their newsletter was initially called "The Udder Side" and later "The Cowrie."

black liberation movements, but because they wanted to define the terms of debate in what they saw as a potentially significant movement. They had been educated by the misunderstandings created by the referent "the Negro problem" which inevitably structured people's thinking in terms of "the problem with Negroes" rather than racism and what to do about it. They were also aware of the historical "women question" and "Jewish question" which led to the same mistake. The problem, they felt, was not one of women, but of women's liberation and the best way to get people to think of the problem in those terms was to label it as such from the very beginning.[11]

These were the people who first conceived the idea of starting a national newsletter for the miniscule movement, and one of them was the first editor. The first issue came out in March 1968 as three mimeographed sheets of paper with no name. Its tag line labeled it "the voice of the women's liberation movement." By the second issue, three months later, it had grown to four sheets offset, and the new editor had elevated the tag line to the name. Under a different editor each issue, the *Voice of the women's liberation movement* served as the main vehicle of communication for the growing movement for the next sixteen months. It represented the national movement to most women receiving it and from it they picked up and used the name. "Women's liberation" became more and more frequent an appellation and "radical women" receded into the background.

Initially, the term "women's liberation" applied only to the younger branch of the movement. Organizations such as NOW considered themselves a part of a women's movement, but not a women's liberation movement. Gradually, however, more and more NOW people and other women not associated with one of the small groups adopted the name until today it has a generic meaning. Some feminists still do not like to be thought of as part of women's liberation and some of the latter do not like the term

---

11. Unfortunately, they did not anticipate that "liberation" would be caricatured as "lib," "libbie," and "libbest" and contribute to the women's movement, like women, not being taken seriously.

feminist, but for most, the two are synonymous. This dual use of the term women's liberation has created some confusion as most of the small groups have no specific names. It is occasionally difficult to tell whether "women's liberation" refers to the whole movement or just to its younger branch.

The original newsletter ceased publication in June 1969, but during its short life it was one of the most useful organizational tools of the movement. Adopting an expansionist policy, its revolving editors gave most issues away free to anyone indicating any interest whatsoever in the women's movement and placed many on bookstore shelves. It was financed by donations, some subscriptions, unpaid labor, and the sale of women's liberation literature at exorbitant prices.[12] Its purpose was to reach any potential sympathizer in order to let her know that there were others who thought as she did and that she was not isolated or crazy. It also functioned to put women in contact with other like-minded women in the same area and thus stimulated the formation of new groups. To do this, all mail had to be answered whether it was simply requests for literature, contacts, or for advice on organizing, as well as news and articles solicited for subsequent issues. This grew to be a herculean task. The *Vwlm* grew from 200 copies the first issue to 2,000 the seventh and last; from 6 pages to 25. It was finally killed because the work of keeping it up had grown too big to handle and because the then editors thought no "national newsletter could do justice to the role of 'voice' at the present time." [13]

At the time of its death there were no other major movement publications apart from an occasional local journal. Three months later, the first women's liberation newspaper, *off our backs*, was published in Washington, D.C. The number of feminist papers and journals increased rapidly thereafter. To date there

---

12. One of the early clashes of women's liberation with the radical movement occurred when the New England Free Press decided to publish women's liberation pamphlets at very low prices. While this made these materials available to a greater public, it undercut the financial base of the newsletter, which was not highly appreciated.

13. *Voice of the women's liberation movement* (*Vwlm*), June 1969, p. 25.

are over 150, and many more were started but did not survive.[14] None of the papers is national in scope though they borrow from one another freely. Magazines range from scholarly to popular to propagandistic, with the majority being literary in nature. Some have a policy of printing literally everything they receive, in the belief that all women have something to say and should be given the opportunity to see their work in print. Some are as exclusive as any professional journal.

Media Hostility

In part this multitude of publications was started out of disillusionment with the commercial press and in the belief that only movement publications would give the movement fair coverage. Young feminists had been hostile to the press from the beginning—significantly more so than other social movements. Some of this fear was traceable to inexperience as even those women with a political background had not done press work before. Much more derived from watching how inaccurately the press had reported the social movements and student protests in which they had previously been active. Unlike blacks, for example, young white women had grown up believing that the press was as objective as it liked to portray itself. When their political experiences made them conscious of the gross discrepancies between what they saw at a particular demonstration and what was reported, they withdrew from any press contact in disgust. Blacks, on the other hand, had never had any illusions about who controlled the press, and saw the media as a tool to be used. Women had wanted to relate to reporters honestly; when the results were not what they expected, they chose not to relate at all.

Most of the media compounded this problem by treating early women's liberation activities with a mixture of humor, ridicule, and disbelief. Some of these early activities did seem funny on the

---

14. *New Women's Survival Catalog* (New York: Coward, McCann and Geoghegan, 1973) lists 163 feminist publications.

surface. Yippies had utilized zap actions and guerrilla theater as a respite from the boring ineffectiveness of mass marches. Women's liberation picked up on this idea as a way of making a political point in an unusual, eye-catching manner. The first major public action, at the 1968 Miss America Contest, featured a "freedom trash can" into which bras, girdles, false eyelashes, and other instruments of female oppression were tossed, and a live sheep was crowned Miss America. This impulse was furthered by the spread of WITCH covens (Women's International Terrorist Conspiracy from Hell) to hex objects of local ire after the first incantation on Wall Street in the fall of 1968 was followed by a five-point drop in the stock market.

Some reporters looked at the serious side of these actions, but most only laughed. Whereas reporters had examined the political message underneath the Yippie spoofs, they just glanced at the surface of the women's actions and used them to illustrate how silly women were.[15] The press treated women's liberation much as society treats women—as entertainment not to be taken seriously.

If they thought it would be funnier, newspapers even made up their own actions, of which the "bra-burning" episode is the most notable. There has yet to be a woman in women's liberation to burn a single bra publicly, but this mythical act was widely reported in the press.[16] "Bra" stories and related nonincidents usually got front page coverage, while serious stories on employment discrimination were always on the women's page. Photographers inevitably depicted feminists with unattractive poses or facial expressions. Reporters commented on interviewees' femi-

---

15. This was not true in all countries. When the Dolleminas of Holland whistled at men on the streets and held other similar actions, their local press was much more sympathetic; but there was a firmer tradition behind these acts. The Provos there had developed the idea of *ludik* actions to a fine art. These actions were intended to make people laugh, but always carried a political message. The press became accustomed to looking for the politics and carried this over to reporting *ludik* actions by women.

16. For details of how this myth developed, see Joanna Foley Martin, "Confessions of a Non Bra-Burner," *Chicago Journalism Review* 4 (July 1971): 11. It should be remembered that draft-card burning was much in the news those days, and many other things were going up in smoke.

ninity, marital status, or style of dress more than their views. Editors ordered production to "get the Karate up front" and writers to "find an authority who'll say this is all a crock of shit." [17] Underground and New Left papers were often the worst of the lot, frequently running women's liberation stories illustrated by naked women and exaggerated genitalia.[18]

Women's liberation dealt with the conflict between desire for coverage and dislike of misrepresentation by refusing to speak to male reporters. First established at the Miss America contest, this practice soon became an informal rule everywhere, and has only partially broken down. There were two main reasons behind this policy, but it had even more unexpected benefits. The first was to compel the media to hire more women reporters and to give others opportunities to do news reporting usually denied to women. The second was to get better coverage. Young feminists had discovered that even sympathetic men were often incapable of understanding what they were talking about because men simply had not had the same experiences as most women. They did not, for example, understand women's anger at being sex objects. With women reporters feminists could communicate their concerns through discussion of experiences common to women that were incomprehensible to men. And in these early stages anecdotes on such experiences were the main means of articulating women's grievances; the ideas had not yet been refined into specific issues.

Even women reporters covered the early movement only with difficulty. Most young activists would not talk to them at all as they saw no value in distorted coverage in the commercial press. Those who would consent to be interviewed often required anonymity and frequently demanded the right to edit the final copy (which was of course denied). Reporters were tossed out of women's liberation meetings when discovered; hung up on when

---

17. Sandie North, "Reporting the Movement," *Atlantic Monthly*, March 1970, p. 105.

18. Sometimes women retaliated. In 1969, Berkeley women held hostage an editor of a new underground newspaper, *Dock of the Bay*, until he agreed to stop publication of a special "sextra" issue planned to raise money for the new paper.

they phoned; saw their notes grabbed from their hands and destroyed at rallies; had their microphones smashed, their cameras threatened, and their films stolen.[19] They also found some sympathetic feminists who would talk to them at length, give them reams of material to read, arrange interviews and group discussions for their benefit, and direct them to good sources of information.

The immediate results of these policies were seen not so much in the quality of the news stories as in their numbers. There was something intriguing about the very difficulty of covering the new movement. Further, the idea that *men* were being excluded from something, especially male *reporters,* generated much more interest than women normally get. People were *curious* why *men* were excluded; and if the stories ridiculed feminists for discriminating, many women read between the lines and flocked to join. Female reporters joined also. Initially skeptical, they often found themselves much more involved in the ideas of the movement than they intended. What many thought would be an ordinary story turned out to be a revelation.

In the fall of 1969 the major news media simultaneously began to do stories on women's liberation, and they appeared steadily for the next six months. Quickly discovering that only women could cover the movement, they tried to pick reporters known for their objectivity and unfeminist views. It made no difference. Virtually all the initial stories in *Time, Life, Newsweek,* etc., are personal conversion stories. These stories had as much effect on the media as they did on the movement. Women writers, researchers, and even secretaries became conscious of their secondary role on their publications and began protesting for better conditions and forming their own small groups.[20]

---

19. North, "Reporting the Movement."

20. *Newsweek* in particular illustrated all these phenomena. The original person assigned to the story was a young writer being "given her chance." Her piece was criticized for unobjectivity, rewritten by a male writer, and finally dropped. In her place a free-lancer who happened to be the wife of one of *Newsweek*'s senior editors was hired. She was paid in advance, specified no undue editing, and wrote the most personal report of all. Despite the fact that it was quite different from

Male Exclusion

The exclusion of male reporters was in conformity with the general policy of excluding men from all movement activities. Initially, this was one of the most controversial aspects of the movement to the outside world, but it was and is one of the most uncontroversial within the movement itself. There was virtually no debate on this policy in any city at any time. Originally the idea of exclusiveness was borrowed from the Black Power movement, much in the public consciousness when the women's liberation movement began. It was reinforced by the unremitting hostility of most of the New Left men. Even when this hositility was not present, women in virtually every group in the United States and Canada soon discovered that the traditional sex roles reasserted themselves in groups regardless of the good intentions of the participants. Men inevitably dominated the discussions, and usually would talk only about how women's liberation related to men, or how men were oppressed by the sex roles. In segregated groups women found the discussions to be more open, honest, and extensive. They could learn to relate to other women and not just to men.

Women continued the policy of male exclusion because they felt men were largely irrelevant to the development of the movement. They wanted to reach women, and found it both frustrating and a waste of time to talk to men. Of course many did talk to men, usually on an individual basis, and many men eventually formed their own groups around the problem of the male sex role.[21] Initially, women's liberation discovered that there was a tactical value in male exclusion. As with the exclusion of male reporters, their activities were taken much more seriously

---

Newsweek's usual style, it was printed. In the meantime, women staffers had watched these developments with great interest and made plans of their own to commemorate the occasion. They chose the day of the special issue's publication to announce their complaint of discrimination filed with the EEOC.

21. Warren T. Farrell, "Women's and Men's Liberation Groups" (Paper given at the 1970 Convention of the American Political Science Association; idem, *The Liberated Man* (New York: Random House, 1974). NOW eventually formed a Masculine Mystique Task Force, headed by Farrell, which held its first convention in New York on June 8–9, 1974.

when they insisted they wanted to speak only with women. The tactic had shock value. A good example, followed many times more, was the organization of a women's discussion group at the August 1968 National Student Association convention at the University of Kansas. To arouse interest in the meeting women stood at the cafeteria lines passing out leaflets to women only. When the man in a couple unthinkingly reached for one, they made a deliberate point of giving it to the woman. When a man took the leaflet from the woman with him, it was taken from him and returned to the woman. The men were indignant, the women curious, and of course everyone wanted to know what the leaflet said. The real purpose of this technique was not to keep men from reading the innocuous leaflet but to catch people's attention and make them think. This it succeeded in doing. It also solved the litter problem; no leaflets were left laying on the floor.

A variation on this theme was used by the sellers of *Notes from the First Year*, a mimeographed magazine of early feminist thought. It sold for $.50 to women and $1.00 to men. One reason for this was that the authors wanted to reach women, thus preferring to keep the price low, but felt men ought to be charged for the privilege of reading the magazine if they insisted on it. They fully realized that a man could get a woman to buy a copy for him at the lower price. That was the second purpose. It was a form of political education to demonstrate to men and women the discomforts of having to go through someone else to fulfill one's desires or needs. It illustrated the true nature of the female role by reverse example as well as the high price of independence.

Rap Groups

The basic form of political education of women came not through the literature, but through the "rap groups." [22] In these, women explore personal questions of feminist relevance by

22. For a thorough elaboration on the function and operation of the rap group, see Pam Allen, *Free Space: A perspective on the small group in women's liberation* (New York: Times Change Press, 1971).

"rapping" to each other about their individual experiences and analyzing them communally. Unlike the male-exclusion policy, the rap groups did not develop spontaneously or without a struggle. The political background of many of the early feminists predisposed them against the rap group as "unpolitical;" and they would condemn discussion meetings which "degenerated" into "bitch sessions." Other feminists saw that the "bitch session" obviously met a basic need. They seized upon it and created an institution. Over time it became the most prevalent activity of the younger branch of the movement. It was easy to organize, required no skills or knowledge other than a willingness to discuss one's own experiences in life, and had very positive results for the women involved in it.[23]

The rap group serves two main purposes. One is the simple process of bringing women together in a situation of structured interaction. The "radical community" served this function in the formative days of the movement, but when the movement outgrew the Left there was no natural social structure equivalent to the factory, the campus, or the ghetto for maintaining interaction among women. The rap group is an artificial institution which provides some degree of structured interaction. This phenomenon is similar to the nineteenth-century development of a multitude of women's clubs and organizations around every conceivable social and political purpose. These organizations taught women political skills and eventually served as the primary communications network for the spread of the suffrage movement. Yet, after the great crusade ended, most of them vanished or became moribund. The rap groups are taking their place and may serve much the same function for the future development of this movement.

Nevertheless, they do more than just bring women together, as radical an activity as that may be. The rap groups have become

---

23. Their use has been adopted by other movements, in particular Gay Liberation. See Kevin J. Burke and Murray S. Edelman, "Sensitivity Groups, Consciousness-Raising Groups and the Gay Liberation Movement" (Paper given at the 1972 convention of the American Political Science Association).

mechanisms for social change in and of themselves. They are structures created specifically for the purpose of altering the participants' perceptions and conceptions of themselves and society at large. The means by which this is done is called "consciousness raising." [24] The process is very simple. Women come together in small groups to share personal experiences, problems, and feelings. From this public sharing comes the realization that what was thought to be individual is in fact common; that what was thought to be a personal problem has a social cause and a political solution. The rap group attacks the effects of *psychological* oppression and helps women to put it into a feminist context. Women learn to see how social structures and attitudes have molded them from birth and limited their opportunities. They ascertain the extent to which women have been denigrated in this society and how they have developed prejudices against themselves and other women. They learn to develop self-esteem and to appreciate the value of group solidarity.

It is this process of deeply personal attitude change that makes the rap group such a powerful tool. "Correct consciousness" is a need of all movements, but it usually does not require such a profound resocialization of one's concept of self. Most women find this experience both irreversible and contagious. Once one has gone through such a "resocialization," one's view of oneself and the world is never the same again, whether or not there is further active participation in the movement. Even those who "drop out" carry the ideas with them and pass them on to their friends and colleagues.

While the rap groups have been excellent techniques for changing individual attitudes, they tend to flounder when their members have exhausted the virtues of consciousness-raising and decide they want to do something more concrete. Some groups

---

24. This technique evolved independently of, but is similar to, the Chinese revolutionary practice of "speaking bitterness." William Hinton, *Fanshen* (New York: Vintage Books, 1966). See also Nancy McWilliams, "Contemporary Feminism, Consciousness-Raising, and Changing Views of the Political," in *Women in Politics*, ed. Jane S. Jaquette (New York: Wiley, 1974), pp. 157–70; and Gerlach and Hine, *Movements of Social Transformation*, pp. 135–36.

take on specific projects, such as working on day care; some constitute themselves as organizer cells and set up other groups; some become study groups and delve more thoroughly into feminist and political literature; most just dissolve and their members look for other feminist activities to join. Because the groups are small and uncoordinated they take up small tasks that can be handled on a local level. Women have set up centers, abortion counseling services, bookstores, liberation schools for teaching courses on women, day-care centers, film and tape production units, research projects, and rock-and-roll bands.[25] Production of a feminist publication is one of the most feasible for a small group to handle, which is one reason why there are so many of them. Development of a project is never the result of any national coordination or planning and thus reflects only the opportunities, needs, and skills of the women engaged in it.

Problems of Structurelessness

This laissez faire philosophy of organizing has allowed the talents of many women to develop spontaneously and others to learn skills they didn't know. It has also created some major problems for the movement. Most women came into the movement via the rap groups; and most go out from there. There is no easy way to move from a rap group to a project; women either stumble onto one or start their own. Most don't do either. Once in a project, participation often consumes enormous amounts of time.[26] The problem is that most groups are unwilling to change their structure when they change their tasks. They have accepted the ideology of "structurelessness" without realizing the limitations of its uses. The rap-group style encourages participation in

25. In the spring of 1973 Susan Rennie and Kirsten Grimsted spent two months visiting movement projects around the country. They found roughly: 163 publications; 18 pamphlet publishers and/or printing coops; 23 rape squads; 5 film coops; 116 women's centers; 35 health clinics or projects; 6 legal services clinics; 6 feminist theater groups; 12 liberation schools; 18 employment services; 12 bookstores; and 3 craft stores. *New Woman's Survival Catalog.*

26. See Jane Mansbridge, "Time, Emotion and Inequality; Three Problems of Participatory Groups," *Journal of Applied Behavioral Science* 9 (May 1973): 351–68.

discussion and its supportive atmosphere elicits personal insight; but neither is very efficient in handling specific tasks. This means that the movement is essentially run, locally, by women who can work at it full time.

Nationally, the movement is not run by anyone, and no public figure commands obedience from any part of it. But because the movement has not chosen women to speak for it, believing that no one could, the media has done the choosing instead. This has created a tremendous amount of animosity between local movement "leaders" (who would deny that they are leaders) and those often labeled "leaders" by the media.

While it has consciously not chosen spokespeople, the movement has thrown up many women who have caught the public eye for varying reasons. These women represent no particular group or established opinion; they know this and usually say so. But because there are no official spokespeople or any decision-making body the press can query when it wants to know the movement's position on a subject, these women are perceived as the spokespeople. Within the movement these women were labeled "media stars" and were often denounced for "making it off the oppression of their sisters." This problem was an inevitable result of having an antileadership ethic in a publicly attractive movement. It had two negative consequences for both the movement and the women labeled "stars."

First, because the movement did not put them in the role of spokesperson, the movement cannot remove them. The press put them there, and only the press can choose not to listen.[27] Thus it is

---

27. A good example of both press "election" and "impeachment" is Kate Millett. She and Shulamith Firestone both published the first new feminist theoretical books within a month of each other (September 1970). Through a combination of Millett's publisher (Doubleday), her own personal predisposition, and *Time* magazine's plan for a special movement issue to coincide with Women's Strike Day (August 26, 1970) her picture appeared on *Time*'s cover. This "established" her as *the* first feminist spokeswoman after Friedan, and subjected her to very severe criticism from the movement. When she subsequently, at a feminist conference, publicly declared herself to be bisexual, *Time* announced that she was now discredited as a movement leader. No movement group had a role in either her ascendancy or dismissal. (*Time*, 14 December 1970, p. 50.)

the press rather than the movement which has control over the selection of national feminist "leaders" as long as the movement believes it should have no representation at all.

Second, from 1969 to roughly 1971 (and still somewhat today), women who acquired any public notoriety for any reason were denounced as "elitists." This name-calling and other forms of personal attacks were the only means of control available to the movement because it had consciously rejected overt structure. As in any group or movement there were certainly power- and fame-hungry individuals who found the movement an excellent opportunity for personal advancement; but in their fear of manipulation, feminists often failed to make a distinction between those who were "using" the movement and those who were "strong" women or had valuable talents. Although the attacks were initially aimed at "media stars," their scope widened to the point that some felt that any individual who had "painfully managed any degree of achievement" was victimized.[28] "Elitist" eventually became used as frequently and for much the same purpose as "pinko" was used by anticommunists in the 1950s. As a result, some of the most talented women in the movement withdrew from it entirely, bitterly alienated. Others remained in, but isolated. Removed from the reaches of group pressure, they were no longer responsible for what they publicly said to anyone but themselves. In June of 1970, women from several cities who had had this experience found themselves coincidentally in New York, and upon comparing notes, sardonically called themselves the "feminist refugees." [29] Thus the movement's greatest fear became a self-fulfilling prophecy. The ideology of "structureless-ness" created the "star system" and the backlash to it encouraged the very kind of individualistic nonresponsibility that it most condemned.

---

28. See especially Anselma Dell'Olio, "Divisiveness and Self-Destruction in the Women's Movement," originally given as a speech in the Congress to Unite Women, New York, Spring 1970. Subsequently appearing in the newsletter of the Chicago Women's Liberation Union, August 1970.

29. Judith Hole and Ellen Levine, *Rebirth of Feminism* (New York: Quadrangle, 1971), p. 161.

Although this ideology damned the idea of leadership, the movement was and is not without leaders in the sense that some people influenced group decision making and activities more than others. Any group of people inevitably structures itself on the basis of the friendship networks within it. If such a network within a larger group is composed of people particularly interested in that group, who share common ideas and information, they become the power structure of the group. And like the "media stars," because the group did not select them as leaders, it cannot remove them. The inevitably exclusive nature of informal communications networks of friends is neither a new phenomenon characteristic of the women's movement, nor a phenomenon new to women. Such informal relationships have excluded women for centuries from participating in integrated groups of which they were a part. In any profession or organization these networks have created the "locker room" mentality and the "old school" ties which have effectively prevented women as a group, as well as many men individually, from having access to the sources of power or social reward. Much of the energy of past women's movements has been directed to having the structures of decision making and the selection processes *formalized* so that the exclusion of women could be confronted directly. It is particularly ironic that the women's movement should inflict upon itself a problem it had been fighting for centuries. Given the movement's ideals, the problem of covert power structures was often exacerbated. When informal elites are combined with a myth of "structurelessness" there can be no attempt to put limits on the use of power because the means of doing so have been eliminated. The groups thus have no means of compelling responsibility from the elites that dominate them. They cannot even admit they exist.

Since movement groups have made no concrete decisions about who shall exercise power within them, many different criteria were and are used around the country. Sometimes the criterion for participation in the elite is adherence to a particular narrow ideological line. Usually, there is conformity to some traditionally female characteristics. For instance, in the early days of the movement, marriage to New Left men was frequently such a prerequisite. This standard did have some reality behind it, however, as the New Left men often had access to resources needed by the movement—mailing lists, printing presses, contacts, and information. While this has altered through time, all informal elites have standards by which only women who possess certain material or personal characteristics may join. They often include: class or educational background, marital or parental status, sexual preference, life style, age, occupation, and especially attractiveness of personal style. As Mansbridge has pointed out, this pattern is not restricted to the women's movement but is common to all groups that stress participatory democracy. "In a participatory system, political resources thus are shifted to the more other-directed. The member who is not subtle or empathic in his relations with people is at a disadvantage in a participatory group." [30]

These and other criteria all have common themes. The characteristics prerequisite for participating in the informal elites of the movement, and thus for exercising power within it, concern one's background, personality, or allocation of time. They do not include one's competence, dedication to feminism, talents, or potential contributions to the movement. The former are the criteria one usually uses in determining one's friends. The latter are what any movement or organization has to use if it is going to be politically effective.

This is not to say that such groups are never effective; merely that effectiveness is often incidental to the functioning of the group. Occasionally, the developed informal structure of the group coincides with an available need that the group can fill. There are almost inevitably four conditions common to such groups:

> 1. It is task oriented. Its function is very narrow and very specific, like putting on a conference or putting out a newspaper. It is the task that basically structures the group. By determining what needs to be done and when it needs to

30. Mansbridge, "Problems of Participatory Groups," p. 358.

be done, it provides a guide by which people can judge their actions and make plans for future activity.

2. It is relatively small and homogeneous. Homogeneity is necessary to ensure that participants have a "common language" of interaction. People from widely different backgrounds may provide richness to a consciousness-raising group where each can learn from the others' experience, but too great a diversity among members of a task-oriented group means only that they continually misunderstand one another. Such diverse people interpret words and actions differently. They have different expectations about the others' behavior and judge the results according to different criteria. If everyone in the group knows one another well enough to understand these nuances, they can be accommodated. Usually, they only lead to confusion and endless hours spent straightening out conflicts no one ever thought would arise.

3. There is a high degree of communication. Information must be passed on to everyone, opinions checked, work divided up, and participation assured in the relevant decisions. This is possible only if the group is small and people practically live together for the most crucial phases of the task. Needless to say, the number of interactions necessary to involve everybody increases geometrically with the number of participants. This inevitably limits group participants to around five, or excludes some from some of the decisions. Successful groups can be as large as ten or fifteen, but only when they are in fact composed of several smaller subgroups which perform specific parts of the task, and whose members overlap with one another so knowledge of what the different subgroups and doing can be passed around easily.

4. There is a low degree of skill specialization. Not everyone has to be able to do everything; but everything must be able to be done by more than one person in order for no one to be indispensable. To a certain extent, people must become interchangeable parts.

These ideal circumstances do not occur often,[31] and when they

---

31. An excellent analysis of one group which appears to meet these criteria is Kennette Mari Benedict, "The Organizational Structure of Participatory Democ-

do, they too tend to coincide with friendship networks. This coincidence is not an accidental one as recruitment into the younger branch is largely through friendship networks and the principles upon which participatory groups operate are largely the norms of friendship;[32] yet when friendship becomes the primary basis of organization, it carries with it several consequences.

1. There are no means of directing participants' energy into productive tasks, or of easily finding people to perform necessary functions. Rap groups are very easy for individuals to form. One can put up a notice on a bulletin board, advertise in the newspaper, or merely pass the word among one's friends. Task groups are not created so easily; especially when one must do so from scratch. It is much more difficult to find and put together the necessary people and to find the necessary resources for one's purposes. A movement that requires every group to start anew does not make it possible for people to build off of others' experiences. Thus the end of consciousness raising leaves women with no place to go and the lack of structure leaves them with no way of getting there. Some just "do their own thing." But the direction into which individual women and/or groups go is determined more by the accident of what's available than by design. This can lead to a great deal of individual creativity, much of which is useful for the movement, but it is not a viable alternative for most women. Many just drift out of the movement entirely because they do not want to develop an individual project and they have found no way of discovering, joining, or starting group projects that interest them.

2. Participatory groups frequently must become closed to new members because of the time and emotional investment required to build up the trust, acceptance, and mutual

racy in the Feminist Movement: A Case Study of the Palo Alto Women's Coalition" (M.A. thesis, Department of Political Science, California State University, San Francisco, May 1974).

32. Jane Mansbridge, "The Limits of Friendship," *Nomos XVI: Participation* (New York: Lieber-Atherton, 1975).

understanding necessary for their successful functioning. But a closed group controlling a project, service, or publication of value to the movement is in effect an oligarchic enclave within the movement. While it can be fairly said that a segmentary, reticulate social structure does not create movement-wide oligarchies, it creates many local ones. Decentralized oligarchies are still oligarchies, and still have all the problems of exclusiveness and emphasis on group maintenance that centralized oligarchies have.[33] Rotation of leadership is minimized and accountability reduced.

3. The need to maintain good interpersonal relationships characteristic of a participatory group tips the balance against instrumental action. A tremendous amount of the participants' time and energy must necessarily be spent on group process rather than group ends. Often group process becomes the group's end. While this greater personal investment in the group can heighten one's commitment to its goals, it also lessens the time and energy available to pursue them. Groups remain together purely for the purpose of remaining together.

4. The incentive structure of the movement becomes heavily weighted in favor of solidary incentives. This in turn favors consummatory activities rather than instrumental ones. In the early days of the movement a major activity was "zap actions" (e.g., witch hexes). These have ceased, to be replaced by service projects. Many of these are useful and interesting, but they are hardly a substitute for political action. Since they are autonomous rather than part of a national political structure, they cannot even function to recruit and channel new members into the action groups that do exist. "The total effect of such actions is comparable to that of the Lady Bountiful of earlier centuries. Individual women's problems will be alleviated for the time being, but no lasting change is produced." [34] The emphasis on service projects does not result solely from the nature of participatory groups. It also reflects an inexperience with and alienation from the traditional forms of political activity, the

---

33. Robert Michels, *Political Parties* (Glencoe, Ill.: Free Press, 1962).
34. Carden, *The New Feminist Movement*, p. 78.

"delegitimacy" of direct-action protest that accompanied the decline of the civil rights and student movements, and the inheritance from its radical roots of the goal of "revolution." The latter led many to believe that *any* cooperation with the "system" was reformist and therefore wrong. Service projects could be set up as "alternative institutions." The paradox of filling holes within the "system's" services as a form of radical activity was not noted by many. The fact that an emphasis on service projects is not purely a result of a decentralized, segmentary structure is illustrated by their predominance in Chicago, Seattle, and the few other cities that have not adhered to the idea of "structurelessness" and have adopted citywide organizations. Nonetheless, service projects are a logical outcome of a primarily solidary incentive system, whether the emphasis on such incentives comes from the remoteness of goals (i.e., revolution) or the greater maintenance needs of a participatory group.

A style of movement organization stressing decentralized, segmentary, participatory groups has both advantages and disadvantages. On the one hand, it is politically inefficacious, exclusive, and discriminatory against those who are not or cannot be tied into the friendship networks. Those who do not fit into what already exists because of class, race, occupation, education, parental or marital status, personality, etc., will inevitably be discouraged from trying to participate. Those who do fit in will develop vested interests in maintaining things as they are. The informal groups' vested interests are sustained by the informal structures that exist, and come to monopolize most of the existing "niches" of movement activity. Concomitantly, the power that they exercise within the movement, while less than that in a centralized organization, is also less responsible.

On the other hand, the very fact that many women are excluded from movement "niches" compels innovation from those who want to relate to it somehow. Its segmentary nature also encourages proliferation, adaptation, and responsiveness to its environment.[35] While expertise is devalued and much labor is

---

35. Gerlach and Hine, *Movements of Social Transformation*, pp. 49–50.

replicated, these aspects in turn create opportunities for individuals to play organizational roles and learn skills that would be limited in a centralized organization. It is not by accident that this branch of the movement has developed several ideological perspectives, much of the terminology of the movement, an amazing number of publications and "counter-institutions," numerous new issues, and even new techniques for social change. The emphasis of this branch has been on personal change as a means to understand the kind of political change desired, and its contribution has been its creativity, not its effectiveness.

As long as the major concern of this branch could be personal change, it did not have to face the problems created by its structure. But from about 1971, consciousness-raising as a major movement function started to become obsolete. As a result of the intense press publicity and the numerous "overground" books and articles that began circulating, women's liberation became a household word. Its issues were discussed and informal rap groups formed by people who had no explicit connection with any movement group. Ironically, this subtle, silent, and subversive spread of feminist consciousness caused a situation of political unemployment. Educational work no longer was such an overwhelming need. Service projects could be only part of the answer. What the movement desperately needed was some sense of direction.

The problem was how to get it. One result of the movement's style was a very broad-based creative movement, to which individuals could relate pretty much as they desired with no concern for orthodoxy or doctrine. Another was a kind of impotency. On a local level most groups could operate autonomously, but the only groups that could organize a national activity were the nationally organized groups. Such groups as NOW, WEAL, and some leftist women's caucuses were the only organizations capable of providing national direction, and this direction was determined by the priorities of these organizations. NOW, for example, organized the August 26, 1970 strike, and in doing so brought many groups into a temporary coalition. WEAL initiated and coordinated the complaints about sex discrimination against colleges and universities filed with the Department of Health, Education, and Welfare. And the Young Socialist Alliance, youth affiliate of the Socialist Workers party, tried to direct the energies of the small groups into mass rallies, demonstrations, and abortion-law repeal.

The SWP/YSA Crisis

The SWP/YSA caused one of the most serious crises within the younger branch of the movement, and also threatened such groups as NOW. The SWP was formed as a Trotskyist split from the Communist party in 1925. A democratic centralist organization, its originators remained in tight control until they began to die off in the mid-1950s. At this time there were at best 1,500 members around the country and the SWP was just one of several small sectarian leftist groups. In the late 1950s, the growing number of younger people within the SWP, and the increase in student activism, prompted the newer SWP leadership to create the Young Socialist Alliance. Throughout most of the 1960s, this too was just one of the many leftist groups competing for members within the youth and student movements. But it had several advantages over most of them, and by the end of that decade it had attained predominance. The Communist party was still tainted from the McCarthy era. The Socialist party was viewed as an arm of the Democratic party. Progressive Labor was seen as narrow-minded in its dogmatic insistence on a worker-student alliance. And SDS was destroyed by PL. It was the latter event which provided the greatest membership boost for the YSA, as the non-PL SDSers often had no other place to go.

SWP/YSA's main purpose has always been to recruit new members. It views itself as the vanguard whose role is to provide political education for other organizations and direction for their activities. This is not achieved by undercover work. SWP/YSA members often openly identify themselves after they have become involved in other organizations in order to utilize every opportunity for private and public debate of their "politics." Extensive group discussions and highly public activities (e.g., mass rallies, marches, and demonstrations) are best suited for this purpose.

At the ninth national YSA convention held December 27–30, 1969, 821 people gathered to discuss the "potential for radicalization" of the women's liberation movement. There reports were made about the success of YSA members in forming feminist groups and "intervening in other groups that do exist and helping to broaden these groups." [36] It was concluded that

> the movement for women's liberation, which has emerged
> rapidly and dynamically in the past years, constitutes an
> extremely important addition to the other social struggles
> going on today, and represents an historic opportunity for the
> revolutionary socialist youth movement. . . . The openness
> of the women involved in the movement, and the
> anti-capitalist thrust of the movement as a whole, offer
> excellent opportunities to the YSA to win the best of these
> women to revolutionary socialism and to the YSA.[37]

YSA clearly felt that the time was ripe for their presence, but that "in order to make our intervention the most successful, we are going to have to step up greatly the amount of national coordination that we've had on the women's liberation struggles." [38]

YSA was correct that the movement was ripe for "intervention," but not because their political line was so attractive. The fact was that the younger branch of the movement often provided no outlets for political action. The process of "conversion" to feminism is often very politicizing. People became aware of the social context of women's situation, and thereby of the interrelated nature of many significant social problems. For the most part, there are no viable political organizations that they can join to work on these problems, especially if they feel alienated from traditional political institutions. This is particularly true on the campus where political activism has shown a sharp decline from previous years. SWP/YSA provides a theoretical framework for

---

36. Statement of Ruthann Miller, YSA Conference report, p. 34.
37. Young Socialist Alliance, "Introduction to the Young Socialist Alliance," April 1970, p. 8.
38. Statement of Kipp Dawson, YSA Conference report, p. 44.

understanding social problems and an active program for working on them. The younger branch of the women's liberation movement provided neither.

The main problem was generated not merely by the recruitment that went on, or even by swp/ysa's contrasting style of action, which often injected some much-needed new ideas into a movement that was getting bogged down in consciousness-raising. The problem came from the alternative power structure naturally created by any small group of people who relate primarily to one another through their common politics. As the swp/ysaers were also part of a tightly organized, national party practicing democratic centralism, the potential was created for minority control not merely of a few groups but of the whole movement.

The mere potential for such control was frightening to most feminists, committed as they were to autonomous groups. Those women with background in the political Left reacted instantly, as they knew from experience what could happen. The first major crisis faced by the newly formed Chicago Women's Liberation Union was over what they called swp's attempt at infiltration and takeover. The battle was fought from roughly the late summer of 1970 to June of 1971, when the swp/ysa was literally forced out. The question raised here, as in many other cities where the same battle eventually ensued, was over the inclusive/exclusive nature of the feminist groups. swp/ysa argued that all groups should be open to all women, that even dues and membership requirements were "elitist." While this position was obviously appealing to the democratic sentiments of most feminists, they quickly learned that such openness of structure could be used by swp/ysa to pack meetings; that the emphasis on mass rallies and demonstrations largely provided them with an opportunity to "push the swp line"; and that groups which could be run largely by those who did most of the work could be easily coopted by the highly disciplined, committed women of swp/ysa.

swp/ysa did their own cause a disservice by engaging in some highly irresponsible behavior. Reports from many groups around the country indicate that they diverted funds to their own use, did not follow policy decisions made in meetings called by them if the decisions were not in their favor, acquired speaking engagements as representatives of feminist groups which were used to talk about SWP concerns, sponsored demonstrations that were not supported or attended by any other feminist groups than their own, and took over mailing lists and office equipment for their own use.[39] Severe conflicts followed in Boston and other cities. While many feminists objected to the "fascist" tactics that both sides were engaging in, and cries of "purge" and "red-baiting" resounded in the feminist media, there was a growing opposition to SWP/YSA around the country. Eventually a large packet on "a series of exposes of the tactics and activities of the Socialist Workers party and Young Socialist Alliance as they relate to the Feminist Movement," ironically labeled the "SWEEP" packet, was compiled and distributed around the country.

During 1972 the SWP/YSA women began to fade out of the movement. From indirect evidence, there appear to be several reasons for this:

1. Independent feminists were organizing against them and even recruiting some of their people into a primary commitment to women's liberation. Needless to say, this created some internal problems within SWP/YSA itself.

2. Because of all the hostility the SWP/YSA had aroused, they did not appear to be making "sufficient progress" within the women's liberation groups.

3. They had found a new movement. During this year the abortion-law-repeal protests were becoming national and of great significance. SWP/YSA was already involved in what many claimed was a front group for it—the Women's National Abortion Action Coalition (WONAAC) which had been founded in July 1971. The SWP/YSA style of mass rallies and demonstrations seemed more viable here.

The experience young feminists had with this highly disci-

---

39. Lucy Komisar, "Confidential Report to the N.O.W. Governing Board [sic] on the Activities of the Socialist Workers Party and the Young Socialist Alliance," undated. Although there was little active "intervention" in NOW, both this report and an August 22, 1972, memo to Massachusetts Chapter presidents on "a forthcoming 'probe' of NOW" indicate a good deal of fear it might occur.

plined, political organization, while disconcerting and disruptive, was not without value. If nothing else, it taught them a lot about politics. The operation of their concepts of sisterhood, consensus, open participation, and equality was threatened for the first time. They were forced to think out how they worked in practice as well as in theory. It was not SWP/YSA politics or program that provided this education, but the realization that they could so easily be controlled by being out-organized.

Those cities and groups that were not threatened by SWP/YSA have been more complacent and have had to deal more with the other problems discussed above. Those few places that already had a structure and program, or could rapidly create one, found themselves more able to resist "intervention" because SWP/YSA in fact commanded the loyalty of very few people. (In 1969, YSA claimed a membership of 1,000, 400 of whom were women, around the country. SWP membership is not known.) For example, many of those in Seattle Radical Women were former SWP members who had learned the virtues of organization as well as grown to dislike SWP. In a public letter, Jill Severn wrote for SRW:

> We have had no problem with YSA members entering our organization because our program delineates our founding principles. . . . Neither the YSA nor the SWP can claim to agree with that program, and since our organizational structure stipulates agreement on program as the basis for membership, none of them would bother even to apply. The conflict between YSA/SWP and many women's organizations is, we think, a conflict between the opportunist and manipulative organizational methods that are the result of the opportunist political program of the YSA/SWP on the one hand, and groups of women with *no* clear program or organization on the other. The vulnerability of these groups to political and/or organizational domination by the YSA/SWP—or anyone else, for that matter—is the result of their own failure to organize themselves in a serious fashion. This failure results not only in the vulnerability of such loose-knit groups to wild changes in direction as new people join them, but also in endless paralysis when there is no

agreed upon method of resolving internal differences about program and policy changes.[40]

The Gay/Straight Split

The "wild changes of direction" and "endless paralysis" of which Severn spoke also characterized the other major crisis in the movement during the years 1970–72. Commonly known as the "gay/straight split," it did not occur in every city, or with the same intensity and conflict in those cities where it was an issue. Its most acerbic forms arose primarily on the East Coast; the more relaxed atmosphere of the West Coast prompted less animosity, and the more conservative Midwest and South inhibited many lesbians from pushing their demands as strongly as in the East.[41]

In a sense lesbianism per se has never been an issue in the younger branch of the movement. The general ethic that women's sexual preference was their own business, that no one should be denied their civil rights, and the feeling that the women's movement should be open to all women, precluded there ever being a debate over the inclusion of lesbians in the movement. The conflict was over the role that lesbians *as lesbians,* not simply as women, ought to play in the movement, and the prominence that lesbian demands ought to have within the spectrum of feminist concerns.

Initially, the issue of lesbianism was to feminism much like miscegenation was to the civil rights movement. On the one hand, the practice of neither was of great relevance as who one sleeps with was not the major thrust of either movement. On the other hand, both occur, and both are logical extensions of central ideas of their respective movements. Just as the acceptability of miscegenation is the logical consequence of the ideal of integration, so lesbianism can cōme from the concept of women learning to relate to other women and not being dependent in any way on men. It is this logical relationship, coupled with our society's

---

40. *Ain't I A Woman,* 19 February 1971.

41. This generalization has some notable exceptions: the feminist newspapers *It Ain't Me Babe* of Berkeley (now defunct) and *Ain't I A Woman* of Iowa City both began strongly to support lesbian/feminism in 1970.

hangups on sex, which made both phenomena potential weapons for the opposition. And it is the fear of their use as weapons, not the phenomena, which created the problems for both movements.

The civil rights movement met this problem by ignoring it. It chose to emphasize the irrelevant aspects of miscegenation rather than the logical ones and thus dismissed it in favor of its main concerns. Those who chose to miscegenate did so without insisting that civil rights organizations take up their cause, or emphasizing that it was one logical consequence of the idea of integration. The women's liberation movement was not let off so easily. The combination of demands for recognition made by lesbians internally and the movement's own emphasis on personal rather than institutional change made the conflict inevitable.

Lesbians have been organized at least since 1955 when the Daughters of Bilitis (DOB) was founded in San Francisco. Many were active in the early days of the movement; their long involvement with the problems of women and divorce from traditional family concerns or dependence upon men made them natural feminists.[42] But within the movement, they remained in the closet. Younger lesbians, however, coming as many did from the counterculture, found DOB far too conservative for their taste, and saw no reason why they should not be active and public both as feminists and lesbians. Many had been involved in the Gay Liberation movement where they had learned to "come out" publicly about their sexual preference. However, "as you might expect, the organizations open to both male and female homosexuals practice the same sort of sexual denigration of women as does the heterosexual society at large." [43] The women's movement was a more hospitable home.

The issue first surfaced at the second Congress to Unite Women, held in New York May 1–3, 1970, when a group of women wearing T-shirts labeled "lavender menace" interrupted a

---

42. Martha Shelley, "Notes of a Radical Lesbian," in Morgan, *Sisterhood Is Powerful*, p. 308.

43. Gene Damon, "The Least of These: The Minority Whose Screams Haven't Yet Been Heard," in ibid., p. 305.

meeting.[44] It was brought up again and again in varying meetings around the country. The movement eventually responded by carrying lesbian analyses in the movement media, by including workshops on lesbianism and sexuality in conferences, by participating in some Gay Liberation movement events such as Gay Pride week or all-women dances, and by passing supportive resolutions at those meetings where such action was appropriate.

But underneath this surface accommodation was a good deal of fear and hostility. Many straight women felt the lesbians wanted all women to be gay or at least to be primarily concerned with gay issues; and many gay women thought that straight women didn't understand them, or were oppressing them as heterosexuals. Straight women often reacted by avoiding the problem; they simply didn't show up for open-discussion meetings on lesbianism or resorted to sarcasm. Some quipped, "In the old days you could only help the oppressed, now you can actually be one." Gays in turn both resented it when straight women ignored them and felt angry at what they thought was a kind of intellectual voyeurism when attention was directed toward them.

All this was compounded by the increasing numbers of women who were "coming out" within the movement rather than before joining it. Some of these "nouveau gays," as they were often called, merely found the movement a safe environment in which to be public about their sexual preferences. Others made a conscious effort to change their sexual orientation due to either group pressure or sincere belief that this was the only proper means to express their politics personally. The latter especially subjected the women's movement to many of the same unpleasant experiences that the newly emerging feminists had put upon their radical brothers when women's liberation was still within the womb of the New Left. Driven by the fervor of the newly converted and the righteousness of their demands, their style was often very totalitarian. For many, lesbianism became redefined to mean much more than merely sleeping with another woman. It

44. Hole and Levine, *Rebirth of Feminism*, p. 240. Also, Sidney Abbott and Barbara Love, "Is Women's Liberation a Lesbian Plot?," in *Woman in Sexist Society*, ed. Vivian Gornick and Barbara K. Moran (New York: New American Library, 1971), pp. 614–15.

developed into a world view which said that women should identify with, live with, and only associate with women. From this premise it was easy to argue that lesbianism was the vanguard of feminism; that a woman who actually slept with a man was obviously consorting with the enemy and could not be trusted. As expressed in a widely circulated paper, "The Woman-Identified Woman," written by the Radicalesbians in 1970:

> Until women see in each other the possibility of a primal commitment which includes sexual love, they will be denying themselves the love and value they readily accord to men, thus affirming their second class status. . . .
>
> It is the primacy of women relating to women, of women creating a new consciousness of and with each other which is at the heart of women's liberation, and the basis for the cultural revolution.[45]

From the advent of consciousness raising, women's liberation had sought to politicize the personal aspects of people's lives. Lesbian/feminists extended this perspective, arguing that the most personal act—sex—was also the most political. Bisexuality was a copout, allowing women to retain the privileges of male association. Celibacy, an option of many women for hundreds of years, was not considered realistic. Products of the sexual revolution of the 1960s, young women of the early '70s assumed that women claiming to be celibate were just repressing their natural urges and limiting their lives. Celibacy did not begin to achieve acceptance as an option until 1974.

The political aspects of lesbian/feminism were elaborated in *The Furies*, a newspaper started in January 1972 by a Washington, D.C. collective of the same name:

> The woman-identified woman commits herself to other women for political, emotional, physical, and economic support . . . not only as an alternative to oppressive male/female relationships but primarily because she *loves*

---

45. Radicalesbians, "The Woman-Identified Woman," in *Radical Feminism*, ed. Anne Koedt, Ellen Levine, and Anita Rapone (New York: Quandrangle, 1973), pp. 243, 245. Also in *liberation now!* (no editor) (New York: Dell, 1971) and many movement publications or anthologies of feminist writings.

women. . . . The Lesbian has recognized that giving love
and support to men over women perpetuates the system that
oppresses her. . . .

Woman-identified Lesbianism is, then, more than a sexual
preference, it is a political choice. It is political because
relationships between men and women are essentially
political, they involve power and dominance. Since the
Lesbian actively rejects that relationship and chooses women,
she defies the established political system.[46]

Like the New Left which spawned it, the younger branch of the
movement has a strong tendency to take every idea to its logical
conclusion, often blindly. The logical conclusion of this idea was
that "in order not to betray women and the feminist movement,
women must give their full love and commitment to women, i.e.,
become lesbian/feminists." [47]

One result of this "vanguardism" ("feminism is the theory,
lesbianism is the practice") was the feeling by many that in parts
of the movement one's sexual preference became the defining
criterion of one's feminist credentials. This situation is both
described and analyzed by Koedt:

If you are a feminist who is not sleeping with a woman you
may risk hearing any of the following accusations: "You're
oppressing me if you don't sleep with a woman"; "You're not
a radical feminist if you don't sleep with women"; or "You
don't love women if you don't sleep with them." I have even
seen a woman's argument about an entirely different aspect
of feminism be dismissed by some lesbians because she was
not having sexual relations with women. . . .

---

46. Charlotte Bunch for the Furies Collective, "Lesbians in Revolt," *The Furies*,
January 1972, p. 8.

47. Mary-Helen Mautner, "Gay Reformism: Almost but Not Quite," *The
Furies*, February 1973, p. 13. This article was a critical review of two major books
on lesbianism published by NOW members—Del Martin and Phyllis Lyon,
Lesbian/Woman (New York: Bantam, 1972); Sidney Abbott and Barbara Love,
Sappho Was a Right-on Woman: A Liberated View of Lesbianism (New York: Stein &
Day, 1972)—which the author felt provided "only half-answers which by
themselves will never destroy lesbian and woman oppression." The gay-straight
conflict within NOW never reached the severity that it did in the younger branch of
the movement.

This perversion of the "personal is political" argument, it must be noted, was not invented by those gay women who may be using it now; the women's movement has had sporadic waves of personal attacks on women—always in the guise of radicalism (and usually by a small minority of women). . . . The original genius of the phrase "the personal is political" was that it opened up the area of women's private lives to political analysis. Before that, the isolation of women from each other had been accomplished by labeling a woman's experience "personal." . . .

However, opening up women's experience to political analysis has also resulted in a misuse of the phrase. While it is true that there are political implications in everything a woman *qua* woman experiences, it is not therefore true that a woman's life is the political property of the women's movement.[48]

The lesbian challenge was particularly difficult for those women who were caught within the web of their own identities as radicals. Given their own personal/ideological need to be in the forefront of social change and the compelling consistency of the argument that the truly radical feminist was a lesbian, they had to conform or drop out. This is exactly what happened to two groups in Washington and Boston, both of which had been composed primarily of former New Left radicals who had been on the politico side of the politico/feminist split. They did not merely split up into separate gay and straight groups as was often the case elsewhere. Those women who were or became gay formed lesbian collectives. Those women who remained straight and still had allegiances to other radical (nonfeminist) organizations became reinvolved in general leftist politics. Those women who remained straight but did not have any other political associations went through a good deal of personal trauma, including a couple of nervous breakdowns, and dropped out of the feminist movement entirely. They could not form or join another group because their identities as radical feminists had been destroyed. Some rejoined when the pressure to become gay began to recede in 1973.

48. Anne Koedt, "Lesbianism and Feminism," *Women: A Journal of Liberation* 3, no. 1 (1972): 33.

This seemingly fundamental demand for personal change had such a strong appeal in part because it offered a definitive means of demonstrating one's political commitment. Social movements require participants to go through a commitment process which involves "an identity-altering experience and a bridge-burning act." [49] The latter may involve a real or symbolic destruction of the old life and/or achievement of the new. A high personal cost of engaging in such acts often serves both to symbolize and to deepen one's commitment to the movement. Thus, those women who chose lesbian/feminism, often at great personal cost, as a means of demonstrating their commitment could easily perceive those who didn't as possessing less conviction, and thus not to be trusted.

While it is hard to say what proportion of the many change-overs from heterosexuality to homosexuality were due to van-guardism and what were the result of personal discovery, it is clear that there were environmental pressures other than political ones. First, the women's liberation movement was having a predictably deleterious effect on many marriages. Men, even the radicals, found it hard to change their own sex-role socialization and their expectations about appropriate male and female behavior. It was especially difficult when their women were not too sure what they wanted out of them. Men often found themselves "damned if they did and damned if they didn't," and the marriage bed became the arena in which unresolved hostility was acted out. Secondly, the movement emphasis on sisterhood and the growing closeness of relationships between women in their political activities made transferring to an all-woman environment an attractive possibility. In sum, women were finding it easier to relate to women and harder to relate to men. Needless to say, this created a good deal of tension, especially for those for whom a sexual relationship was a central part of their lives. A glimmer of a solution appeared when homosexuality was legitimated by the Gay Liberation movement. When lesbianism became touted as the avant-garde life style, its appeal was enhanced.

---

49. Gerlach and Hine, *Movements of Social Reform*, p. 135.

In addition to relief from environmental pressures, lesbian/feminism had a strong appeal because it offered a personal means of political action with immediate results. While the younger branch of the movement has been very creative in its analysis of present conditions and its proposals for the future, it has provided only the vaguest outlines of a strategy for change. Traditional strategies (e.g. demonstrating, lobbying, running elections, petitioning, legislating, litigating, advertising, etc.) either required resources these small, autonomous groups did not have or were considered "sell-outs to the system." Even among those young feminists who did not consider themselves Leftists were many who had imbibed the concept of radicalism to the point where they found any form of political action to be reformist. Lesbian/feminism provided a strategy for action. Further, it was a strategy which fused purposive and solidary incentives more fully than almost any other conceivable set of ideas. One did not have to wait for the revolution; one could revolutionize one's own life now. And in the process of doing so one could eliminate onerous counter-pressures (i.e. men) from one's life without having to give up intimate relationships. This was a compelling idea in part because it was a means of action which provided a very traditional solution. Most women have been trained to seek their fulfillment through personal relationships. Thus many found it easier to demonstrate their feminist commitment by changing their relationships than other aspects of their lives.[50] The appeal of lesbian/feminism was that it was an overt act of commitment which provided a political strategy which was consonant with women's traditional style but avoided the onus of traditional institutions.

For the movement at large, it was also easier to spend one's energies on the essentially personal nature of the gay/straight

---

50. Charlotte Bunch argues further that "women have adopted at least four substitutes for individual self-identity: building identity around (1) oppression, (2) the movement, (3) ideal models, and/or (4) relationships." She feels that a woman "needs a sense of her own self-worth based on what she can do and be—on her work. The women's movement's concentration on feelings and relationships often shields and diverts us from this part of the hard but crucial struggle to develop each woman's sense of self." "Perseverance Furthers: Woman's Sense of Self," *The Furies*, February 1973, pp. 3, 4.

conflict rather than deal with the harder political questions. Underlying many conflicts in the movement was a basic difference in ideology which was never sharply defined and never by itself became the focus of a major split. One perspective saw the ultimate goal of the movement as the annihilation of sex roles. By its nature this view includes the liberation of men with that of women. Thus, while sex is seen as political and men as privileged by the current sex-role system, the complete rejection of men is not a valid position.

The other perspective can best be described by the term "cultural nationalism." This view sees men at worst destructive and at best irrelevant. The goal of the movement should be to affirm and strengthen female attributes and culture. Integration with men is neither possible nor desirable; the only alternative is female autonomy.

Many women and many groups in the movement articulate a mixture of these perspectives without ever having analyzed their fundamental premises. However, the lesbian/feminists expressed the latter view in its purest form. Not surprisingly, they have also become the largest component of those women engaged in feminist cultural activities. Because most other feminists were not sensitive to this basic ideological difference, they found it hard to defend rationally the politics of their personal lives. Consequently, real issues were avoided, and the real challenge of lesbian/feminism for the movement to define its goals was never met.

The Consequences of Structurelessness

There were two major results from all the tensions and conflicts the movement experienced in these years. One was to create a forum for new ideas and to provide a political education for many young feminists. The other was to tear apart, slowly but surely, the reticulate interstices of the movement. The segmented groups were becoming fragmented groups; increasing in number and decreasing in communication. The feminist media continued to provide some sort of common milieu, but so many people were no longer speaking to so many others that intergroup personal contact was lost. Late in 1972 a revival appeared to be occurring in many cities. Fragmented groups were coming together again, new national communications networks were being set up among people with common projects (e.g., health clinics, media, theater groups), and the ideology and consequences of "structurelessness" were being seriously questioned in such diverse places as New Haven, Chapel Hill, and Berkeley.

One reason for the movement's dissolution is that it had been limited by its own origins. A product of the counterculture and New Left, it had within a few short years expanded to the boundaries of that culture, transformed and/or integrated most of its organizations and institutions, and then turned in on itself as it had no place else to go. The new relationships and activities that were tentatively emerging in late 1972 involved many people who had not been part of the youth and student movements, whether by age or inclination.

However, these new relationships did not appear to include a new sense of direction and it is upon the rock of lack of direction that the younger branch of the movement has been floundering for so long it has practically become a way of life. There is a phoenixlike quality to the movement—different groups simultaneously dying, reforming, and emerging—so that it is hard to get an accurate reading on the state of its health. Although the resurgence of feminism tapped a major source of female energy, the structure of the younger branch has not been able to channel it effectively. Some women are able to create their own local action projects, study groups, or service centers. Most are not, and the movement provides no coordinated or structured means of fitting them into existing projects. Instead, such women either are recruited into NOW and other national organizations, or drop out of organized activity altogether. The latter rarely cease to be feminists; instead they apply their new ideas to their personal lives and individual concerns. The consequence, however, is that new groups form and dissolve at an accelerating rate, creating a good deal of consciousness and very little concerted action. To a certain extent the movement is expanding but not building; forging into new areas while failing to consolidate its gains in old.

The average life of most movement activists is about two years, after which they retire in exhaustion to be replaced by new converts who try to make up in enthusiasm what they lack in experience. While this high rate of turnover continuously adds new blood to the movement, it also means old issues have to be continuously refought. Thus, internal education consumes a good deal of the movement's energy, and only some organizations—primarily in the older branch—have been able to avoid becoming bogged down by that task.

Gerlach and Hine argue that a decentralized, segmented movement is the most viable way of developing new means of social change as their flexibility permits greater use of

> the time-honored method of social innovation—trial and error. A bureaucratic, centrally directed organization is obviously ill adapted to this type of approach. It is within the context of a decentralized, segmented structure that such innovation can most easily take place.
>
> In a polycephalous movement, the errors of one group or one leader have little, if any, effect on the others. Group members can disband, re-form under new leadership, or simply be absorbed into other groups, and the movement goes on. An attempt at innovation which fails affects only those most closely associated with it; in fact, such failure may aid others by its demonstrations of what will not work.[51]

As applied to the women's liberation movement, their judgments about the increase in innovations are correct. There have certainly been a lot of new ideas. Nevertheless, one could dispute whether the development of these new ideas represent progress or merely fashion. That is, whether they are founded upon past experience in an attempt to improve it, or are pursued upon the assumption that anything new is automatically better. It is perhaps too soon to make that kind of assessment. But what is clear is that new ideas without organizational direction often go nowhere. This does not mean that the ideas do not spread. Given a certain amount of interest by the media and the appropriateness

51. *Movements of Social Transformation*, p. 77.

of social conditions, the ideas will still be diffused widely. But diffusion of ideas does not mean they are implemented; it only means that they are talked about. Insofar as they can be applied individually, they may be acted on; insofar as they require coordinated political power to be implemented, they will not be.

This is why the younger branch of the movement can at one and the same time be so innovative ideologically, and so conservative in practice. Its debates, disputes, and ideas provide new food for feminist thought. Its segmented oligarchies and service projects restrict its activities to politically innocuous ones. Gerlach and Hine obviously failed to appreciate the political implications, or lack of them, in this kind of structure, however appealing its other aspects may be. It is good for personal change; it is bad for institutional change.

Fortunately, the younger branch is not the sum total of the women's liberation movement. There exist some national, somewhat centralized organizations capable of coordinated political action. It is these organizations that usually develop the ideas fermented by the small groups. While it is likely true that NOW and other national organizations would not be as innovative without the ideological pressure these groups provide, it is also true that their new ideas would have few avenues for implementation if it were not for NOW. This symbiotic relationship between varying, even differing, movement groups is typical of other movements, and is perhaps a condition of movement success.[52]

The irony is that it is not the centralized social-movement organization, NOW, that has moved toward conformity with the Weber/Michels model of oligarchization, conservatization, and goal transformation. It is the nonbureaucratic, noncentralized small groups. They are the ones run largely by oligarchies, who have sufficiently accommodated themselves to their environment to have transformed their goals, in practice if not in theory, from radical social change to ameliorative service projects. It would seem that here the inherent tension between goal-achievement

---

52. Zald and Ash, "Social Movement Organizations," pp. 332–36.

needs and group-maintenance needs comes full circle. A group that has too little structure devotes itself as disproportionately to the latter just as does a group that has too much. One can conclude that what is necessary for movement survival is to opt for neither the apotheosis of efficiency nor the apotheosis of participation, but to maintain a balance between them both.[53]

---

53. The problem of participation versus efficiency is an old one. See V. I. Lenin's 1901 classic "What Is to Be Done?" in *Collected Works*, vol. 4, bk. 2 (New York: International Publishers, 1929).

5

"The Mushroom Effect": A Partial Profile

T*HE MUSHROOM EFFECT* IS THE NAME OF A 16-page tabloid directory of several hundred women's liberation groups. Published in late 1970, it was outdated the day it was printed. Its name and its datedness both accurately reflect what happened to the movement in its first few years. Three years later, *Women Today*, an independent national newsletter, published a directory of several thousand groups.[1] The women's liberation movement may have had two distinct origins, but like the branches of two neighboring trees, its progeny have spread over both trunks so thickly that one cannot easily detect the roots of specific leaves.

According to the diffusion-of-innovations literature, adoption of a new idea follows a fairly predictable bell-shaped curve.[2] This

---

1. Myra E. Barrer, ed., *Women's Organizations and Leaders: 1973 Directory* (Washington, D.C.: *Women Today*, 1973).

2. Herbert F. Lionberger, *Adoption of New Ideas and Practices* (Ames, Iowa: Iowa

curve does not explain the absolute rate at which a new idea will
be adopted, if it is at all, but it does hypothesize the relative rate
of acceptance of one segment of the population compared to the
other. Rogers classifies people under it into five categories:
Innovators (2½ percent), Early Adopters (13½ percent), Early
Majority (34 percent), Late Majority (34 percent), and Laggards
(16 percent).[3]

The crucial moment in this curve is the inflexion point, when
the rate of increase shoots radically upward. In an economic
context this has been called the "takeoff point."[4] The women's
liberation movement "took off" in 1970. It was during that year
that the accelerating influx of new people became too great for
the groups and organizations to handle, and that new groups were
formed more quickly than anyone could keep count. Of great
importance in this development was what has been called the
"grand press blitz," which took place primarily but not exclusively between January and March of that year. Women's
liberation became the latest fad. Virtually every major publication and network in the country did a major story on it. While the
evidence abounds that the media alone do not induce people to
make a commitment to a new innovation or a new movement,[5]
they do provide information of its existence and to some extent
legitimate what would otherwise be seen as an outlandish idea.

The question that this raises is why so much of the press
responded at almost precisely the same time. One reporter
commented on this coincidence that "It's New York groupthink.
You can hear them all mooing like a herd of cattle when they are
on to the same trend."[6] Although descriptive, this comment

State University Press, 1960), p. 37. Everett M. Rogers, *Diffusion of Innovations* (New
York: Free Press, 1962), p. 152.

3. Rogers, *Diffusion of Innovations*, p. 162.

4. W. W. Rostow, *The Stages of Economic Growth* (Cambridge, England: Cambridge University Press, 1960).

5. Luther P. Gerlach and Virginia H. Hine, *People, Power, Change: Movements of
Social Transformation* (Indianapolis: Bobbs-Merrill, 1970), p. 90; Lionberger, *New
Ideas and Practices*, pp. 43–46.

6. Interview with Bernice Buresh, formerly of the Chicago *Newsweek* bureau,
currently head of the Boston bureau, January 1973.

requires some elaboration. It is true that most of the national media are located in New York, but does that automatically mean they all think alike?

Two possible hypotheses present themselves. (1) People in positions to make policy decisions could be responding to the same sequence of public events by feminists. (2) Since reporters are part of the same and/or overlapping social groups, an idea by one could be quickly spread "over the grapevine" and be picked up by others. The possibility that one publication "scooped" the others, who then followed suit, is precluded by the short period of time in which the major stories appeared. To ascertain which of these hypotheses was the more valid, I interviewed people who had been involved in the relevant policy decisions on four of the major national media: NBC, CBS, *Time*, and *Newsweek*. In all cases, respondents were somewhat vague about where they got the idea due to the three-year time lapse between the events and my interviews. Nevertheless, while neither hypothesis was proved conclusively, the former received the greatest support.

In the case of NBC and *Newsweek*, the idea for a women's liberation story could be traced to one person, who proposed and nurtured the idea. The then executive producer of the "Huntley/ Brinkley Show," for reasons of personal history, was very conscious of the problems of women. He had also spent much of his reportorial career covering civil rights and "once you throw yourself into the business of reporting on civil rights, it is easy to see the similarities."[7] Although he does not remember what events might have influenced his decision, since NBC seems to be the first national medium to begin working on the story[8] he is less likely to have picked it up from the others.

During the previous year the New York groups, including NOW, had been very active. NOW had sponsored several picket lines; besides that of the *New York Times*, WITCH had hexed many venerable institutions; and the second Miss America protest was

---

7. Interview with Wallace Westfeldt, NBC, February 1973.

8. An NBC interoffice memo in August 1969 is the first written proposal for a story on the movement that I could find.

held in Atlantic City, N.J. in early September 1969. These events were reported widely in the underground press, soon in the *Village Voice*, and eventually in more establishment places such as the *Times*. There was a growing crescendo both of activity and of attention. Much of it was patronizing, but it was attention nonetheless. Reporters read these media[9] and feel that "our business is to be aware. We are enormously sensitive to what is going on." [10]

Free-lance stories on women's liberation were also appearing in such magazines as *New York*, the *New York Times Magazine*, and the *Nation*. It was a negative story on the movement in *New York* which prompted a young writer at *Newsweek* to make her suggestion, but as it was a timely story, she had no trouble getting it picked up by her superiors. In the process of discussing the story with her female colleagues, she discovered that several had already written the EEOC for material on how to file a complaint. They coordinated their efforts and both the story and the complaint were made public on the same day.[11]

Whether the close timing of the stories was because "it is a journalistic function to try and sense a change" [12] and all the reporters were equally sensitive, or because "all are interchangeable with people at the other media; at this level, everybody knows everybody else," [13] the cumulative impact of the series of stories was tremendous. Within the short space of a few months the movement went from a struggling new idea to a national phenomenon. It accelerated even more the multitudinous splits.

The pluralistic nature of the women's liberation movement is a characteristic that has not been adequately appreciated either by the movement's participants or by its critics. The latter usually attack specific organizations for being too homogeneous in composition without realizing that the movement as a whole is

---

9. Interview with Ruth Brine, *Time*, 5 March 1973 and Peter Goldman, *Newsweek*, February 1973.
10. Interview with Kermit Lansner, *Newsweek*, February 1973.
11. Interview with Lynn Young, *Newsweek*, February 1973.
12. Interview with David Culhane, CBS, February 1973.
13. Interview with Peter Goldman, *Newsweek*, February 1973.

becoming more and more heterogeneous. The primary means by which feminism enters new segments of the population is by the formation of new groups rather than by more women joining established groups. Black women, older women, trade-union women, office workers, etc., have all created new organizations to deal with the implications of feminism for their particular situations—even though some individuals in these groups are active in established feminist organizations. Members of the earlier organizations despair about appealing to a wide sector of the population, without understanding that no purpose would be served by having an identical base for every organization within the movement. Another extreme to which feminists, especially in the younger branch, often go is that of vanguardism—deprecating anyone (especially anyone white, middle-class, college-educated, and heterosexual) who cannot be identified as among the "most oppressed," as though only the latter could make a significant contribution.

Historically, American movements have thrived best when they were highly pluralistic, with each group within them having a solid identity and sense of purpose rather than trying to be everything to everyone. The result is a division of labor of both appeal and activity that permits a great deal of flexibility. It is often necessary and valuable for different groups to play different roles, with pressure coming from one and conciliation from another, without any having to be directly responsible for the actions of any other. Further, it is difficult for a single organization, unless it is severely decentralized, to meet the needs of a very diverse membership. Homogeneity facilitates agreement on action. Thus, different groups are better off having their own organizations that can deal with their own particular needs, without having to secure approval from everyone else. A broadly based organization (which few feminist groups are) is not the same as a broadly based movement (which feminism is).

The unceasing fission of the movement has been both its strength and its weakness. With the formation of each new group an entirely new segment of the female population is brought under its umbrella and a correspondingly new segment of men and women have the reality of feminist revolt brought into their everyday lives through the activities of their colleagues, friends, and relatives. Conversely, this diversity makes the possibility of a united movement more and more impossible and agreement on common issues more and more difficult. It usually means that while each separate feminist effort has the existence of the movement to give it moral strength, it lacks any powerful organization behind it to give it material strength. Apart from NOW, most feminist organizations still consist of a handful of dedicated people and a large penumbra of hesitant sympathizers.

Predictably, the lines of fission have been along ideological differences, personality conflicts, and the other social cleavages of our society, especially occupation.[14] Some of the former have been described in earlier chapters, and personality conflicts are too numerous and too specific to pursue. Therefore, what follows is a rough breakdown of some of the major new areas of feminist action and organization of a nonideological character. The purpose of this cataloguing is twofold: (1) to give some idea of the scope of the movement, both its major institutionalized activities and the diverse corners into which it has penetrated; (2) to introduce organizations, some of whose activities will be discussed later, not described elsewhere.

Specifically Feminist Organizations

The Women's Equity Action League (WEAL) was founded by an Ohio lawyer, Dr. Elizabeth Boyer, as a result of one of NOW's splits in the fall of 1968. Its initial membership was concentrated in Ohio. At first, its purpose was deliberately restricted to economic and educational discrimination and tax inequities. A conservative image was established specifically in order to recruit people already occupying positions of power. WEAL called itself the "right wing of the women's movement" and at one time every new member was required to have a sponsor.

WEAL was especially attractive to those women who wanted

---

14. Gerlach and Hine, *Movements of Social Transformation*, p. 42.

organizational involvement in the movement but viewed NOW as too radical and/or unconventional. It served for many as "an entry way into feminism." One of the new members was Dr. Bernice Sandler, then of the University of Maryland and now of the Association of American Colleges. Largely through her efforts, WEAL initiated and sustained a campaign to charge colleges and universities with sex discrimination under Executive Order 11375. On January 31, 1970, WEAL made a class-action complaint against all colleges and universities holding federal contracts with the Department of Labor's Office of Contract Compliance. Accompanied by over 80 pages of documentary material, it charged an "industry-wide pattern" of discrimination against academic women. This was followed by subsequent specific complaints against over 250 institutions, extensive lobbying for federal investigations into their discriminatory practices, and organizing of local campus pressure groups. This project put WEAL on the feminist map and attracted into it a large number of women, especially academic women, of a less conservative bent than the founders. During 1972 power shifted from the conservative Ohio chapters when a national office was opened in Washington, D.C. In the next few years WEAL expanded its projects to include the elimination of sex-role stereotyping in elementary and secondary schools, the promotion of women in sports, an analysis of credit and banking practices, and a study of divorce reform. At its December 1972 convention it even reversed its previous avoidance of the abortion issue and came out for repeal.

Partially because of the success of its higher education project and partially due to the nature of its membership, 10 percent of whom live in the Washington, D.C. area, WEAL views itself more and more as the primary political pressure group in the feminist movement. It puts out a monthly report on the congressional progress of legislation relevant to women and focuses much of its energies on the administrative implementation of feminist legislation already passed. It feels that its local chapters can provide a means of pressuring key congressmen while it coordinates a national effort. The potential problem this creates is that of becoming "top-heavy," with local chapters atrophying because they feel no purpose beyond that of the national organization. This has not yet become acute, and in the meantime WEAL is moving to assume the "pressure group" role.

The *Women's Action Alliance* was conceived by Gloria Steinem and her friend Brenda Feigen Fasteau, at about the same time as *Ms.* magazine, in response to the overwhelming number of requests for information and contacts they and others received. *Ms.* was to be its self-supporting newsletter, and foundation support was sought. It was viewed as "sort of a complement to the National Women's Political Caucus" to deal with nonpolitical activities. The two projects acquired separate identities as they grew; *Ms.* emerged in April 1972 as a profit-making slick magazine, while WAA received $30,000 from the Stern Foundation in November 1971 to set up an information-referral system. Housed in a large office three floors above *Ms.*, which pays half its rent, WAA's staff of six paid and two volunteer women maintain a large card catalog of addresses and information and answer about two hundred letters a week. This clearinghouse function is no different from that performed by many unpaid feminist organizations for years and illustrates how acceptable credentials can facilitate the use of establishment resources for movement activities. It is also an indication of the "institutionalization" of some movement functions, though it is too early to assess the impact of such a development.

In addition to information referral, WAA also puts out information packets on such subjects as Women's Centers, how to start consciousness-raising groups, elimination of sex-role stereotyping in child-care centers, and cooperates with several local feminist projects on the East Coast. Seeing itself as service-oriented and educational in nature, it would like to teach feminists how to appeal to foundations for support of special projects. As it is oriented primarily toward the younger branch of the movement, viewing NOW and WEAL as "closed clubs," if it succeeds in achieving a national role as an information and funding center, it will impose on the younger branch that national direction and organization it has been avoiding so assiduously.[15]

The *Women's Lobby Inc.* was begun by Carol Burris and Flora Crater out of mutual lobbying efforts for the Equal Rights Amendment. From their experiences they perceived that a permanent lobby for women's issues would be a valuable addition to the movement. Composed of from thirty to forty people, at least a rotating dozen of whom spend every Wednesday making the congressional rounds, it seeks to educate congresspeople on issues of concern to women and keep records on their attitudes and voting patterns. Most of the lobbyists are married women who live primarily on their husband's incomes, thus permitting them weekday time to lobby. The lobby has been financing itself largely through Burris's independent income and contributions by participants, but it is looking for other sources. Working from a list of 5,000 names accumulated by Burris and Crater during their ERA work, the Lobby hopes to set up state coordinators and support groups.[16]

Human Rights for Women was born at the same time as WEAL, but much less intentionally. When two disgruntled lawyers walked out of NOW in the fall of 1968, they carried with them a sizable check from Alice Paul of the *National Women's Party* to finance the two feminist legal cases they were working on. At the bank to deposit the money, they did not want to put it in their personal accounts; on the spur of the moment they invented the name "Civil Rights for Women" as an account name. Discussing what they had done with friends, they decided to make the name permanent but changed it to the more general HRW. Further thought convinced them that what the movement needed was not another action organization but a nonprofit, tax-exempt foundation which could research and finance relevant legal cases and other activities. Since then, HRW has sought to assist women in sex-discrimination cases, to raise money to finance feminist

---

15. Information and quotes from interview with Carol Shapiro of the Women's Action Alliance, 6 April 1973.

16. Information and quotes from interview with Carol Burris, Carol Douglas, and Flora Crater, Women's Lobby, February 1973.

research projects, and to produce an educational newsletter. Its major activities have been legal research in two major Title VII cases[17] filing *amicus curiae* briefs in other sex-discrimination and abortion cases, and the production of pamphlets on the legal remedies to sex discrimination. Its current focus is on the situation of single women.

The *National Black Feminist Organization* emerged out of a meeting of 30 women in New York in May 1973. After it announced its existence at a press conference on August 15, it received over 300 phone calls. Spurred by this response, NBFO convened its first East Coast conference in November 1973, and over 500 women attended. For the next year it operated out of the Women's Action Alliance office, before acquiring its own headquarters in New York. During that time it expanded to more than 2,000 members in over 10 cities. The membership of the NBFO is much more heterogeneous than that of any other feminist organization, including women from a wide range of ages and occupations. Its statement of purpose defines its major concerns as self-definition and the development of a positive image for black women:

> The distorted male-dominated media image of the Women's Liberation Movement has clouded the vital and revolutionary importance of this movement to Third World women, especially Black women. The Movement has been characterized as the exclusive property of so-called "white middle class" women, and any Black women seen involved in this movement have been seen as "selling out," "dividing the race," and an assortment of nonsensical epithets. Black feminists resent these charges. . . . Black women have suffered cruelly in this society from living the phenomenon of being Black and female, in a country that is *both* racist and sexist. . . . *We*, not white men or Black men, must define our own self-image as Black women and not fall into the mistake of being placed upon the pedestal which is even being

---

17. *Bowe* v. *Colgate-Palmolive Co.* 416 F.2d 711 (7th Cir. 1969); *Mengelkoch* v. *Industrial Welfare Commission* 442 F.2d 1119 (9th Cir. 1971).

> rejected by white women. . . . We must together, as a
> people, work to eliminate racism from without the Black
> community which is trying to destroy us as an entire people,
> but we must remember that sexism is destroying and
> crippling us from within.

The wide variety of movement organizations are far too numerous to list.[18] Nonetheless, a few have achieved a sufficient national role to justify an honorable mention. The *Women's History Research Library* was begun by Laura X in her home in Berkeley in 1969. A private, nonprofit archive of everything collectible by or about the current feminist movement, it employed ten to twenty work-study students and/or volunteers. It was financed primarily by the independent income of its founder, partially by contributions and sale of literature. It soon had to close to the public because of scarcity of resources, but its files were available to movement scholars and it arranged for Bell and Howell to microfilm its extensive collection of feminist publications and newsletters. In 1974 money ran out and its collection was donated to the libraries of Northwestern University and the University of Wyoming.

Know, Inc., The Women's Free Press, is a nonprofit, tax-exempt corporation founded in the fall of 1969 by Pittsburgh NOW members to reprint feminist articles at cost for wide distribution. They describe themselves:

> Housed in a member's garage and later in a basement, we
> began to flourish, supported by volunteer labor, donated
> supplies and money, good faith and growing sales. We
> quickly added many original articles, several longer works
> and books. Each step in our development brought us closer to
> the status of feminist publisher.

Know, Inc. now provides a wide range of publication services at only slightly above cost, including a national news bulletin, women's studies syllabi, bibliographies and lists of special projects.

---

18. The best current attempt to list and describe them is *The New Woman's Survival Catalog* (New York: Coward, McCann and Geoghegan, 1973).

Operating as a collective, it now pays its staff and has acquired a storefront office. With typical movement optimism, it is attempting to be a low-cost publisher, an information network, an experimental collective workgroup and a successful business all at the same time.

The Feminist Women's Health Centers of California are only three of many such clinics throughout the country which seek to provide gynecological and abortion care for women by women at very low cost within the political context of women controlling their own bodies. What makes them distinctive is that they started what has become known as the "self-help movement." Their leaflet describes it:

> The first step toward gaining control of our own bodies must come by tearing down the walls of ignorance. . . . We have gross misinformation given to us by the male medical profession who have been the sole repositors of gynecological knowledge. . . .
>
> The Self Help clinics are small groups of women who meet to learn more about their bodies through self examination. The group observes cervical changes, common infections, ranges of normality, effects of birth control methods, and thoroughly discusses the myths, misconceptions and hangups we as women are all prey to. It compares what "authorities" say about our women's bodies to what is really going on. In these ways women come to know the workings of their bodies in a matter-of-fact common sense way. . . .
>
> For better than two years, the Self Help Clinic women have been working on a feminist strategy to help women to take control of our bodies. One such very successful strategy was in the development of menstrual extraction. . . . With a great deal of self-taught knowledge about the workings of our bodies, . . . great expenditures of money and time to travel, . . . we invented a safe, portable menstrual extraction kit that would give women the technology and power to take control of our menstrual periods.

Although word of the technique has spread far and wide, the kits are not easily available, and there is still a good deal of debate over their safety.

Government and Politics

Although they would be reluctant to apply the term "feminist" to themselves, the State Commissions on the Status of Women were the first women's groups in the government. They still operate in forty-nine states (all except Texas), the District of Columbia, Puerto Rico, and the Virgin Islands, although some exist in name only. Local commissions have also been formed by some counties and cities.

For many years their members met informally at annual Women's Bureau conferences, until they decided to create their own organization on June 11, 1970. Operating as a federation of autonomous commissions, each of whom has one vote, the *Interstate Association of Commissions on the Status of Women* has functioned as an information network and testified at legislative hearings on bills of interest to women. Ratification of the Equal Rights Amendment is currently its main priority, though it is also setting up a tax-exempt fund for educational projects. Although composed of official groups, the IACSW is a private organization and thus must fund itself from annual dues. These amount to $150 per state commission and $75 for local ones. A constitutional convention to reorganize the Association is planned for March 1975.[19]

Federally Employed Women was founded by Allie Latimer-Weeden in 1968. She and other women who attended a series of seminars on executive opportunities for women offered by the Department of Agriculture Graduate School were searching for some means of keeping in touch with one another because women executives are often quite isolated. At a luncheon of 35 women in June 1968 they decided what they really needed was a nongovernmental organization that would fight sex discrimination in the government and promote women into its higher echelons. The result was aptly named FEW. Headquartered in Washington, but with chapters in fifty-six cities, FEW directs most of its energies against the Civil Service Commission. Under a separate provision of Executive Order 11375 the Commission is charged wih alleviating discrimi-

19. Interview with Joy Simonson, president, Interstate Association of Commissions on the Status of Women, October 1974.

nation within the government and encouraging the active search and promotion of qualified women to higher positions. FEW charges the Commission is not seriously enforcing the provision and that, as it also practices extensive discrimination within its own ranks, it is a compromised prosecutor, judge, and jury of discrimination complaints. FEW is also working for child-care centers and other benefits for government employees.[20]

In addition to FEW, several women's organizations have appeared in the different departments and agencies including the Departments of Health, Education, and Welfare, Agriculture, Housing and Urban Development, Commerce, State, and Labor. Some were casual meeting groups, others formal organizations. The efforts of most were directed at the improvement of women's positions within their agencies, through meetings with officials, registries of women available for promotion, and the establishment of communications networks. None has organized specifically to effect national policy, but that potential is certainly there.

Outside government, women have been forming women's caucuses within their parties and local organizations or working independently in campaigns. Democratic women received a tremendous boost by the McGovern guidelines which specified that women, minorities, and youth be represented in the convention delegations according to their percentage in the population. While only 13 percent of the 1968 delegates were female, they were 40 percent of those attending the convention in 1972. Although the Republican women were not under the same kind of pressure, their percentage of the delegates also improved, from 17 percent to 29 percent.

These tremendous jumps were due in part to the Women's Education for Delegate Selection (WEDS) project of the *National Women's Political Caucus*, which held several state conferences for women on the rules and procedures of delegate selection. In conjunction with these conferences, meetings were held with the

---

20. Interview with Helen Dudley, 4 June 1974. Judith Hole and Ellen Levine, *Rebirth of Feminism* (New York: Quadrangle, 1971), pp. 98–101.

National Committees of the parties and with the various Presidential candidates to elicit from them statements of support. At the conventions women delegates were further supplied with informational material on issues, challenges, credentials and procedures. In the Democratic convention the NWPC helped to prepare a "women's plank" for the platform, changed the rules to alternate the convention chairmanship between the sexes at successive conventions, and participated in a number of credentials challenges and platform fights.

The NWPC was formed on July 10 and 11, 1971, at a Washington meeting of 324 women instigated by Bella Abzug, Gloria Steinem, Betty Friedan, and Shirley Chisholm. Its major aim is to get more women elected and appointed to public office and to support women's issues. This meeting chose a National Policy Board of thirty members, who were subsequently replaced at the 1973 convention by a National Steering Committee of State, Regional, At Large and Special Interest representatives. Initially the NWPC was structured much like a political party: as a coalition of state and local organizations. However, the Steering Committee decision in 1974 to require national as well as chapter dues will provide the independent financial base necessary for a national organization to emerge.

Currently the NWPC services rather than directs the organization, with newsletters and educational materials. It has solicited support for some issues, such as the ERA, the Equal Employment Opportunity Act of 1972, and child care, by mailings, but it cannot compel support.

There are caucuses of some sort in 47 states, and the staff estimates that two-thirds of these are effective; 36 are state organizations, more or less, and the others are purely local. There are 37,000 names on the national mailing list, which is the only available estimation of NWPC support as there is no national membership.

The biggest difficulty of the NWPC is that it attempts to be a coalition of probably the most diverse combination of women in the movement. It is predominantly Democratic and independent, with Republicans claiming special-interest representation on the

National Steering Committee as a minority group. Republican participation tends to be stronger in those states where they are a minority party, such as the South. Initially, feminist participation was stronger in those states which did not have NOW or WEAL chapters and the NWPC was the only outlet for feminist activities. As all three feminist organizations have grown, overlapping memberships have become common. The staff estimates that about half their numbers are already feminists when they join and "the others learn pretty quickly." While 75 percent have had some political experience, only 50 percent consider themselves party women, and "a lot [of the latter] come in thinking of themselves as missionaries in the Congo—they have to impart political knowledge to the poor ignorant souls." [21]

One of the potentially more important NWPC chapters exists among the female staff on Capitol Hill. In November 1971, Bella Abzug and the NWPC held a reception for all women staff members to which more than a hundred came. Out of this occasion the Capitol Hill chapter of the NWPC was organized with the help of Arvonne Fraser, new president of WEAL and wife of a congressman from Minnesota. While the main concerns of this chapter are improving the job opportunities and working conditions of women on the Hill, rather than effecting policy, they have still met with a hostile reception from the legislators. Their main problem is lack of continuity, as the Hill job turnover is normally high, and unlike civil service, there is no job security. Consequently, those women who do the work of the chapter are reluctant to have their identities made public and are constantly changing. There are also conflicts between the differing interests of the professional (about two-thirds) and the clerical staff members. The result of these difficulties is that the chapter has had to reorganize itself three times and has not yet been able to accomplish much more than making members aware of one another and sharing information about job availability.[22]

---

21. Interview with Jane McMichels, NWPC staff member, 29 March 1973.
22. Interview with Olga Grakavac, NWPC Capitol Hill Chapter, February 1973.

The Church

There are many women's caucuses, boards, and special organizations within the Catholic Church and the Protestant denominations which have turned their interest to sex discrimination in and out of the church since the advent of the women's liberation movement. One, *St. Joan's Alliance*, was founded in Britain during the suffrage movement and started a U.S. branch in 1965. *The National Coalition of American Nuns* was formed in July 1969 "to speak out on human rights and social justice" as well as to urge the ordination of women and "protest any domination . . . by priests, no matter what their hierarchical status." *The Joint Committee of Organizations Concerned with the Status of Women in the Church* is working for the creation of an official Office of Women's Affairs with the U.S. Catholic Conference. *The Unitarian-Universalist Women's Federation* is the most militant of the Protestant groups. Such organizations as *Church Women United* of the National Council of Churches and the *Women's Board* of the Methodist Church have been quite active on women's issues and the status of women. A 1969 statement of the latter group reads: "When organized women's groups have been removed from a visible policy-making and power-sharing role, the following things tend to occur: (a) Male chauvinism increases, (b) The status of women declines." [23]

The Professions

Professional women have been the most prolific in the production of women's caucuses and even separate women's organizations created to advance the status of women within each profession. Too numerous to name here, many have joined together in the *Federation of Organizations for Professional Women*. There is also an omnibus organization called the *Professional Women's Caucus* (PWC) which attempts to represent the more general interests of professionals. Founded in April 1970, it hoped

---

23. Hole and Levine, *Rebirth of Feminism*, pp. 277–83. See also Sarah Bentley Doely, ed., *Women's Liberation and the Church* (New York: Association Press, 1970).

to attract women who felt they did not fit in elsewhere but was originally dominated by NOW members. As the major feminist activity of women professionals on the status of women in the professions is largely within their separate organizational caucuses, PWC wanted to provide a means for women in different professions to communicate and share their ideas for action.

Labor

Although several trade-union women were active in the formation of NOW, the movement did not spread rapidly among the ranks of the female blue-collar working force. This was partially the result of an extreme lack of union organization among women workers which not only leaves them unprotected economically but also precludes the obvious network through which feminist ideas could spread. However, even those women in unions have not used them for organizing on women's issues extensively. They have largely not been able to. Even when women predominate on a local level, their unions are run by men on the regional and national level. Consequently, according to one union woman,

> while organizations of women in other areas have been
> growing rapidly in recent years, trade union women
> generally did not have an inter-union framework for the
> exchange of information and for plans of action to fight for
> the solution of problems affecting all women in the labor
> force.[24]

What happened instead was that individual women seized upon Title VII to file sex-discrimination cases against both their employers and their unions. And by filing those cases they became conscious of the economic discrimination other women faced and the need to organize to alleviate it. In Indiana, for instance, women involved in a suit against the Colgate Palmolive Co. formed the League of American Working Women (LAWW) to

24. *Women Today*, 23 July 1973, p. 5.

lobby against so-called protective legislation, and for the ERA and other laws beneficial to working women. Through the lawyers who handled their case they became aware of sex discrimination cases in other states, handled by the same volunteer feminist attorneys, and are trying to form chapters elsewhere.

On the West Coast some women formed their own separate unions when they found it impossible to buck the Local's male power structure. A group called *Women Inc.* struck Crown Zellerbach and Fiberboard plants in Northern California in 1969 over the regular union's objection. They borrowed their idea from women who closed down a paper mill near Seattle the previous year in protest of its discriminatory hiring practices and separate seniority lists. The latter group of women was refused recognition by the national union, so they decided to name themselves— Local 36-22-36.

The one union that does have a long record of activity on women's issues is the United Auto Workers which formed a Women's Department in 1944. Subsequently the UAW has funded several research projects, lobbied for laws against sex discrimination, and passed strong women's rights resolutions at all UAW national conventions.[25] Though the UAW once opposed the ERA, it reversed its stand when Women's Department studies indicated that "protective" laws were more discriminatory than beneficial. In 1971 the Women's Department organized a Network for Economic Rights (NER) in several states as a coalition of social action groups from several spheres to work on legislation prohibiting social and economic discrimination against women and other disadvantaged groups.[26] For the next two years, women leaders in some large unions, especially the Communications Workers, the United Auto Workers, the Amalgamated Clothing Workers, the Meatcutters, and the Teamsters, lobbied within their unions for support of women's issues and for greater organization of women workers.

Their efforts came to fruition in two major ways. In October

---

25. Hole and Levine, *Rebirth of Feminism*, p. 80.
26. *Spokeswoman*, 1 October 1971, p. 6.

1973, at its annual convention, the AFL-CIO finally reversed its historic opposition to the Equal Rights Amendment. And on March 22–23, 1974, more than 3,200 women from 58 unions met in Chicago to form the Coalition of Labor Union Women (CLUW). The latter development, by far the most significant effort of trade-union women to organize as a group since the ill-fated Women's Trade Union League early in this century, was preceded by a series of meetings to test sentiment for such an organization. Over a year before, representatives from several major unions with significant numbers of female members had met at O'Hare Airport near Chicago to discuss a coalition. Then on June 30, 1973, more than 200 trade-union women from 20 unions and 18 states, most of them in the Midwest, met in Chicago to discuss their common problems and the possibility of forming a national organization. Similar meetings were held in Philadelphia, on the West Coast, and in the South during the next nine months, in preparation for the national CLUW meeting.

CLUW's purposes are: to organize women not yet in unions in conjunction with established unions; to support legislation of benefit to working women; to increase the participation of women in union leadership; and to encourage affirmative action and the upgrading of women in their jobs.

Academia

The campus reflects the movement in microcosm, and usually sports separate groups for the separate strata of women in the university community. The first campus women's groups to emerge in late 1968 and 1969 were primarily undergraduates who had some relationship to varying leftist organizations. Movement organizers found it much more difficult to organize feminist groups on campus than they had more typically "political" organizations. They explained this by saying that the undergraduate years were the most egalitarian of a woman's life and it was not until she left school for marriage and/or job that she became personally aware of women's true situation. Almost in defiance of this rationalization, a year later campus women's liberation groups had become practically ubiquitous. For undergraduates this was primarily a consequence of the rising national awareness of the movement and the decline of most leftist groups. As with the movement in general, however, numerous women who had not been attracted to leftist groups were attracted to women's liberation, so the undergraduate groups often lost their leftist identity.

As a rule, undergraduate groups, like the younger branch of the movement, are primarily rap groups concerned with working out the many personal conflicts a young woman faces between her ascribed role and the new possibilities of her college environment. Additionally, many have worked in efforts to get free campus child-care centers for the children of all employees, faculty, and students; easy availability of contraception and abortion by student health; and the formation of courses on women.

On many campuses, graduate women have formed separate groups, usually confined to their particular department or professional school. Although many of these serve much the same functions as rap groups, they also reflect the increasing concern of women graduates for their future careers. Women are often excluded from the informal networks of communication among male faculty and students through which most information necessary to proper professional socialization is passed. The graduate caucuses give women a chance to share what bits of information they have, thus forming their own network. Similarly, they function as support groups for women who are discouraged and/or isolated by the male faculty and students. More concrete concerns are demonstrated by passing information on jobs and fellowships, lobbying their departments for more women faculty, and doing research on women for dissertations. Many have gone further than this and filed formal complaints of discrimination with their professional associations. The women's law school caucus at The University of Chicago sued the law school under Title VII of the Civil Rights Act charging that in their function as an employment agency, the law school allowed firms that overtly refused to hire women graduates to use the school's premises. The League of Academic Women (LAW) at the University of California at Berkeley filed a federal court suit charging sex discrimination on February 15, 1972, to compel the university to have a percentage of women on the faculty and in administrative positions within thirty years, that is approximately equal to the percentage of women in the qualified labor force.

Faculty women have not often been able to form their own groups on campus; usually, there are too few women to do so. Although some statewide organizations are emerging, faculty generally join with the graduate women, form a contingency in the local NOW or WEAL chapter, or confine their feminist activity to their professional association's women's caucus. The first three caucuses were formed in September 1969 at the national conventions of the Sociological, Psychological and Political Science Associations. Today over seventy-five professional associations have women's caucuses, and many have split to form separate organizations.

The caucuses have had three major functions. The first has been to provide incisive criticism of a discipline's concept of women, or lack of one. Through symposia, papers, panels, and forums the *content* of a discipline has been severely questioned, and tentative steps have been made toward the development of new concepts. The other functions have been largely practical. The caucuses have become organized interest groups to urge an end to discrimination, professional sanctioning of institutions that do not hire many women, and provision of facilities of interest to women faculty and students. The latter include child-care centers on campus and at conventions, an end to nepotism rules, increased research money devoted to the study of women, acceptance of courses on women, and a concerted effort to hire and place women Ph.D.s. Additionally, the caucuses form the basis of communications networks for the exchange of information on jobs, complaints, and other matters of common interest.

Associations of nonfaculty employees have been fewer in number and much more concentrated on job-related disabilities than any of the other groups. Their major interest has been better pay and working conditions and an end to discrimination. Thus, many employee associations have focused their interests on organizing unions—with or without a feminist approach.

Despite their differences and diversity (Yale, for example, has six separate women's groups), all campus groups have been able to join together in charging their universities and colleges with violations of Executive Order 11375. While some campus groups were formed specifically to compel an HEW investigation, many have seen this as only a part, albeit a major one, of their activities. Concern with contract compliance has caused coalitions among women who were heretofore not at all aware of the commonality of their problems.

In the meantime, universities themselves had not been insensitive to the potential power of female organization. Many appointed official committees on the status of women, though their impact varied from campus to campus. The first two reports were begun at the University of California at Berkeley and the University of Chicago in the spring of 1969. They were followed by almost a hundred reports at other campuses within the next two years.[27] Similarly, professional associations appointed their own official committees to look into the situation. The quality of these investigations varied considerably. Many were obvious attempts at whitewashes, but others were quite incisive in their implications. Whatever the conclusions and interpretations of the committees, the facts quite clearly showed one thing feminists had been saying all along: the number of women thinned out toward the top. As with the caucuses, the main effect of these reports was to increase the awareness of both women and men to the reality of female subordination. Concrete institutional changes have yet to be made.

27. A review of the early reports was made by Lora H. Robinson, "Institutional Variation in the Status of Academic Women" in *Academic Women on the Move*, ed. Alice Rossi and Ann Calderwood (New York: Russell Sage Foundation, 1973), pp. 199–238.

6
The Policy Impact of the Women's Liberation Movement

Wᴴᴇɴ ᴛʜᴇ ᴡᴏᴍᴇɴ's ʟɪʙᴇʀᴀᴛɪᴏɴ ᴍᴏᴠᴇᴍᴇɴᴛ emerged in 1966 and 1967, there was no national policy on the status of women. There were a plethora of state laws restricting women's opportunities and freedoms in keeping with traditional mores and a few providing for equal and fair employment practices—the latter more often ignored than enforced.[1] The President's Commission on the Status of Women had issued its report in 1963, but its effects on policy per se had been negligible. While it indirectly contributed to the formation of the State Commissions on the Status of Women, and with them to part of the women's liberation movement, it did not lead to any concrete

---

1. Jo Freeman, "The Legal Basis of the Sexual Caste System," *Valparaiso Law Review* 5 (Spring 1971): 302, gives a more complete analysis.

legislation. The only federal legislation at that time, the 1963 Equal Pay Act[2] and the addition of "sex" to Title VII of the 1964 Civil Rights Act,[3] had been idiosyncratic occurrences (see supra, pp. 53–54. The latter had not even been supported by the Women's Bureau and was largely ignored by the EEOC. If anything, the various civil rights agencies within the government and the people in and out of government concerned with civil rights were hostile to the addition of sex discrimination as a legitimate concern. Women had it pretty good, they thought, and their demands should not be allowed to compete with those of minority groups for a share of the slim federal pie.[4]

By 1972 this picture had changed radically. Three-fourths of the demands in NOW's 1968 Bill of Rights had been at least partially attained, including the two then so controversial they caused splits within the organization (legalized abortion and congressional passage of the Equal Rights Amendment). While the President had yet to make a major statement on the status of women a new Task Force Report issued in 1970 had made numerous administrative and legislative suggestions many of which had had results or were well on their way to enactment. A federal policy of equal opportunity, if not total equality, was clearly emerging in piecemeal fashion, and the legal and administrative tools were being forged with which feminist groups could viably work toward equal opportunity.

What is striking about this new policy is not simply that there is still a long way to go, but that the notoriously cumbersome governmental apparatus has done so much so quickly. When one compares the strenuous, conflictual efforts of the black civil rights movement to the relatively peaceful endeavors of feminists, the road to progress clearly appears to have been much smoother. That this greater ease is not due purely to racism is evident from

---

2. Public Law 88–83, *U.S. Code*, vol. 29, sec. 206(d) (1964).

3. Public Law 88–352, *Statutes at Large*, vol. 78, sec. 241 (1964), *U.S. Code*, vol. 42, secs. 2000(a) et seq. (1965).

4. For an example of this thinking, see U.S. Commission on Civil Rights, *Jobs and Civil Rights*, by Richard P. Nathan, Clearinghouse Publication No. 16 (Washington, D.C.: Government Printing Office, April 1969), pp. 50–55.

the similarly strenuous battles other white movements—antitrust, temperance, suffrage, and the Townsend movement immediately come to mind—have had in the past. It is even more striking when one realizes that this new policy is basically redistributive in nature, although it often uses regulatory techniques, and thus involves conflict between large classes of people over the redistribution of social resources from one group to another.[5]

As Lowi points out,[6] there have been very few case studies of redistributive policy decisions; thus there are not really any adequate models for analyzing the ones we are concerned with here. I would argue that a main reason so few studies have been made of this important arena is because the development of these major new policy areas has often been the result of social movements. Political scientists have paid little attention to social movements as relevant political phenomena, concentrating primarily on the interest groups into which they occasionally evolve. Thus they have not been able to see the intimate relationships between many new redistributive policies and the emergence of new organized interests in society.

This lack of awareness is exacerbated by the fact that redistributive policies are often only in the broadest sense conflicts between major classes; the immediate battles are between specific groups within the more powerful classes whose own interests are not always congruent. The fact that major redistributive decisions can be made as a result of intraclass conflicts adds an element of confusion to the decision-making process as well as greater room for maneuvering. For example, in the broadest sense civil rights policy reflects a decision to redistribute "life chances" from whites to blacks. But if it was perceived as that, it is highly unlikely that whites as a class, who control social resources to a greater degree than blacks, would have allowed this to happen. As Dye describes it, civil rights policy was

---

5. For an analysis of the three major categories of public policy—distributive, regulatory, and redistributive—see Theodore J. Lowi, "Distribution, Regulation, Redistribution: The Functions of Government," in *Public Policies and Their Politics*, ed. Randall B. Ripley (New York: W. W. Norton, 1966), pp. 27–40.

6. Ibid., p. 34.

an effort of established liberal elites to insure that the benefits of the American system would be available to those blacks who accept the prevailing consensus and exhibit middle-class values. Opposition to civil rights is centered among white masses; virtually none of the progress in civil rights since World War II (Brown v. Topeka, Civil Rights Act of 1964, Fair Housing, etc.) would have taken place if white masses rather than white elites determined public policy.[7]

In other words, the whites who made the new policy were not those who lost because of it. Basically, the upper-middle class was making policy for the lower and lower-middle classes[8] and, at least in the beginning, the North was making policy for the South.[9] The specific issues of conflict were much more narrow than implied by the redistributive nature of the overall policy. Similarly, efforts to improve the status of women can ultimately be viewed in the short run as taking away opportunities from men and giving them to women (though both feminists and liberals would argue that in the long run men will benefit, as whites will benefit from black equality). But the specific targets are largely employers, unions, and educational institutions; and the specific techniques are regulation of how they distribute their occupational and educational opportunities.

In the pages to follow the major national policies on the status

---

7. Thomas R. Dye, *Understanding Public Policy* (Englewood Cliffs, N.J.: Prentice-Hall, 1972), p. 22. For an extensive analysis of civil rights policy, see Dye's *The Politics of Equality* (Indianapolis: Bobbs-Merrill, 1971).

8. The economic aspects of this point are aptly illustrated by Barbara Bergman in her study of "The Effect on White Incomes of Discrimination in Employment," *Journal of Political Economy* 79 (March/April 1971): 294. Her projection of the consequences of a nondiscriminatory world indicated that "those whites in the lowest education bracket—those who had not achieved an elementary school education—would bear the brunt of the change. These white males might suffer losses on the order of 10 percent with losses running up to 20 percent very unlikely. While for white males the heavy damage will probably be restricted to those who did not achieve an eighth-grade education, for white females the damage would extend to all those who did not graduate from high school, and would be greater" (p. 310).

9. This also explains why the most provocative and far reaching civil rights changes have been promulgated by federal judges and the least and fewest by local legislature. The former are least likely to be affected either personally or by adverse constituent pressure.

of women are described and analyzed.[10] The first three—the Equal Pay Act of 1963, Title VII of the 1964 Civil Rights Act, and Executive Order 11375—were declared prior to or in the early days of the women's liberation movement. Thus enough time has elapsed to focus on their implementation and the response of their enforcement agencies to the new movement. The other policies, including congressional passage of the Equal Rights Amendment, have all occurred since 1971.[11] Thus the major impact of the movement has been in their actual passage, not their administration, and it is these efforts that are examined.

The Equal Pay Act

As Nelson Polsby points out, "there is often a hiatus of years—sometimes decades—between the first proposal of a policy innovation and its appearance as . . . a law." [12] Such innovations require *"incubation"* (italics his), a function usually assumed by the Senate whose members propose "bills that they know will not pass, make speeches, make demands for support . . . from interest groups favoring the proposal." [13] This process was certainly necessary for passage of the Equal Pay Act, the first piece of federal legislation on women since the Nineteenth Amendment. By the time it was passed in 1963 a number of states had equal-pay acts so it was hardly innovative. Federal action, however, did generate an even greater passage of similar laws by many more states and, in this sense, can be said to have catalyzed a local concern with the economic problems of women.[14]

---

10. This chapter discusses only the major developments affecting the private sphere. For a concise description of all federal laws, regulations, and programs to combat sex discrimination, see U.S. Commission on Civil Rights, "A Guide to Federal Laws Prohibiting Sex Discrimination," Clearinghouse Publication No. 46 (Washington, D.C.: Government Printing Office, 1974).

11. There were sex-discrimination prohibitions added to two minor bills in 1970: The Intergovernmental Personnel Act, 42 *U.S.C.* §§4701–4772 and the Disaster Relief Act, 42 *U.S.C.* §4419.

12. Nelson W. Polsby, "Policy Analysis and Congress," in *American Politics and Public Policy*, ed. Michael P. Smith (New York: Random House, 1973), p. 102.

13. Ibid., p. 103.

14. Leo Kanowitz, *Women and the Law* (Albuquerque, N.M.: University of New Mexico Press, 1969), p. 102, note 16.

The Equal Pay Act came about more out of a concern for men than for women. First proposed in 1868 at the National Labor Union Convention, equal pay did not become an issue until World War I. Prior to that time women were a relatively small proportion of the labor force and found primarily in sex-segregated jobs. Under such conditions equal pay was simply not relevant. During the national emergency many women were encouraged, even required, to move into jobs that had formerly been held by men. Since women traditionally worked for less money than men, the 2 million to 4 million women suddenly added to the work force created a concern that they would depress the wage rates and that men would be forced to work at the lower rates after the war. Several actions were taken by the government, of which the March 1918 report by the War Labor Conference Board is typical. It said: "If it shall become necessary to employ women on work ordinarily performed by men, they must be allowed equal pay for equal work." [15]

Some of this momentum carried over after the war and in 1919 Montana and Michigan enacted the first state equal-pay laws. It was many years before others followed their lead, but some federal agencies, in particular the Women's Bureau, pushed the "rate for the job" principle. In 1938 the Fair Labor Standards Act[16] set a statutory floor to wages for covered workers. It also provided for appointment of industry committees to recommend minimum-wage rates above the basic statutory minimum and specified that "no classification shall be made under this section on the basis of age or sex."

World War II saw a repeat of what had happened in the first war. In 1942 the War, Navy, and Labor Departments issued a joint statement saying "Wage rates for women should be the same as for men, including the entrance rate." The National War Labor Board applied this principle on a mandatory basis in

---

15. This discussion is taken primarily from a pamphlet of the Women's Bureau, U.S. Department of Labor, *Action for Equal Pay* (Washington D.C.: Government Printing Office, 1966). See also Morag MacLeod Simchak, "Equal Pay in the United States," *International Labour Review* 103, no. 6 (June 1971): 541.

16. Public Law 75–718, *Statutes at Large*, vol. 52, sec. 1060 (1938).

disputes coming before it. The war period also saw the introduction of the first equal-pay bills into Congress, though it was not until 1945 that a major bill with broad coverage was debated. Despite strong testimony in its favor, the bill was not adopted, but every succeeding session of Congress saw another one introduced. Finally, after "eighteen years of persistent, unsuccessful efforts to get an equal pay bill to the floor of Congress" [17] the federal government was added to the roster of nineteen states that prohibited wage differences on the basis of sex.

Throughout all the early agitation for equal pay, the major concern of Congress and the supporting unions was the "prevention of women's wages from undercutting the wages of men." [18] Women's unions and feminists supported equal pay out of dedication to principle and feelings of working-class solidarity but always with the proviso that there be training programs for "working girls" to avail women of the same opportunities as men to earn decent wages.[19] For the most part, they never achieved decent wages because male unions continued to exclude women from membership and apprenticeship programs while employers,[20] when faced with a choice between male and female employees, chose women only if they would work for lower wages. Then as now, equal pay was irrelevant without equal job opportunity. If anything, the Equal Pay Act *"increased job security for men* by discouraging the replacement of men with lower paid women" (italics author's).[21]

Because the Equal Pay Act was passed as an amendment to the Fair Labor Standards Act, its coverage was restricted to those 61

---

17. Bessie Margolin, "Equal Pay and Equal Employment Opportunities for Women," *New York University Conference of Labor* 19 (1967): 297.

18. Elizabeth Baker, *Technology and Women's Work* (New York: Columbia University Press, 1964), p. 412.

19. Alice Henry, *Women and the Labor Movement* (New York: George H. Doran, 1923), p. 129; Edith Abbott, *Women in Industry* (New York: D. Appleton, 1910).

20. See Gail Falk, "Sex Discrimination in Trade Unions," in *Women: A Feminist Perspective*, ed. Jo Freeman (Palo Alto, Calif.: Mayfield, 1975), pp. 254–76.

21. Caruthers Gholson Berger, "Equal Pay, Equal Employment Opportunity and Equal Enforcement of the Law for Women," *Valparaiso Law Review* 5 (Spring 1971): 331.

percent of all wage and salary earners covered by the FLSA. Thus administrative, executive and professional positions were not covered until the act was amended again in 1972 as part of the Education Amendments Act.[22] Although its coverage was limited, its implementation was quite effective for those few situations where men and women did perform the same work. Administered by the Wage and Hour Division of the Employment Standards Administration of the Department of Labor, the FLSA provides for anonymity to complainants and rapid handling of complaints. As periodic routine reviews are made of employers without a specific complaint, unreported violations can be found, and the possibility of employer retaliation against a complainant is mitigated. Although voluntary compliance and conciliation is preferred, a vigorous litigation program by the Department of Labor serves as a spur to corrections. When there has been litigation, the courts have been generally liberal in their interpretation, ruling that work need only be "substantially" equal to qualify for equal pay.[23] By the end of fiscal 1974, the Equal Pay Act had recovered in back pay alone over $84 million for over 171,000 employees— all but a few of them women.[24] While feminists have found little to complain about in the implementation of the EPA, it should be realized that its "success" is not due so much to a great concern with women's pay as the fact that it is included in the overall efforts of the Wage and Hour Administration to enforce the multifaceted FLSA. The salary statistics it reviews are just one part of its general investigation into covered employers and unions.

Title VII and the Equal Employment Opportunity Commission

The main redistributive decision on sex discrimination, i.e., its

---

22. Public Law 92–318, *Statutes at Large*, vol. 86, sec. 235 (1972).

23. *Schultz* v. *Wheaton Glass Company*, 421 F.2d 259 (Third Circuit, 13 January 1970), certiorari denied, 398 U.S. 905 (1970). *Schultz* v. *American Can Co.—Dixie Products*, 424 F.2d 356 (Eighth Circuit, 1970).

24. Internal Department of Labor figures given out in phone interview of July 1974. They do not include the $15 million in back pay gained by the AT&T settlement (infra, pp. 188–90).

addition to the pantheon of public concerns, did not take place until 1964. However, the circumstances under which it took place clouded the fact that it had taken place at all. It came about not as a result of authoritative decision or public commitment after long debate, but as a combination of historical accident and coattail riding. The event was the addition of "sex" to Title VII of the Civil Rights Act, prohibiting discrimination in employment. The incidents surrounding its surprise addition were described earlier. What is more relevant here are the incidents surrounding the creation of Title VII's enforcement agency, the Equal Employment Opportunity Commission (EEOC), and the power which it was, or was not, given to act.

Title VII was among the most strongly opposed provisions of President Kennedy's omnibus draft civil rights bill. The House acted on 47 amendments to it and adopted 18 of them before it passed a substitute bill on February 10, 1964, under pressure from the new Johnson administration. Because the Senate Judiciary Committee was known to be hostile, it was bypassed by the bill's leadership to avoid delay and watering down of the act. Nonetheless, during the subsequent three months of floor debate, involving over 500 proposed amendments, a substitute bill was hammered out in informal conferences which succeeded in doing both.[25] The results satisfied no one.

Providing equal job opportunity was the intention of Title VII of the 1964 Civil Rights Act, but its means of carrying out this intention involved little more than a stated prohibition against job discrimination by employers, employment agencies, unions, or joint labor-management apprenticeship committees. Even a perfunctory glance at Title VII revealed that it was intended to create more of an appearance than a reality. The act stated the admirable goal of eliminating employment discrimination while providing absolutely no viable means of doing so (sec. 2). This

---

25. For a description of the official proceedings which led to this "Mansfield-Dirksen Compromise," see the Equal Employment Opportunity Commission, *The Legislative History of Titles VII and IX of the Civil Rights Act of 1964* (Washington, D.C.: Government Printing Office, 1967), p. 10.

"forked tongue" approach is reminiscent of the first protective legislation to institute the ten-hour day among factory workers passed in the first half of the nineteenth century. It too stated a policy of concern in order to pacify the striking workers while providing many loopholes and few enforcement mechanisms to calm the irate manufacturers.[26] As it finally emerged from Congress, the basic principles upon which Title VII relied to eliminate discrimination in employment were individual initiative on the part of the discriminatee and goodwill on the part of the discriminator. These principles are not likely to be useful in enforcing any policy decision, certainly not one as far-reaching as job discrimination.

In attempting to carry out its stated functions, Title VII suffered from a high degree of structural schizophrenia. It provided little substantive power and then distributed this power in such a way that it would do the least good for those who were victims of discrimination. On the one hand it created the EEOC as its main regulatory agency (sec. 4). On the other hand it emasculated it. What power Title VII created was allocated elsewhere. All the EEOC could do to directly effect employment discrimination was to listen to and conciliate complaints, file *amicus curiae* briefs if the unconciliated complainant should go to court, and recommend that the attorney general prosecute the most serious cases (secs. 4f, 5, 6).

Originally, as proposed by the Kennedy administration, the EEOC was modeled after the National Labor Relations Board and possessed "cease and desist" powers common to the NLRB and various state Fair Employment Practices Commissions. By the time it had survived the House Judiciary Committee, this power had been changed to a provision requiring the EEOC, if conciliation failed, to bring civil suit for the defendant unless it felt such a case was not in the public interest. The final Senate version, as agreed upon by the House, removed even this modicum of power and put the burden of bringing suit on the individual complainant.

---

26. Alice Henry, *The Trade Union Woman* (New York: D. Appleton, 1917), pp. 14–15.

The result was that Title VII's enforcement agency, the EEOC, was itself without power. The only meaningful authority lay in the individual, who alone could initiate investigation or civil suit; the courts, who alone could make binding decisions and impose sanctions; and the attorney general, who was the only government representative that could bring suit under Title VII. Yet, even in this situation, the attorney general was not required to act on the recommendation of the EEOC and the cases to be prosecuted could be selected independent of Title VII's creation. The attorney general had absolute discretion, provided there be "reasonable cause" to believe there existed a "pattern or practice of resistance to the full enjoyment of any of the rights secured." [27]

As the EEOC itself realized, most people are either ignorant of Title VII and the processes involved, or if aware, hesitant to file complaints because of fear of reprisal, a reluctance to solicit intervention from a seemingly remote federal agency, and the desire to avoid the time-consuming and potentially costly process involved in a legal suit.[28] According to one expert:

> As the experience of all the anti-discrimination commissions has shown, most victims of discrimination never complain to them. To reach the great bulk of discriminatory practices, commissions must take the initiative themselves.[29]

The only way this difficulty can even partially be overcome is by the existence of active, functional organizations working in the interest of the different "minority groups" mentioned in the act. Individuals rarely have the resources or the tenacity to confront corporations. Only organizations with the political motivation to see the gain for the group inherent in the individual complaint are capable of bringing action. For most of the "minorities" listed in the act, such organizations do not exist or are not sufficiently viable to undertake this task.

---

27. The Civil Rights Act, *U.S. Code*, vol. 42, sec. 2000e–6 (1964).
28. Equal Employment Opportunity Commission, *Third Annual Report* (Washington D.C.: Government Printing Office, 1968), p. 16.
29. Michael I. Sovern, *Legal Restraints on Racial Discrimination in Employment* (New York: Twentieth Century Fund, 1966).

This need reveals the pluralist assumptions about the structure of the political system that are implicit in the act. Government was not prepared to enforce its own law; rather, it had to wait until organized interests forced it to do so. Since those interests which are the most organized are the most likely to be in violation of the law—and those individuals who are their victims least likely to be organized as interests—this practice ensures a minimal effect. Implicit in the law itself was the requirement that there be active social-movement organizations to mobilize support for the victims of employment discrimination. Thus, the enforcement mechanisms themselves serve as a barometer of social pressure. As political consciousness and organization of a particular minority group grows, so does its ability to prosecute complaints in the courts. But as long as the EEOC had no power itself, when such organizations faltered, or where they had not yet developed, the status quo practices could regain possession of the field.[30]

If individual initiative is the prerequisite for bringing the machinery of the EEOC into operation, employer goodwill was the necessary ingredient for resolving the conflict. In the final version of Title VII, the most potent weapon given the EEOC after it had investigated and found reasonable cause to believe discrimination existed was to "endeavor to eliminate any such alleged unlawful

---

30. The women's movement has only recently created the machinery to systematically assault the legal channels as the NAACP Legal Defense and Education Fund did, but has not yet plotted the strategy for so doing. NOW has been plaintiff in cases and some of its members who were attorneys have handled cases or at least written *amicus* briefs for several others. However, most cases have been sporadically handled by dedicated lawyers who donated their time out of a commitment to the issue. Over 300 sex-discrimination cases have been sponsored by the ACLU, and some feminist law firms, with and without foundation financing, have been created to handle other sex-discrimination cases.

Nonetheless, there have been some significant decisions. One of those came about because another social movement organization had the enlightened self-interest to extend a helping hand to their less organized colleagues. When Ida Phillips wanted to file suit in the Fifth Circuit against the Martin Marietta Corporation for refusing to hire her because she was the mother of a pre-school child, she was not too sure where to turn. Her case was eventually handled by the NAACP Legal Defense and Education Fund despite the fact that she is white. (411 F.2d 1, 416 F.2d 1257 [5th *U.S.C.A.* 1969] and 400 *U.S.* 542, [1971]).

employment practice by informal methods of conference, concilia-tion, and persuasion." [31] Nor could any findings from this limited process be made public which might lead to informal social sanctions if conciliation failed. This sweetness-and-light approach is not only absurd in theory but also had proved useless in the states many times over.

> By 1964 it was quite evident, upon the basis of the experience
> of states and municipalities having civil rights legislation,
> that the reliance upon administrative techniques of
> persuasion and conciliation to secure voluntary compliance
> with prohibitions against discrimination in employment were
> almost certainly doomed to failure.[32]

The results of the EEOC's lack of enforcement powers were clearly evident in its lack of results. Prior to amendment, of the 15,000 cases wherein the EEOC had found "reasonable cause" that there was discrimination, only about half had been successfully conciliated. Nationally, about 20 percent of these cases involved sex discrimination through 1972, though they ran as high as 60 percent in some regions. (Of the 48,898 new charges filed in fiscal 1973, 35 percent charged sex discrimination.) Of the several hundred cases that have been brought to the courts by individual complainants, less than a handful have been adjudicated. As one authority states: "individual lawsuits, without the aid of other enforcement techniques, are not an adequate way of dealing with the widespread violations of law existing in the civil rights field.[33]

The EEOC's lack of power has been further complicated by administrative difficulties. As its own Fifth Annual Report valiantly commented: "Born in compromise and limited by budgetary restrictions, the Equal Employment Opportunity Com-mission exercises its few powers to their fullest in attacking discrimination." [34] Although both budget and staff have ex-

---

31. *U.S. Code*, vol. 42, sec. 2000e–5(a) (1964).
32. Joseph P. Witherspoon, *Administrative Implementation of Civil Rights* (Austin, Tex.: University of Texas Press, 1968), p. 138.
33. Ibid., p. 11.
34. Equal Employment Opportunity Commission, *Fifth Annual Report* (Washington, D.C.: Government Printing Office, 1971), p. 1.

panded steadily since its formation—close to $56 million and 2,124 staff members in 1974—the backlog of cases has expanded even more rapidly. It was projected to reach over 90,000 by the end of 1974.[35] One analysis concluded:

> Structural deficiencies have been compounded by acute staffing problems, most notably long vacancies in key positions, and high rates of turnover at all levels, including major policy making and supervisory positions, and, as a result of small appropriations, and insufficient personnel. Consequently, the Commission has suffered from a critical lack of continuity and direction whereby its ability to operate efficiently and to fulfill its mandate under Title VII have been seriously impaired. . . .
>
> The Commission's operations have also been hampered by haphazard programming, which is frequently on an ad hoc basis. Means of making maximum use of the agency's limited resources have not been devised and methods to measure its overall effectiveness have not been instituted. . . .[36]

According to the U.S. Commission on Civil Rights' 1973 assessment, the "EEOC is just beginning to take a systematic approach to handling its responsibility." [37] Thus its minimal effectiveness was only partially accounted for by its lack of significant enforcement power. The latter problem was partially remedied in 1972 by the latest compromise in the long struggle between civil rights groups seeking major federal weapons to attack employment discrimination and business interests led by the U.S. Chamber of Commerce who wanted to see as little disruption as possible.[38]

---

35. Interview with Bill Monahan, EEOC Office of Public Information, 12 July 1974.

36. U.S. Commission on Civil Rights, *The Federal Civil Rights Enforcement Effort* (Washington, D.C.: Government Printing Office, 1971), pp. 88, 135.

37. U.S. Commission on Civil Rights, *The Federal Civil Rights Enforcement Effort—A Reassessment* (Washington, D.C.: Government Printing Office, 1973), p. 78. The Civil Rights Commission was preparing a new comprehensive enforcement assessment while this book was in press.

38. For an account of the opposing sides and their positions, see D. Culhane, "Labor Report/Battle Over Enforcement Powers for the EEOC Pits Business Against Labor, Civil Rights Groups," *National Journal*, 13 November 1971, pp. 2249–59.

The two alternative approaches debated during the first session of the Ninety-second Congress had both been defeated in the original framing of the act. The Hawkins (D.-Calif.) Bill [39] would have given the EEOC cease-and-desist powers while that of Congressman John Erlenborn (R.-Ill.)[40] would only have authorized the Commission to bring civil suit if conciliation failed—taking this power away from the Justice Department. Other provisions in the latter bill were opposed by civil rights forces, and a five-week filibuster led to a compromise in favor of the civil suit approach with the other provisions removed.[41]

In its final form, the Equal Employment Opportunity Act of 1972 (PL 92–261) expanded the EEOC's jurisdiction as well as its powers to include three new classes of employers previously exempted: public and private educational institutions, state and local governments and their agencies, and employers and unions with fifteen or more members (twenty-five was the previous limit). After a two-year period of mutual cooperation, it removes from the attorney general the right to bring civil suits in all cases except those against government agencies and gives it to the EEOC if thirty days of conciliatory efforts are not successful. Within six months of passage, the EEOC had filed five suits, and by the end of 1973, 147 more. The right of an individual to go to court was retained and a provision added permitting an individual or organization to file a charge "on behalf of" an aggrieved party.

It is too early to assess the effect of these increased EEOC powers. Thus it is within the context of minimal civil rights enforcement for *all* covered groups, due to limited powers, restricted budget, and administrative problems, that the progress of women must be assessed. It is not the achievement of equal employment opportunity, but equal consideration by the Equal Employment Opportunity Commission that has been the short-range goal of feminist organizations. In this effort women started from way behind. As

---

39. H.R. 1746, 92nd Cong., 1st sess., 1971.
40. H.R. 9247, 92nd Cong., 1st sess., 1971.
41. Richard R. Rivers, "In America, What You Do Is What You Are: The Equal Employment Opportunity Act of 1972," *Catholic University of America Law Review* 22 (Winter 1973): 460–62.

the U.S. Civil Rights Commission's 1971 Report makes clear, the EEOC began and remained for a long time a black-oriented agency. "The Commission's three priority anti-discrimination activities have been concerned with blacks, and Spanish Americans, and women, in descending order of priority." [42] This despite the fact that sex discrimination is the second-largest category of complaints, and women the largest group of "minority" members.

The early guidelines of the EEOC did not find much favor with feminist groups. The sole exception to this was the Commission's interpretation of the "bona fide occupational qualification" (bfoq) exemption to the sex provision of Title VII. A 1965 ruling asserted that

> An employer cannot justify the refusal to hire women on the basis of assumptions of the comparative employment characteristics of women in general, or stereotyped characterizations of the sexes, or because of his own personal preferences or those of his employees, customers or clients. The principle of nondiscrimination in employment requires that applicants be considered on the basis of individual capacities and not on characteristics generally attributed to a group." [43]

While this interpretation was subsequently upheld in the courts, it is clear from the language that it derives from an understanding of some of the rationales for race discrimination rather than indicating any early concern with sex discrimination. Thus, it was the only one of three recommendations made by the Citizens Advisory Council on the Status of Women to the EEOC which was accepted. [44] Recommendations on eliminating

---

42. Civil Rights Commission, *Enforcement Effort*, p. 97.

43. Commission guidelines of 22 November 1965. The EEOC has said that the only situations in which the bfoq would apply are those in which authenticity or genuineness (actor, actress) is a factor, it is dictated by community standards of morality or propriety (restroom attendant, lingerie sales clerk), and for jobs in the entertainment industry in which sex appeal is an essential qualification. Equal Employment Opportunity Commission, *Toward Job Equality for Women* (Washington, D.C.: Government Printing Office, 1969), pp. 5–6.

44. Letter of 2 November 1965 from Franklin Delano Roosevelt, Jr., first chairman of the EEOC, to Secretary of Labor Willard Wirtz.

sex-segregated want ads and the importance of enforcing the sex provision of Title VII were ignored.

The Citizen's Advisory Council (CACSW) was the permanent body of prominent women which replaced the President's Commission in 1963.[45] While its participants have not been noted feminists, many have over the years become sympathetic to the feminist position. Its staff in particular have been strong supporters of feminist objectives and organizations. Thus the Council and its reports have been able to function as a feminist voice within the government. It was the combined impact of the Council reports, feminists within Congress such as Martha Griffiths, and feminist organizations such as NOW and WEAL in conjunction with a small coterie of staff within the EEOC, that led to its final favorable interpretation of the want-ad issue. However, it is evident from the fact that these guidelines were not enforced while the cases are in court that the EEOC has given only verbal support (see infra, pp. 76–79).

Guideline interpretations disavowing "protective legislation" took considerably longer. Here, the major influence toward change was neither internal nor external pressure but the decisions of the courts. Initially the EEOC ruled that

> the Commission will not find an unlawful employment practice where an employer's refusal to hire women for certain work is based on a state law which precludes the employment for such work, provided that the employer is acting in good faith and that the law in question is reasonably adapted to protect women rather than to subject them to discrimination.[46]

In keeping with this ruling the EEOC refused to investigate several complaints made by women when their denial of job opportunities was justified by employers on the basis of state protective laws. Many of them took their cases to court, where repeatedly the decisions were in their favor. Concomitantly, the

---

45. Executive Order 11126 (1 November 1963) as amended by EO 11221 (6 May 1965).

46. Commission guidelines of 22 November 1965.

attorneys general of several states ruled that their states' protective laws were succeeded by Title VII and therefore void.[47] As a result, the EEOC was forced to change its interpretations to keep them in accord with judicial rulings on Title VII. According to then Commissioner Elizabeth Kuck:

> This Guideline revision followed the reasoning of the case of *Rosenfeld* v. *Southern Pacific Company* (293 F. Supp. 1219 [C.D. Calif. Nov. 1968] appeal pending Nos. 23,983 and 23,984) in which a Federal District Court, relying upon the Supremacy Clause of the Constitution, voided the California hours and weight law upon which an employer based his refusal to promote a female charging party because the law was found to be discriminatory on account of sex and violative of the Civil Rights Act of 1964.[48]

Consequently, new guidelines were promulgated on August 19, 1969, which stated that

> . . . the Commission has concluded that such laws and regulations conflict with Title VII of the Civil Rights Act of 1964 and will not be considered a defense to an otherwise established unlawful employment practice or as a basis for the application of the bona fide occupational qualification exception.[49]

This interpretation of Title VII, and its subsequent confirmation in the courts, has had a devastating effect on state protective legislation. For example, in 1964 forty states and the District of Columbia had maximum-hours laws for women. Today, only Nevada has neither repealed nor severely restricted their applicability.

In the last few years there have been no major objections by feminists to the guidelines and there has been a growing feeling that the EEOC has become at least as active on sex discrimination as on race in the area of interpretations and legal work. It is in the

---

47. Equal Employment Opportunity Commission, *Laws on Sex Discrimination in Employment* (Washington, D.C.: Government Printing Office, 1970), p. 10.

48. Speech of 10 November 1969.

49. Commission guidelines of 19 August 1969.

areas of technical assistance, affirmative action, and research that deficiencies still remain. The acceptance of sex discrimination as a legitimate area of concern rather than as a competitor for scarce resources with race discrimination was in part due to the changing climate of opinion stimulated by the women's liberation movement, in part to the hiring of many young attorneys, especially women, who were open to new ideas, and in part to the impact of the cases themselves. As one lawyer in the office of the General Counsel expressed it: "You can't take your job seriously without beginning to see there is a problem in this area." [50]

Both a consequence and a contribution to this change in attitude was the EEOC's decision to go after the single largest private employer of women in the United States—the American Telegraph and Telephone Company. According to then EEOC Chairman William Brown III, "We found through a study we did back in the fall of 1970 that about seven percent of our work load was devoted to AT&T cases. But we lacked the power to act." [51] That same fall the AT&T was petitioning the Federal Communications Commission for a 9 percent rate increase. In a moment of inspiration, one EEOC lawyer saw an opportunity to get at AT&T by intervening and requesting the FCC to deny the increase on the grounds that the corporation's discriminatory employment practices were not in the public interest.

Brown gave this idea his full support and a special task force was created (of four white men) which filed the first petitions with the FCC on December 10, 1970.

> The F.C.C. saw no relationship between rate levels and company's employment practices, but on January 21, 1971, it agreed to establish a separate docket to consider the question of discrimination, which was illegal under F.C.C. regulations.[52]

---

50. Interview with Sonia Pressman Fuentes, then head of the Trial Litigation Division, EEOC, February 1973.

51. Harvey D. Shapiro, "Women on the Line, Men at the Switchboard: Equal Employment Opportunity Comes to the Bell System," *New York Times Magazine*, 20 May 1973, p. 27.

52. Ibid.

After a year of investigation, the EEOC presented over 30,000 pages of testimony and documents attesting that the Bell System systematically discriminated against minorities and women. According to the head of the task force, Dave Copus, in this endeavor

> . . . we were advancing the really revolutionary view of sex discrimination. We took more or less hook, line and sinker the feminist view as espoused by the National Organization for Women—their view of institutionalized sex discrimination—and we said we wanted to attack it at its roots in the Bell System. Not just equal pay for equal work, etc. We wanted to present the whole sociology and psychology of sexual stereotypes as it was inculcated into the Bell System structure.[53]

The task force members had originally been educated to this "revolutionary view" by feminist lawyers within the EEOC. Once convinced of its value they had held meetings with NOW leaders arranged by Catherine East of the CACSW. The impact of these meetings is evident not so much in the final financial settlement (which NOW denounced) as in the final insistence that future Bell System employment practices integrate men into women's jobs as well as advance women into men's. Previously, the orientation of the EEOC had been solely to advancing minorities and women into better jobs, while ignoring those poorly paid jobs held primarily by minorities and women. It was NOW that convinced them that any job category that remained solely female (or black) would contribute to the maintenance of sex-role and race stereotypes and with that the psychological aspects of discrimination.[54]

The EEOC's final report concluded that "the Bell monolith is, without doubt, the largest oppressor of women workers in the United States." [55] Their analysis showed that sex discrimination

---

53. Quoted in ibid.
54. Interview with Dave Copus, EEOC, 23 May 1973.
55. Equal Employment Opportunity Commission, " 'A Unique Competence': A Study of Equal Employment Opportunity in the Bell System," Washington, D.C., undated, p. 173. Manuscript.

alone accounted for a difference of $500 million per year in wages.[56] This viewpoint and others were expressed during the year of sporadic public hearings and cross-examination that took place in 1972. At the same time negotiations were proceeding between the Bell System and a coordinated effort by the EEOC, the Labor Department's Office of Contract Compliance and Wage and Hour Divisions. Lack of cooperation and even lack of communication between the diverse federal agencies responsible for alleviating discrimination had led to many problems in this and other cases. The final settlement agreed to on January 18, 1973, was due in part to the successful collaboration of these government agencies.

Although there were some striking victories in this agreement, financial compensation was not one of them. The $38 million which AT&T must pay in back pay and wage increases falls far short of the $3.5 billion in back pay due since discrimination became illegal. Nonetheless, according to Dave Copus, it still represents a greater monetary gain for more people than the sum total of all the EEOC's efforts since it was created. This success led to a reorientation of the EEOC's overall strategy. It set up an entirely new National Programs Division to investigate cases of national significance where there are multiple complaints. Currently under investigation are four major corporations and their employees' unions, and a major construction union in conjunction with the contractors with whom it has collective bargaining agreements.

Now that the EEOC has the power to go to court, it does not have to restrict itself to those corporations regulated in the public interest by other federal agencies. Too, it has also learned that efforts to secure an end to race and sex discrimination do not necessarily have to compete with each other. A concerted attack on the elimination of both in the same companies can be mutually reinforcing.[57]

---

56. Ibid., p. 176.
57. Interview with Dave Copus, EEOC, 23 May 1973.

Executive Order 11375 and the Higher Education Campaign

Such a multifaceted attack has been partially incorporated into the policies of the Office of Federal Contract Compliance—but only within certain industries. The OFCC was set up by Executive Order 11246, signed by President Johnson on September 24, 1965, to supervise and coordinate the compliance activities of contracting agencies of the government. Under this order all employers holding federal contracts—covering one-third of the labor force—must not only agree that they will not discriminate in employment practices, but must also undertake affirmative action programs to rectify the effects of past discrimination. While the OFCC oversees general implementation of the order and issues the relevant regulations, specific authority to investigate complaints lies with the federal agencies issuing the contracts. Eighteen agencies have been allocated compliance responsibilities at one time, and, needless to say, this has led to very spotty enforcement. Each designated agency has the entire responsibility for all of a contractor's facilities, even though some of them may not have contracts with it, or may have contracts with other agencies. Thus, the Department of Health, Education, and Welfare is responsible for all colleges, universities, museums, and insurance agencies, while the General Services Administration governs the compliance activities of electric, gas, and sanitary services, among others) and the Department of Defense oversees 75 percent of all federal contracts.[58] Due to the administrative unwieldiness of overseeing so many agencies, OFCC is in the process of reducing the number with compliance responsibilities, eventually, to five or six.

The OFCC has available to it very strong sanctions to enforce compliance—the cancellation of all government contracts and debarment from future contracts. However, its enthusiasm for enforcing the Executive Order has been noticeably absent. It did

---

58. See the Civil Rights Commission's 1971 report on *Enforcement Effort*, p. 61, for a list of agencies and their jurisdictions prior to a reassignment in July 1974. The new list is available as Order No. 1 (revised) from the OFCC.

not issue regulations until two and a half years after it was created (May 28, 1968). It took it even longer to define explicitly what was meant by "affirmative action" with the result that for a long time the order was meaningless. Nor did it aggressively require contracting agencies to comply with their responsibilities under the order. In many cases, it was unaware that the agencies were ignoring its regulations. For years, employment data on applications, hiring, and promotions by race, let alone by sex, was just not systematically collected from the contractees.

> The ineffectiveness of the program, however, was due at least as much to failure to impose sanctions on known noncomplying contractors, as to the lack of staff of OFCC and the agencies and OFCC's lack of leadership. All contract compliance efforts prior to Executive Order 11246 had been characterized by volunteerism—designed to achieve compliance by consultation and mediation without resort to sanctions.[59]

Although the OFCC indicated a preference for enforcement over volunteerism, in practice it largely continued this policy.

> The lack of utilization of sanctions by contracting agencies forced OFCC to become involved in some of the most difficult negotiations of major noncompliance situations. For several reasons, including the paucity of OFCC's staff, this deference to OFCC in enforcement actions caused many to believe that sanctions would be imposed only in exceptional cases and only with OFCC involvement. Failure to make sanctions appear a likely result of noncompliance undermined all enforcement efforts in the early stages of implementing the order.[60]

During this time the only major use of the Executive Order was to create what became known as the "Philadelphia Plan" to improve minority hiring in the construction industry. By 1973 there had been some improvement; the OFCC had issued eighteen

---

59. Ibid., p. 52.
60. Ibid., p. 53.

orders specifying the nature of affirmative action plans and some of the compliance procedures to be used. Nonetheless, the Civil Rights Commission still reported in January of 1973 that the "OFCC has not yet provided Federal agencies with adequate mechanisms for resolving compliance problems, thus weakening the impact of these agencies upon employment discrimination." [61] This is in part due to the attitude of the Department of Labor which delayed approval of policy directives and in other ways "emphasized contract compliance's low priority." [62]

As with the EEOC, it is within this general context of apathetic enforcement of civil rights policy that the inclusion of women must be considered. Again, it is the achievement of parity with blacks, not actual implementation, that has been the consequence of the movement so far. However, such parity is not evident in all compliance agencies so sex discrimination cannot yet be said to have caught up with race discrimination as a legitimate policy concern in all areas of enforcement. The idea of adding sex discrimination to the Executive Order was one of the first major policy goals of NOW, and was expressed in a letter to President Johnson in the fall of 1966. This was followed by meetings with the Justice Department and the Civil Service Commission. In the meantime, Catherine East made copies of NOW's letter available to Esther Petersen, former director of the Women's Bureau and then assistant secretary of labor, who had long approved of the idea, and persuaded Secretary of Labor Willard Wirtz to do likewise. She also persuaded prominent members of some of the more respectable women's organizations, the Business and Professional Women (BPW) and the General Federation of Women's Clubs, to write supportive letters. With support from these groups, the secretary of labor, the Citizen's Advisory Council on the Status of Women, and the Interdepartmental Committee on the Status of Women, the staff of the CACSW was directed to draft a new order and send it to the Office of Management and Budget for approval. Its clearance by OMB and other government agencies

---

61. Civil Rights Commission, *Enforcement Effort*, p. 64.
62. Ibid.

encountered no opposition and Executive Order 11375, amending No. 11246, to include sex discrimination, was signed by President Johnson on October 13, 1967, to become effective one year later.

According to some sources, this relatively easy success was largely due to the precedent of Title VII. Since sex was now added to race, religion, and national origin in one piece of major legislation, its addition to others was facilitated. All EO 11375 did was bring the policies of the executive branch of government into conformity with those of Congress.[63]

Apart from fights with the Labor Department over guidelines, it was over two years before any use was made of the Executive Order by feminist groups and when it was resorted to it was an accident of circumstances. In 1969, Bernice Sandler, a member of WEAL, was not considered for any of seven openings in the Department of Counseling and Personnel Services of the University of Maryland despite the fact that she was as well qualified as the other candidates, held a doctorate, and had been teaching there part time for several years. When she asked why, she was told it was because she "came on too strong for a woman." That phrase stuck in her head, and when her husband assured her that sex discrimination was indeed the most likely reason rather than merely an excuse, she began looking for a legal remedy.[64]

This search was initially unproductive as all the obvious federal laws did not apply to sex discrimination against faculty. Title VI of the 1964 Civil Rights Act, which prohibited discrimination in all federally assisted programs, including education, applied only to discrimination on the basis of race, color, and national origin and didn't cover employment. Title VII prohibited sex discrimination in employment but specifically exempted the teaching personnel of educational institutions (until amended in March 1972). And the Equal Pay Act did not cover administrative, executive, and professional employees (until amended in June 1972).

---

63. Interview with Mary Eastwood, attorney for the Department of Justice, 27 March 1973.

64. Interview with Dr. Bernice Sandler, February 1973.

While reading an analysis of the laws prepared for the U.S. Commission on Civil Rights,[65] Sandler found a footnote on EO 11246 and from it developed the idea of using contract compliance as the means of legal redress. Unlike the laws that covered employment discrimination, it did not exempt educational institutions or professional employees. Further, it allowed for both individual- and class-action complaints and applied to the entire institution, not just the specific area of complaint. More important, a complaint could be based on very general data showing a *pattern* of discrimination rather than detailed documentation of instances of sex discrimination. And such a complaint could request a complete investigation of *all* hiring practices.

In consultation with Sandler, an OFCC official suggested an appropriate strategy and helped draft the initial complaint. On January 31, 1970, WEAL began a national campaign to end discrimination in higher education by filing a class-action complaint of sex discrimination against all universities and colleges with the Department of Labor. Over 90 percent of these institutions hold at least one federal contract, worth a total of over $3 billion. Charging an "industry-wide pattern" of discrimination,

> WEAL asked that the Department of Labor investigate the following areas: admission quotas to undergraduate and graduate schools, discrimination in financial assistance, hiring practices, promotions, and salary differentials. More than eighty pages of materials documenting these charges were submitted with the complaint to the Secretary of Labor. WEAL requested an immediate "class action" and compliance review of all institutions holding federal contracts. At the same time, specific charges were filed against the University of Maryland. Charges against more than 250 other institutions (about 10 percent of the nation's institutions of higher education) were subsequently filed by WEAL as word went out to women throughout the academic community. Among the institutions charged by WEAL were the University

---

65. Civil Rights Commission, *Jobs and Civil Rights.*

of Wisconsin, the University of Minnesota, Columbia University, the University of Chicago, and the entire state university and college systems of California, Florida, and New Jersey. In October WEAL filed a class action against all the medical schools in the country. A similar class action against the nation's law schools also was filed by the Professional Women's Caucus in April 1971. The National Organization for Women has also filed charges against Harvard University and the entire state university system of New York. Additional complaints . . . have brought the number . . . to more than 360.[66]

When the initial complaint reached the Contract Compliance office of the Department of Health, Education, and Welfare (HEW), their reaction was to dismiss it. Since they had no women among their professional staff, Rose Brock of the Office of Civil Rights was asked to deal with the complaints by women's groups "in order to calm them down. HEW gave the women's organizations six months to run out of steam." [67] Instead, six months later, "they were up to their ears in Congressional mail." [68]

If all WEAL had done was to file complaints, HEW's prediction would probably have been correct. Certainly, HEW would have done nothing to encourage any other possibility. But the WEAL complaint was able to catalyze an entire incipient structure of action created by the women's liberation movement. There were already feminist groups on many campuses. More significantly, there were several women's caucuses and/or separate women's organizations among the academic disciplines. These women were already angry about sex discrimination but, often isolated and vulnerable on their own campuses, had found no way to fight it individually. All they had done so far was to meet together periodically to compare notes. Bernice Sandler attended many of these academic meetings, either as an invited speaker or on her

66. Bernice Sandler, "A Little Help from Our Government: WEAL and Contract Compliance," in *Academic Women on the Move*, ed. Alice Rossi and Anne Calderwood (New York: Russell Sage Foundation, 1973), pp. 440–41.

67. Interview with Rose Brock, 28 March 1973.

68. Ibid.

own initiative. At the women's caucuses she told what she had done and encouraged women from different schools to collect the basic data necessary for WEAL to file additional complaints. The data necessary were minimal–statistics showing that women were underrepresented in various departments at various levels was adequate. Often that data had already been collected by the official Committees on the Status of Women established by many universities in response to internal pressures. Since WEAL would do the official filing, anonymity could be maintained; and since, apart from individual complaints, WEAL could request institution-wide investigations, the individuals who supplied the data could be protected.

Although Sandler, as head of the WEAL task force, did the bulk of the work in the ensuing onslaught, it was not a one-woman campaign. Academic women picked up the idea from her and spread it themselves in a continuous chain reaction. If Sandler was not present at a particular meeting, someone would be sure to announce the word and give out her address. Sandler's correspondence quickly became so voluminous that answering it became a full-time job. In the meantime, WEAL was well aware that just filing complaints would not lead to action. What HEW was most sensitive to was congressional pressure, especially from members of the Education committees. So WEAL developed a packet of materials on sex discrimination and sent it with personal notes pointing out the applicability of the Executive Order to about forty congresspeople. They were asked to write a note to the secretary of labor requesting that EO 11375 be enforced in the academic community; about half complied within a few weeks. On March 9, 1970, Representative Martha Griffiths (D.-Mich.), a member of the Ways and Means Committee and the WEAL Advisory Board,

> gave a speech in the House of Representatives detailing sex discrimination in education, describing WEAL's complaint, and criticizing the government for not enforcing its own rules and regulations as contained in the Executive Order. Some three weeks after Representative Griffiths' speech, the first

investigation concerning sex discrimination began at
Harvard University.[69]

For the next year campus feminist groups mobilized themselves
in the national effort. It was national not in direction but in scope.
Neither WEAL nor Sandler had any authority over any of the
groups that participated in the effort. What mobilized them was
not any kind of organizational directive, but their own dedication
to the issues and the opportunity for action created by the
Executive Order and WEAL. Sandler estimates the entire campaign cost less than $400, mostly for postage and phone calls.

Many groups of course did not participate. The idea of doing
something so mundane as petitioning the federal government for
a redress of grievances was not an activity they could relate to.
The government was too remote, and its response too distant.
Many however, did so anyway, despite their radical rhetoric and
alienation from traditional political activity. Former members of
SDS and women so politically apathetic they had never even voted
found themselves writing their congressional representatives to
encourage an HEW investigation and gathering data to assist the
government investigators if and when they came. They found
themselves "working within the system," occasionally to their
dismay, because the system gave them a way of working within it.

As the WEAL strategy was to stimulate many letters from
congressional offices to HEW, they asked local feminists to write
their own representatives. Since students are not always registered
to vote in the districts where they go to school, they also wrote
those representatives of their home districts.

> At one point the Office for Civil Rights at HEW was receiving
> so much Congressional mail that one person was assigned
> full-time to handle the correspondence. Similarly, at the
> Department of Labor more than 300 Congressional letters
> were received within a short period of time. Letters to
> legislators serve a dual function: they sensitize Congressional

---

69. Sandler, "WEAL," p. 443. Griffiths' speech was largely written by Sandler
from the voluminous material she had gathered.

staffs to the problems of sex discrimination, and they are an
effective prod to bureaucratic inaction. . . . Five months
after filing, in June 1970, there was a double pay off. HEW
issued a memorandum to all field personnel requiring them
to routinely include sex discrimination in all contract
compliance investigations, . . . [and] the Department of
Labor issued its long-awaited "Sex Discrimination
Guidelines" for federal contractors.[70]

The investigation of sex-discrimination charges on college
campuses was not without its effect on HEW. Partially in response
to pressure and partially due to the devastating nature of the field
reports, the HEW office of Contract Compliance expanded from
roughly twenty to sixty people nationally within two years, and a
special Higher Education division was set up in it in the summer
of 1972. Guidelines for implementation were also issued for the
first time. Rose Brock was put in charge of all compliance reviews
on sex discrimination and

her dedication, experience, and persistence led to extensive
documentation of sex discrimination charges in the early
investigations, and she helped set the pattern for later
compliance reviews. Her findings also helped to convince
some of the HEW staff of the extent of discrimination against
women, and the blatant violations of the Executive Order on
the campus.[71]

Nonetheless, according to Brock, the investigations are more
thorough than the actual implementation. "HEW is highly lenient.
It allows schools lots of time to comply and rarely takes them to
the hearings stage." [72] At best, two dozen schools have had
contracts slowed down and none have had them terminated.
Brock says all HEW really demands is "affirmative motion, not
action" because HEW officials and university administrative
personnel operate in the same social networks and with the same
frame of mind.

---

70. Ibid.
71. Ibid.
72. Brock interview.

By the end of December 1972, HEW was beginning to build up a sufficient backlog of complaints to request from the House Appropriations Committee money for extensive staff expansions. They had received 544 complaints against higher educational institutions, of which 350 concerned sex discrimination. Many of these were class actions. Of the 183 still pending, 154 involved sex discrimination. Thirty university affirmative-action programs had been accepted, 51 rejected, and 60 were pending review. In an attempt to cut down on the work, HEW worked out an arrangement with the EEOC whereby individual complaints would be sent to it and HEW would handle only class complaints. Needless to say, with the EEOC's enormous backlog and its two-year-average investigation period, this put individual complainants at a disadvantage.

How much of a disadvantage became apparent when the backlash began in early 1972. Although a plethora of established academicians opposed affirmative action, ironically, at the vanguard of the backlash were neither conservative nor professional organizations, but those of another minority group—the Jews. Their efforts were originally stimulated by an extensive investigation by the City University of New York into sex discrimination within its institutions. The target of the attack was the goals and timetables requirement of Revised Order No. 4. This concept was developed as part of the "Philadelphia Plan" and has become the heart of all affirmative-action plans. Although it has been argued by the OFCC that goals are merely objectives which a contractee must show good-faith efforts to achieve in contrast to quotas which are fixed restrictions that are discriminatory in intent, many have confused the two. As Jews comprise a substantial proportion of the white males in the CUNY system, the American Jewish Congress took up the banner against "quotas or preferential employment practices." [73]

In May 1972 representatives from six Jewish organizations—

---

73. Letter from Theodore J. Kolish, chairman of the American Jewish Congress New York Metropolitan Council, to Luis Quero-Chiesa, president of the New York Board of Higher Education, cited in *Women Today*, 7 February 1972, p. 4.

the Anti-Defamation League, the American Jewish Congress, the American Jewish Committee, the Jewish Labor Committee, Agudath-Israel, and the Jewish War Veterans—met with then HEW Secretary Elliot Richardson to voice their concern about abuses of affirmative-action guidelines. That summer they filed over thirty complaints with HEW charging that white males were denied either jobs or promotions due to preferential treatment given to women or minorities by colleges attempting to meet the federal regulations. In October several New York congresspeople met with the head of HEW's Office of Civil Rights to urge that an outside investigator look into the reverse discrimination charges on the ground that they were the result of governmental action. Consequently, a temporary "ombudsman" was appointed, who found that over three-fourths of the complaints had no validity. During the same period that these complaints were receiving priority treatment from HEW, many individual complaints from women and minorities were referred to the EEOC where they were added to the statistics on backlog.[74]

Although these groups have jointly filed over 150 complaints of reverse discrimination, and have not shown equal concern for the plight of Jewish women suffering from sex discrimination, their interests are not identical. They run the spectrum from seeking to rectify abuses of the regulations while accepting the desirability of affirmative action to seeing any effective affirmative-action plan as a threat to Jewish interests. Despite this divergency, the emergence of Jewish groups in the service of backlash efforts does not bode well for those desiring to see strong affirmative-action programs. With their liberal backgrounds these groups are in a much better position publicly to argue down goals and timetables as legitimate means of improving minority hiring than institutions of higher education or professional associations. It is still too early to see whether the portending conflict of interest-groups this new

---

74. Brock interview. Interview with Samuel H. Solomon, executive assistant to the director, Higher Education Division, Office for Civil Rights, HEW, 20 September 1974. See also *Women Today*, 25 December 1972, p. 4, and 5 March 1973, p. 5.

development represents will succeed in stalemating federal enforcement efforts. However, the nonaggressive attitude of HEW's understaffed compliance division and the lack of sympathy for minorities and women of the current Secretary Weinberger make such stalemating a distinct possibility. Redefining the conflict from one of "affirmative action" to one over "preferential hiring" could well undermine the ameliorative intent of the Executive Order by transforming what is essentially a fight over access to resources into one over ideology.

The Ninety-second Congress

The Ninety-second Congress passed a bumper crop of women's rights legislation—considerably more than the sum total of all relevant legislation that had been previously passed in the history of this country. In addition to the 1972 Equal Employment Opportunity Act discussed previously, there were:

1. Anti-sex-discrimination provisions in the Comprehensive Health Manpower Training Act of 1971 (PL 92–257)[75] and the Nurses Training Act of 1971 (PL 92–258).[76] Affecting some 1,400 academic institutions and hospitals that received over $600 million in federal funds in fiscal 1972, these bills prohibit sex discrimination in all training aspects of health-profession programs.

2. A Child Development Act that would have provided free day care for children in families of four with less than $4,300 annual income and a sliding fee scale for families with higher incomes (H.R. 6748 and S. 1512). Although many Republicans supported the bill in the belief that it met with the approval of the administration, Nixon vetoed it on December 9, 1971. He said the bill showed "fiscal irresponsibility, administrative unworkability, and family-weakening implications."

3. The Revenue Act of 1971 included an amendment to the Internal Revenue Code of 1954 which allows parents

---

75. 42 *U.S.C.* §2952–9.
76. 42 *U.S.C.* §2986–2.

with combined incomes of up to $18,000 per year to make income tax deductions for child care up to $400 a month. However, taxpayers are required to itemize all personal deductions in order to claim this one, and most low-income parents do not normally do so.

4. After a long and bitter fight, both Houses passed the Equal Rights Amendment with overwhelming majorities and without any of the crippling amendments that had threatened its passage many times before. This will be discussed in greater detail later on.

5. The Educational Amendments Act (PL 92-318)[77] that became law on July 1, 1972, included a title (IX) which prohibits sex discrimination in all federally aided education programs. Single-sex schools, private undergraduate colleges, and military academies are exempted from the admissions provision, and those schools going coeducational are allowed a transitional period to complete the process. Closely paralleling Title VI of the 1964 Civil Rights Act, its provisions will also be administered by the Office for Civil Rights of HEW as will those of the Health Manpower and Nurses Training Acts.

6. The U.S. Commission on Civil Rights is a temporary, independent bipartisan agency originally established by Congress in 1957 as a study group on minority problems. As of October 14, 1972, its jurisdiction has been expanded to include sex discrimination (PL 92-496).[78] This was done contrary to the desires of the Commission, which felt it had enough to do dealing with minority problems and saw additional responsibilities as a dilution of its resources. While the Commission has no enforcement powers, it is able to issue subpoenas and take testimony under oath at public hearings, collect and disseminate information, and appraise federal civil rights enforcement efforts in order to make recommendations to the President and Congress. This watchdog function in particular makes resources available for analysis of civil rights policy that would otherwise have to be provided by minority and/or feminist groups.

---

77. 20 *U.S.C.* §1681–1686.
78. §86 Stat. 813 amending 42 *U.S.C.A.* §1975c(a) (1957).

7. A bill equalizing employment benefits for married women federal employees (PL 92–187) was passed in late 1971.[79] Additionally, antidiscrimination prohibitions were added to several federal programs: Revenue Sharing (PL 92–512);[80] Public Works, Economic Development, and Appalachian Redevelopment Act (PL 92–65);[81] and the Water-Pollution Act (PL 92–500).[82] The latter two were added during committee by Bella Abzug, a member of the Public Works and Government Operations Committee. She makes it a policy to carry in her floor file a standard anti-sex-discrimination amendment which she introduces into every bill she can. Abzug has encouraged others to do so in their committees and the addition of similar provisions to the Revenue Sharing, Health Manpower, and Nurses Training Acts was largely due to this semiautomatic response.[83]

Abzug and Griffiths between them were also responsible for most of the more than twenty other bills of relevance to women considered during the Ninety-second Congress. They included several different abortion bills, and ones on social security, credit, extension of the minimum wage to domestics, and several miscellaneous bills. These and many more, including a new child-care bill, were immediately reintroduced into the Ninety-third Congress. Although sponsorship of relevant bills diversified in the Ninety-third Congress the fact that almost all of the approximately two dozen bills relevant to women originated in the House, with few comparable ones as yet introduced into the Senate, illustrates the importance of having sympathetic *women* in Congress, rather than merely sympathizers.

The major exception to this pattern was the Equal Credit Opportunity Title proposed by Senator William Brock (R.-Tenn.) as an amendment to the Fair Credit Billing Act (S.2101) and passed by the Senate 90–0 on July 23, 1973. Nonetheless, it

---

79. Amendments to 5 *U.S.C.* §§2108, 5924, 7152.

80. 31 *U.S.C.* §§1221–1263.

81. 42 *U.S.C.* §1321 et. seq. and 40 *U.S.C.* §101 et. seq.

82. 33 *U.S.C.* §1251 Note.

83. Interview with Marilyn Markison, legislative assistant to Bella Abzug, February 1973.

too had feminist origins, as it was the brainchild of Emily Card, a feminist political scientist serving on Brock's staff as a research fellow in 1973. Technical assistance was provided by Sharyn Campbell, head of NOW's national Task Force on Credit. The Senate bill failed to get out of House Committee, but Brock relentlessly supported his anti-sex-discrimination provision and eventually attached it as an amendment to H.R. 11221, the Depository Institutions Amendments which was signed into law in late 1974.[84]

While several male legislators have sponsored women's legislation, there is usually a feminist in the background someplace. But staff support is hardly sufficient to gain congressional support, as illustrated by the many members of the Capitol Hill Women's Political Caucus who work for male legislators who have not actively supported or sponsored feminist bills.

The Nixon Administration

As a general rule, most congressional legislation, especially that which gets out of committee, originates with the administration.[85] This has certainly not been the case with women's rights legislation, as all but a handful of it has been sponsored by Democrats. Yet, for the most part, it was not opposed by the administration either, and many Republican congresswomen and female Nixon appointees have worked actively for it. Rather, the attitude of the Nixon administration was one of patronizing neglect; giving a supportive gesture when actively pushed to do so, but otherwise pretending that women's issues don't exist.

It was in large part this apathetic attitude which stimulated many Republican women to become active in the cause of women's rights. They expected Nixon to appoint at least one female cabinet officer and were angry when he did not. When he

---

84. Interviews with Emily Card, August 1974; Sharyn Campbell, July 1974; and Eleanor Bachrach, legislative assistant to Senator Proxmire of Wisconsin, July 1974.

85. Harold Wolman, *Politics of Federal Housing* (New York: Dodd, Mead, 1971), p. 109.

publicly invited the cabinet wives to attend an occasional meeting as an apparent substitute for appointing women, they got very angry. "This was a slap in their face. You could almost feel women's hostility rise," one commented.

At a press conference early in 1969, Vera Glaser, a reporter for the North American Newspaper Alliance, asked Nixon why he had appointed no women to high positions and duly reported his answer that he had been unable to find any qualified ones. In response to this story, Catherine East sent Glaser a packet of material on women and the women's liberation movement and subsequently met with her. With this material and in response to Nixon's obvious uninterest in women, Glaser gave the newly emerging movement its first national media coverage in five stories syndicated by her employer. She and East subsequently met with a presidential assistant, Arthur Burns, in April of that year to propose an administration legislative program for women.

On July 8, 1969 four Republican congresswomen sent a strongly worded six-page memo to President Nixon in which they berated his administration because it had "done absolutely nothing of significance in the field of women's rights, responsibilities and opportunities." They went on to assert that

> its record represents a retreat from the inadequate action of
> past Administrations. Not a single important policy decision
> or legislative recommendation has been made. . . . Not only
> have fewer women been appointed to responsible positions,
> . . . but the number of existing women officeholders replaced
> by men has [made] the net record a minus one. . . .
> . . . even the rhetoric has been negative. . . .
> Administration officials have not only avoided the issue, but
> several are known to be positively anti-woman.

The congresswomen followed this diatribe with a list of seventeen recommendations including presidential support for new legislation, recruitment of women to top government positions, and thorough investigation into and correction of all sex discrimination in and out of government. They also urged the enactment of the Equal Rights Amendment and proposed "the construction of multi-purpose day care centers for the children of working mothers."

The congresswomen later met with the President, and to illustrate their point about neglect, protested that Helen Bently had not been given an appointment for which she was clearly the most qualified individual. Shortly thereafter, Bently was appointed head of the Maritime Commission, the highest administration appointment of a woman at that time; 125 other women were subsequently appointed to high-level positions in the first Nixon administration. In August Nixon issued Executive Order 11478 which directed all federal agencies and departments to "establish and maintain an affirmative action program of equal employment opportunity for all civilian employees and applicants." However, this Order merely added emphasis to the prohibition against sex discrimination in federal employment contained in EO 11375.[86]

The only other administration response was the creation of the President's Task Force on Women's Rights and Responsibilities in September. This idea was proposed by Arthur Burns who was in charge of setting up task forces. Vera Glaser was a member, and the CACSW staff became the task force staff and provided most of its research material. The report was submitted on December 16, 1969, but was held up for six months by the administration because it was "too strong." Many thought it would never be released publicly at all. Events, however, dictated otherwise as the report was leaked to the Miami *Herald* which not only published it in toto but sold reprints to the public as contraband. It was finally released in June 1970 in conjunction with the fiftieth anniversary of the Women's Bureau.

Though not as strong as rumor had it, the tone and recommendations of the Task Force Report compared favorably with the longer 1963 Report of the President's Commission. Explicitly

---

86. Mary M. Lepper, "A Study of Career Structures of Federal Executives," in *Women in Politics*, ed. Jane Jaquette (New York: Wiley, 1974), pp. 109–30, reports that "the movement of women into the federal hierarchy is not really rapid nor is it quiet" (p. 126).

stating that women "are now denied their full constitutional and legal rights," it went on to lay out a plan which it hoped would prove a deterrent to "accelerating militancy." The crux of this plan was that there be "a national commitment to basic changes that will bring women into the mainstream of American life." Included in the legislative proposals were passage of the Equal Rights Amendment, several amendments to the Civil Rights Acts of 1964 and 1957 to extend parts of their coverage to women, and liberalized social security, child-care and income tax provisions. Demanding that the federal government be "as seriously concerned with sex discrimination as with race discrimination" the task force also recommended the White House put its own house in order with more appointments for women, a "sensitivity" among the different federal employment programs to sex discrimination, suits by the attorney general where appropriate, and a good deal of research into the problem.[87]

Despite the fact that task force reports are a major way in which legislative recommendations enter the President's program[88] most of this report's suggestions were largely ignored. Although there was subsequently some mild support for a few of the proposals, for the most part the Nixon administration acted as though production of the report itself was as much support as it cared to give. A White House Office of Women's Programs was established in February 1973 but by May 1974 all the staff had resigned. Their feeling was that Nixon was too preoccupied with Watergate to be concerned with special interest programs.[89] Major support for women's issues from within the administration came not from the White House, but the Women's Bureau, especially in the efforts to revise the OFCC guidelines.

The Women's Bureau is a direct descendant of the Women's Division of the Ordinance Department set up to look after the needs of women entering the munitions industry during World

---

87. President's Task Force on Women's Rights and Responsibilities, *A Matter of Simple Justice*, April 1970.

88. J. Clarence Davies III, *The Politics of Pollution* (Indianapolis: Bobbs-Merrill, 1970), p. 63.

89. *Women Today*, 27 May 1974, p. 70.

War I. Renamed the Women in Industry Service, the division was shifted to the Labor Department in July 1918 and in June 1920 was renamed again and made a permanent Bureau.[90] Its new purpose was "To formulate standards and policies which shall promote the welfare of wage-earning women, improve their working conditions, increase their efficiency, and advance their opportunities for profitable employment."

Throughout its history, a major activity of the Women's Bureau had been to promote state protective legislation for women through its pamphlets, conferences, and staff speaking engagements. Its directors during those years had strong ties to the AFL–CIO which favored protective legislation, and, like it, strongly opposed the Equal Rights Amendment which was seen as a potential threat to special protection. Women's Bureau opposition was often cited by opponents of the ERA in Congress.

The first Nixon appointee was Elizabeth Duncan Koontz, a former president of the National Education Association and a Democrat. Her appointment was largely due to the influence of George Schultz, who had known her prior to his becoming secretary of labor. After careful consideration, Koontz favored the ERA, and held Bureau staff meetings during 1969 to discuss it. Although the staff was hardly unanimous, most were inclined to support it, especially since the courts were rapidly declaring state protective laws to be preempted by Title VII. This support continued after Koontz's replacement in 1973 by Carmen Maymi.

The Equal Rights Amendment

The Equal Rights Amendment was first proposed by the National Women's Party in 1923, because the courts maintained that sex, unlike race, color, creed, national origin, or religion, was a legitimate basis for class legislation and the NWP did not expect the courts to change their views. In the words of one judge,

---

90. Marcia Hovey, "A Doughty Lady Turns 50," *Manpower*, official publication of the Department of Labor's Manpower Administration, March 1970.

sex-based classification "had always been made, and, unless prohibited in express terms in the Constitution . . . is a natural and proper one to make." [91] This judicial position was solidly maintained until 1971 when a few cracks began to appear. Previously, the doctrine that sex was a "reasonable basis of classification" had been definitively spelled out as recently as 1961 in *Hoyt* v. *Florida*[92] where the Court explicitly refused to apply the "equal protection" clause of the Fourteenth Amendment. In two sex-discrimination cases in 1971 and 1973, the court tentatively moved toward the position that sex was an inherently "suspect classification" but in a 1974 decision the majority of the Court backed away.[93]

---

91. *Salt Lake City* v. *Wilson*, 46 Utah, 60, 69, 148, pp. 1104, 1107 (1915).

92. 368 U.S. 57, 59–62, 68 (1961). In this case a woman convicted by an all-male jury of murdering her husband challenged a Florida law stating that women were not required to serve on juries unless they registered such a desire with the clerk of the circuit court. The Court said: "We of course recognize that the Fourteenth Amendment reaches not only arbitrary class exclusions from jury service based on race or color, but also all other exclusions which 'single out' any class of persons for different treatment not based on some reasonable classification. . . . In neither respect can we conclude Florida's statute is not based on some reasonable classification, and that it is thus infected with unconstitutionality. Despite the enlightened emancipation of women from restrictions and protections of bygone years, and their entry into many parts of community life formerly considered to be reserved to men, women are still regarded as the center of home and family life. . . . This case in no way resembles those involving race or color in which the circumstances shown were found by this Court to compel a conclusion of purposeful discriminatory exclusions from jury service. . . . There is present here neither the unfortunate atmosphere of ethnic or racial prejudices which underlay the situations depicted in those cases, nor the long course of discriminatory administrative practice which the statistical showing in each of them evinced." The Court reversed the Hoyt decision in January 1975 in *Taylor* v. *Louisiana*, #735744.

93. *Reed* v. *Reed* (401 U.S. 71 [1971]) challenged an Idaho law which gave preference to men over women as administrators of estates. The Court unanimously ruled that the statute was not relevant to the purposes of administration, but avoided the question of whether sex was a suspect classification. In *Frontiero* v. *Richardson* (411 U.S. 677 (1973)), the Court voted 8–1 to invalidate a military fringe-benefits' scheme automatically available to the wives of military men, but which required military women to prove that they provided over half their husband's support. Four justices agreed that "classifications based on sex, like classifications based on race, alienage, or national origin, are inherently suspect, and must therefore be subjected to strict judicial scrutiny." Three justices said the statute was unconstitutional, but that it was not necessary to rule all sex classifications inherently suspect. The eighth judge merely said that sex was not

Because of this attitude by the Court, resolutions have been introduced in every Congress since 1923 proposing an equal rights amendment. The original version stated, "Men and women shall have equal rights throughout the United States and everyplace subject to its jurisdiction." This was revised by the Senate Judiciary Committee in 1943 to read: "Equality of rights under the law shall not be denied or abridged by the United States or by any State on account of sex." Passage of the original version may have had an effect on nongovernmental activities, but the revised language applies only to laws and governmental activities. The Senate Judiciary Committee has frequently reported the amendment favorably, most recently in 1964,[94] and the ERA passed the Senate in 1950 and 1953. Both passages however, were marred by the addition of the "Hayden rider" that the amendment "shall not be construed to impair any rights, benefits, or exemptions now or hereafter conferred by law, upon persons of the female sex." [95] This rider killed the amendment both times as it was totally unacceptable to women's groups who had seen women denied opportunities under the guise of "protection" and "benefits."

The major opponents of the ERA feared that it would abolish all "protective" legislation which restricted the number of hours women could work per week, the amount of weight they could be allowed to lift, and occasionally provided for special benefits such as chairs and additional rest periods. This legislation was supported by most unions, including most women's unions. The belief by working-class women was that the amendment might provide benefits to professional and/or upper-class women by equalizing the laws governing marriage, but would be only detrimental to them.

---

relevant in this case. However, in *Kahn* v. *Shevin* (No. 73–78, April 1974) six justices upheld a Florida statute which exempted $500 worth of property from taxation for widows but not for widowers on the grounds that it bore a fair and substantial relation to "the state policy of cushioning the financial impact of spousal loss upon the sex for whom that loss imposes a disproportionately heavy burden." Three justices maintained that the law was in violation of the "equal protection" clause of the Fourteenth Amendment.

94. Senate Report No. 1558, 88th Cong., 2nd Sess.
95. 96 *Cong. Rec.* 872–3 (1950); 99 *Cong. Rec.* 8954–5 (1953).

By 1970, however, this picture was beginning to change. One effect of Title VII of the Civil Rights Act was numerous court rulings that voided state protective laws. Employers and unions had used these laws to deprive women of jobs, promotions, and overtime on the grounds that women could not legally lift the required weight or work the required hours of the better-paying positions. The women had taken them to court and won. Research was also making it apparent that "state labor laws applying to women only are discriminatory and harmful." [96] As a result, not only the Women's Bureau but many unions, including the Teamsters, the United Auto Workers, and the Communications Workers, had changed their minds about the ERA.

Among those groups with a renewed interest in the ERA was the Citizen's Advisory Council on the Status of Women. On February 7, 1970, it officially endorsed the ERA, "sensing that the time had come to advance the cause of justice and equality for men and women." [97] With this endorsement it published a definitive legal analysis of the ERA and transmitted both to Nixon with an appropriate press release. This analysis was written by a lawyer in the Justice Department, Mary Eastwood, who had been a founder of NOW, and had originally written the paper in the summer of 1967 for NOW. On March 26, Martha Griffiths entered it into the *Congressional Record*.[98]

These events made what was originally a feminist analysis of the ERA for a feminist organization an official part of its legislative history. What was significant was that the analysis made it clear that "equal rights" did not admit of special exceptions on the basis of sex alone, and it clarified certain confusing aspects of protective legislation. For the latter it argued that only those laws which served to restrict freedoms or deny rights to one sex would

---

96. Susan Deller Ross, "Sex Discrimination and 'Protective' Labor Legislation," in *The "Equal Rights" Amendment*, Hearings before the Subcommittee on Constitutional Amendments of the Committee on the Judiciary, U.S. Senate, 91st Cong., 2nd Sess., 5–7 May 1970, p. 408.

97. Citizen's Advisory Council on the Status of Women, *Women in 1970* (Washington, D.C.: Government Printing Office 1970), p. 2.

98. 116 *Cong. Rec.* 2nd Sess. (1970).

be voided, while those which actually conferred benefits on women would be extended to men. This interpretation mitigated some of labor's disagreements with the feminists by opposing an across-the-board elimination of all sex-specific laws.

That same month, roughly two dozen NOW members disrupted hearings on the eighteen-year-old-vote amendment being held by the Senate Judiciary Subcommittee on Constitutional Amendments, demanding that hearings be scheduled on the Equal Rights Amendment. As momentum gathered, the Senate Judiciary Subcommittee called hearings on the ERA for May 5 through 7, 1970, and the White House released the Task Force report with its endorsement of the ERA. At the fiftieth-anniversary conference of the Women's Bureau on June 13, Secretary of Labor-designate James D. Hodgson added the Labor Department's endorsement. Two days before, Martha Griffiths had filed a petition to discharge the House Judiciary Committee from further consideration of the amendment as it had not been considered during the previous twenty years. Bottling up the amendment in committee had been the major tactic to deter it from House consideration.

Griffiths had filed the petition in part at the suggestion of Catherine East as a commemorative event, but once done, she threw all her enormous energy into getting it out of committee and passed. In this effort she had several resources to draw upon.

1. Griffiths had sat for several years on the powerful Ways and Means Committee. In this position she had accumulated a lot of political favors which she had not used up for home district bills. As Griffiths expressed it, "There is a better fraternity among chairmen than among unions." When she called in her favors, fifteen out of seventeen chairmen signed her discharge petition, despite the fact that committee chairmen normally oppose discharge petitions as undermining of their power.

2. Among her many activities, Griffiths spoke at a D.C. consciousness-raising group which included many employees of the Hill among its members. When she asked their support for the discharge petition, twenty or so formed the National Ad Hoc Committee for the ERA. This committee became the

nucleus of what was to be the major lobbying group for the ERA. They accumulated innumerable lists of individuals and organizations and sent them mailings requesting women to wire their representatives. They also began a personal and telephone campaign of the House members, and instituted lobbying efforts of the Senate Judiciary Committee. To help their escalating efforts, the Ad Hoc Committee was able to use the mailing lists and newsletters of the many national women's organizations (not necessarily feminist groups), the WATS telephone lines of the congressional offices, and the research materials of the CACSW and Women's Bureau.

3. A major assist in the discharge campaign came from the 180,000-member Business and Professional Women's association which was holding their annual convention in Hawaii that July. Three former BPS presidents were members respectively of NOW, the Task Force, and the CACSW. They persuaded women attending the convention to write, wire and call their representatives immediately. Since many of these women had been active in congressional campaigns or had made large contributions, and an election was coming up in the fall, their influence was very great at this point.

4. In its forty-seven years of lobbying effort, the National Women's Party had secured the sponsorship of the ERA of 248 members of the House and 81 members of the Senate. Most of these people had sponsored the amendment in the firm belief that they would never have to vote on it, and now they were put in the bind of having to support it or appear as hypocrites. Since the only active opposition to the amendment at this time was the AFL–CIO and their main argument had been rendered obsolete by a combination of Court decisions and the CACSW paper, the easiest course for most congresspeople was to bend in the direction of public pressure.

Consequently, Griffiths got the necessary 218 signatures on her discharge petition by July and the House passed the amendment on August 10, 1970, by a vote of 350 to 15. The Senate, however, proved more obdurate. Opponents forced further hearings in early September[99] in hopes of delaying action on the amendment until fall election campaigning would guarantee the absence of many senators. When the resolution came before the Senate on October 13 it was amended by a vote of 36–33 to permit Congress to exempt women from the draft, and a rider was added to permit prayer in public schools. To get around this block, Birch Bayh proposed a substitute amendment on October 14, but it was opposed by feminist groups as inadequate and later withdrawn.[100]

During the interim, the Ad Hoc Committee met with leading women officials of the Democratic and Republican parties and many feminists and women's organizations to plan strategy for the coming Congress. One of the first problems that had to be dealt with was the question of the draft. While lobbyists could argue that women ought to have the same right as men to make their own decisions without special exemption, the congresspeople could also point out that all the women making this argument were well over the draftable age. They were answered February 10, 1971, at hearings by the Senate Armed Services Committee on the administration's proposal to extend the draft for two years. There, representatives from George Washington University Women's Liberation read a statement decrying the use of the draft as a means of intimidating women seeking equal rights especially while the Senate was also discussing abolishing the draft.

> If it is their intent to have us believe that the draft is a
> permanent institution, then we again attest to our equality

---

99. *Equal Rights 1970, Hearings Before the Senate Committee on the Judiciary*, 91st Cong., 2nd Sess., 9, 10, 11, 15 September 1970.

100. Most of the above and following information on the passage of the ERA not otherwise cited comes from a combination of sources including interviews with: Martha Griffiths, Representative from Michigan, February 1973; Val Fleishhacker, an aide to Representative Don Fraser of Minnesota, February 1973; Flora Crater and Carol Burris of the Women's Lobby, formerly of the Ad Hoc Committee, February 1973; Mary Eastwood, attorney with the Justice Department, April 1973; Catherine East of the CACSW, February 1973; and from *The Woman Activist: An Action Bulletin for Women's Rights*, vol. 1, no. 1 (January 14, 1971) through vol. 2, no. 4 (April 1972); *Women in 1970, Women in 1971, Women in 1972*, and *Women in 1973*; annual reports of the CACSW; and from various newspaper clippings.

and demand equal application of the Selective Service Law. Sex exemption from the draft is a negation of our ability to face the most onerous self-determination question of our time. We are not asking to be spared from making critical decisions. If the passage of the Equal Rights Amendment means that both men and women will be subject to involuntary induction, we claim the right to answer for ourselves. . . .

For long enough we have been given an easy out solely because we are females. We did not ask for this easy out, and we will accept it no longer. Neither will we have our credibility diminished, our need for equal rights demeaned by senators who seek to deny us this equality with the tactic of fear.[101]

The fact that radicals from a local university were working with congressional offices; administrative bureaus; and a potpourri of feminist, women's, establishment, and liberal organizations ranging from the Americans for Democratic Action to the National Republican Committee illustrates the scope of the ERA campaign. The ERA could command this diverse following in large part because it was a moral issue that cut across political lines, in part because it cost nothing and therefore was not overtly redistributive, and in part because it attracted the allegiance of an enormous number of "woodwork" feminists.

As the women's liberation movement became public, its ideas struck a responsive chord in women from various walks of life. These women had often been isolated from one another, assuming their latent feminist ideas were peculiar to themselves, and to be talked about only at the risk of social opprobrium. As the movement emerged, and the concept of feminism lost some of its taint, some joined feminist organizations or worked actively for women's issues within their own organizations. Most, however, did not, due in large part to the bad publicity women's liberation

---

101. The statement was written by Beverly Fisher and Carol Vance, both of draft age and employees of George Washington University, and read by Vance. Their testimony was repeated at the House Judiciary Subcommittee hearings the following April 5.

had received and the radical image it had acquired. They were still waiting an appropriate moment to "come out of the woodwork."

The Equal Rights Amendment brought them out in droves. It was simple, straightforward, consonant with traditional American values, and didn't cost anything. There was no organized opposition except for that of labor, and that was breaking up. Although the ERA had been around for years, the fact that it had only recently become "public" meant that it had not acquired any politics. With few exceptions, people could not determine their attitude toward the ERA by virtue of who else was for or against it. The initial alliance formed against it was a rather unholy one. The opposition included not only the AFL–CIO, but the John Birch Society, Phyllis Schlafly, the National Council of Catholic Women, and the Communist party.

This opposition had not yet coalesced during the Ninety-second Congress and the ERA was still very much a nonpartisan issue. As Clausen points out, there is no simple explanation of congressional decision making. He isolates five major policy areas and analyzes the major forms of influence in each one. He asserts that for civil liberties and civil rights policy, the major influence is the constituency.[102] While women's issues are not included in his analysis as it ended before the Ninety-second Congress, it is reasonable to assume that as they are basically civil rights issues, they would follow the same pattern. If the constituency is the major influence on congresspeople in civil rights voting, the constituency pressure for the ERA was enormous.

The more than 50 national organizations that supported it did not just give verbal support. They weren't permitted to. The Ad Hoc Committee alone sent out over 40,000 letters to presidents of varying organizations asking them to write their congressmen and publish items on the ERA campaign in their newsletters. All of Common Cause's 215,000 members received a letter to do the same, and a battery of volunteers made over 51,000 phone calls

---

102. Aage R. Clausen, *How Congressmen Decide: A Policy Focus* (New York: St. Martin's Press, 1973), p. 221.

on Common Cause's WATS lines. The Business and Professional Women's Clubs sent at least 100,000 letters to state officers and local club presidents, and served as the spearhead of the pass-ERA drive in many locales where feminist organizations were anathema. The result was that some congresspeople received as many as 1,500 letters a month and congressperson Tip O'Neill of Massachusetts was quoted as saying that the ERA had generated more mail than the Vietnam war. The coordinated effort worked so well that, according to one key member of the Ad Hoc Committee, "Toward the end, it got so you could make twelve phone calls and get five to ten thousand letters." [103] The lobbying effort was similarly intense, with 20 to 35 full- and part-time volunteers literally living in the halls of Congress. A couple of women devoted a full two years of their lives to the ERA campaign.

The occasion for the renewal of the ERA fight was the hearings scheduled on the omnibus Women's Equality Act proposed by Abner Mikva (D.-Ill.) to enact the proposals of the President's Task Force. Held in late March and early April of 1971, Don Edwards (D.-Calif.) included the ERA as well. Unfortunately, the committee decided that it could report only one of the two bills, so the Mikva bill was killed. At those hearings, then Assistant Attorney General William H. Rehnquist testified for the administration, giving what can at best be described as lukewarm support:

> The President in 1968 endorsed the Equal Rights
> Amendment, which is presently embodied in H.J.Res. 208.
> . . . While the Department supports the enactment . . .
> there is no denying that opponents of that amendment have
> raised significant questions which deserve serious
> consideration of the Committee. . . . The Department of
> Justice feels that the amendment, no matter how construed,
> would not be a substitute for the Statute (H.R. 916). . . . In
> pointing out the shortcomings of the amendment, we do not
> wish to be understood as either condemning its purpose or

103. Interview with Val Fleishhacker, aide to Representative Don Fraser of Minnesota, February 1973.

suggesting that statutory method of accomplishing the same goal would necessarily be preferable.[104]

The ERA was recommended by the subcommittee, but the full committee chose to amend it by the addition of Section 2:

> This article shall not impair the validity of any law of the United States which exempts a person from compulsory military service or any other law of the United States or of any State which reasonably promotes the health and safety of the people.

Under the leadership of Griffiths, Don Edwards, and Robert McClory (R.-Ill.) the full House rejected the committee's amendment by 265 to 87 after debate on October 6 and 12, and passed the ERA by a vote of 354 to 23.

The House resolution was sent to the Senate to meet the tender mercies of its time-honored foe, Senator Sam Ervin (D.-N.C.). Through a combination of filibuster, multiple amendments, and prevention of quorums, Ervin had prevented the ERA from getting out of committee for years. But Ervin's efforts were met with greater and greater opposition from senators whose constituent pressure was beginning to exceed his. Ervin won the first round in the Subcommittee on Constitutional Amendments of the Senate Judiciary Committee, which on November 1971 reported his substitute amendment reading as follows:

> Sec. 1. Neither the United States nor any State shall make any legal distinction between the rights and responsibilities of male and female persons unless such distinction is based on physiological or functional differences between them.

---

104. Testimony at *Equal Rights for Men and Women, Hearings Before the House Judiciary Subcommittee #4,* 24, 25, 31 March and 1, 2, 5 April 1971. The 1968 reference is to a casual statement by Nixon while campaigning that he supported equal rights for women. Although Nixon sent a letter to Senator Hugh Scott (R.-Pa.) endorsing the ERA on 18 March 1972, he did not publicly speak in favor of it until after it had passed Congress. The written version of his 1973 State of the Union message contained the statement that "Additionally, in the year ahead, we will continue to support ratification of the Equal Rights Amendment to the Constitution so that American women . . . need never again be denied equal opportunity." *Cong. Rec.,* 93rd Cong., 1st sess., 1 March 1973, House 1273.

He lost the second round when the full committee made its decision, the following March. As several members of the subcommittee changed their votes and reported the unamended ERA by 15 to 1. On the Senate floor debate was short and uneventful. President Nixon belatedly added his support in a personal letter to Senator Hugh Scott of Pennsylvania the day after debate began. Finally, on March 22, 1972, under the leadership of Birch Bayh (D.-Ind.) and Marlow Cook (R.-Ky.), the Senate voted 84 to 8 for the amendment after rejecting 9 amendments offered by Ervin. After 49 years of effort, the ERA was sent to the states for ratification. Its final passage showed the necessity of multifaceted attack that could only have been mounted by an emerging social movement. It involved a combination of congressional allies, administrative resources, intensive lobbying by volunteers, and grass-roots pressure that could not have been replicated for an issue that did not symbolize so much to so many. As Martha Griffiths summed it up, "In the House we won by logic; in the Senate we won with lobbying."

Unfortunately, this coalition could not be quickly replicated in the states, and it was there that the ERA stimulated a well-organized, determined opposition. For the first year it appeared to have clear sailing as twenty-eight states quickly ratified it. Then, in January of 1973 a national "Stop ERA" campaign surfaced, headed by noted right-winger Phyllis Schlafly. What had looked like a sure thing began to seem more and more problematical under the assault of a well-financed and well-organized right-wing opposition. Although Schlafly denies her campaign is backed financially by far-right organizations, groups such as the John Birch Society, Pro-America Incorporated, the Christian Crusade, and the Young Americans for Freedom have thrown their organizational resources into the fight.[105] Raising the specter

---

105. Eileen Shanahan, "Opposition Rises to Amendment on Equal Rights," *New York Times*, 14 January 1973. Nick Thimmesch, "The Sexual Equality Amendment," *New York Times Magazine*, 24 June 1973, p. 8. See also *Homefront*, newsletter of the Institute for American Democracy, February 1973, and Lisa Cronin Wohl, "Phyllis Schlafly: Sweetheart of the silent majority." *Ms.*, March 1974, pp. 55ff., for a thorough review of the right-wing backing of the stop-ERA campaign. The NOW Legislative Office also has material available on this topic.

of drafting women, denying wives the support of their husbands and mothers the custody of their children,[106] the Schlafly forces have organized mass mailings to the legislators of southern and rural states, bused in women to lobby, and testified at ratification hearings. The kind of constituent pressure that congresspeople had felt at the national level local legislators felt at the state, but for the opposite position. Despite the fact that the AFL-CIO, once the ERA's most formidable opponent, had voted unanimously in its October 1973 convention to support ratification, by the end of 1974 only five more states had ratified the amendment and two others—Nebraska and Tennessee—had voted to rescind their ratification.[107] Responding to this crisis, the members of the ERA Ratification Council, a coalition of over two dozen national organizations, redoubled their lobbying efforts for ratification. In the states which had not acted definitively one way or the other on the amendment, a major battle between opposing interest groups was shaping up.

The Emerging Policy System

Regardless of the outcome of the ERA, the two-year final battle to get it through Congress had some very beneficial side effects.

---

106. *The Phyllis Schlafly Report*, "What's Wrong With 'Equal Rights' for Women?" February 1972, and "The Right to Be a Woman," November 1972.

107. According to J. William Heckman, counsel to the Senate Subcommittee on Constitutional Amendments, in a letter to Nebraska State Senator Shirley Marsh of February 20, 1973, "Once a state has ratified an amendment, it has exhausted the only power conferred on it by Article V of the Constitution, and may not, therefore, validly rescind such action." In the only such case to come before it, the Supreme Court ruled that the question was a political one, and therefore only Congress could decide whether to accept or reject rescission (*Coleman v. Miller*, 307 U.S. 433 [1939]). In the prior instances where states have later rescinded their ratifications, Congress has ignored their attempts. In 1868 Ohio and New Jersey first ratified then rescinded the Fourteenth Amendment. In 1868 New York ratified the Fifteenth Amendment, then withdrew that ratification a year later. In the congressional proclamation that declared these amendments part of the Constitution, the rescinding states were included. See also J. Franklin Jameson, *On Constitutional Conventions: Their History, Powers, and Modes of Proceeding* (Chicago: Callaghan, 1887) and Lynn A. Fishel, "Reversals in the Federal Constitutional Amendment Process: Efficacy of State Ratification of the Equal Rights Amendment," *Indiana Law Journal* 49 (Fall 1973): 147–66.

Primary among them was the climate it created in Congress that there was serious constituent interest in women's rights. The ERA was probably the easiest of all the legislative issues to generate mail about from a wide cross section of the population. Once the question of the value of "protective" legislation was out of the way, courtesy of Title VII, there was something vaguely immoral about the inequitable application of the Constitution. As there was as yet little organized opposition to women's rights legislation in general, this mail created the impression that there was strong constituent support for the whole policy area. Both the mail and the numerous respectable organizations which backed the ERA helped to dispel the negative impression of the women's liberation movement created by the press. As Martha Griffiths expressed it, "The ERA created a moral climate for reform. Once it was put through, everything else became logical." [108]

The other major side effect was the establishment of liaisons between feminist organizations and congressional staff. The ERA lobbying effort both provided an excellent excuse to establish working relationships with and educate staff, and exposed many of the "woodwork" feminists on the Hill. The incipient network this created made it easier to know who to approach for what kind of support and/or information for other bills.[109]

This incipient network, however, was not entirely due to the ERA. Much of it was already emerging around education legislation. Of all the many policy areas in which women's rights legislation has been submitted, it has achieved its greatest success in the area of education. This is partially because the equal right to as much education as one has the potential for is perhaps the most widely accepted value of the American egalitarian ethic. Secondly, there were a lot of feminists in the House Education and Labor Committee. Edith Green was chair of the Subcommittee on Education; and Shirley Chisholm, Patsy Mink, and Ella Grasso were members. Thus it was easy to set up a symbiotic

---

108. Interview of February 1973.
109. Interviews with Val Fleishhacker, Martha Griffiths, and Ann Scott, Legislative Vice-President for NOW, February 1973.

relationship between feminists interested in education and committee members interested in women's rights. The first major women's rights bill (apart from the ERA) was proposed by Edith Green in 1970 to prohibit discrimination against women in federally assisted programs and in employment in education; and to extend the jurisdiction of the U.S. Commission on Civil Rights to include sex.[110] The first hearings on women's rights legislation in over a decade were held on this bill in June of that year.

Green's proposal came about in part as a result of the efforts of WEAL to file complaints with HEW and the interest this aroused. Green's office had contact with Sandler of WEAL who suggested many of the people invited to testify at the hearings and supplied her office with abundant data on discrimination against women in higher education. While the bill died at the end of the Congress due to lack of time, its provisions were later enacted in subsequent bills. Additionally, the printed committee hearings have proved one of the most thorough compilations of material on women in higher education and have often been used by feminists as a textbook—published at government expense.

This symbiotic relationship was extended when it became apparent that HEW was dragging its heels on enforcement of the Executive Order. As chair of the Ad Hoc Subcommittee on Discrimination Against Women of the House Education and Labor Committee, Green called oversight hearings on the Office of Education in April and May of 1972.[111] When the proposed hearings became public knowledge, Green's office was "flooded with calls from HEW employees wanting to offer anonymous information. But they were reluctant to testify publicly because their jobs were unprotected." With Green's office playing a brokerage role, this information could be given to feminist organizations and individuals who could afford to testify publicly and did so.[112] While such oversight hearings often do not result in

---

110. Section 805 of H.R. 16098, 91st Cong., 2nd sess.

111. *Oversight Hearings on Discrimination Against Women Before the Ad Hoc Committee on Education and Labor of the House of Representatives*, 92nd Cong., 2nd Sess., 26–27 April; 3, 10 May, 1972.

112. Interview with Sue Black and Sally Kirkgasler, aides of Congresswoman Edith Green, February 1973.

any specific legislation, they are a major way for

> administration witnesses [to] have an opportunity to assess
> the attitudes of committee and subcommittee members on
> administrative programs. . . . Such attitudes compel
> administrative spokesmen to view the agency role through
> the eyes of the committee or subcommittee.[113]

Since the first congressional hearings in response to pressures by new feminist groups were held in May 1970, the number of hearings held on topics relevant to women has been considerable. The women's liberation movement has had a major impact on the Government Printing Office, if not necessarily on the government. While the role of hearings in influencing congressional decision making is debatble, they do serve other functions. Truman lists three:

> First, the hearing is a means of transmitting information,
> both technical and political, from various actual and
> potential interest groups to the committee. . . . A second use
> is as a propaganda channel through which a public may be
> extended and its segments partially consolidated or
> reinforced. A third function is to provide a quasi-ritualistic
> means of adjusting group conflicts and relieving disturbances
> through a safety valve.[114]

A fourth function, peculiar to newly emerging interests, is that of legitimation. Incipient interest groups, especially those created by social movements, are often perceived suspiciously by more "established" groups and institutions. Attention by Congress through the hearings process and public airing of the issues help provide an aura of legitimacy to new ideas and newly public problems which can facilitate their acceptance elsewhere. Certainly, the hearings on sex discrimination have served the legitimation, propaganda, and informational functions. It is too

---

113. William L. Morrow, *Congressional Committees* (New York: Charles Scribner's Sons, 1969), p. 162.

114. David B. Truman, *The Governmental Process* (New York: Alfred A. Knopf, 1951), p. 372.

early to assess whether they are merely providing a "safety valve" by allowing spokespeople to "blow off steam" by expressing themselves publicly. The ERA hearings during the 1950s perhaps served this purpose, but at this point, even if hearings on women's rights issues do not result in the immediate passage of legislation, the propaganda and legitimation functions are sufficient to make such hearings valuable to feminists. It is after an issue becomes "old," with most of the main points and positions public knowledge, that hearings can become merely a substitute for action.

Fortunately, Congress is not the only federal body that can hold hearings, and other agencies can do so without needing the excuse of legislation. In particular the Civil Rights Commission has this as a primary function. Its complementary functions as an informational clearinghouse on matters relating to civil rights and its periodic appraisal of federal civil rights enforcement efforts make it an excellent source of propaganda and legitimation. Like the Women's Bureau, which serves some similar purposes for working women, it cannot operate effectively in a vacuum of interest; but given a reasonably supportive atmosphere, it can well serve as an advocate of minority and women's interests within the government. The problem from the perspective of feminist groups is whether the Commission can overcome its hostility to its expanded jurisdiction as a threat to its concern with racism. The Commission has shown some perceptiveness in this regard and as early as 1971 created a Task Force on Sex Discrimination to propose a possible program in this area. The report suggested that the new jurisdiction should be utilized to make connections between the operation of sexism and racism as well to encourage an alliance between feminist and minority civil rights groups for legislation of mutual interest.[115] To this end, the Commission set up a special program unit on women's rights within the national office; began work on the sex discrimination

---

115. Interview with Carol Kummerfeld, then special assistant to the staff director, now head of the Women's Rights Program Unit, U.S. Commission on Civil Rights, 29 March 1973.

aspects of federal civil rights enforcement efforts; planned and/or published several studies and articles on women's issues,[116] held hearings on "Women and Poverty" in Chicago, June 17–19, 1974, sent some of its staff to the national conventions of feminist organizations; submitted statements on proposed laws and regulations involving sex discrimination and women's rights, and developed liaisons with numerous feminists and feminist organizations about how the movement and the Commission can be of mutual help to each other.

The Civil Rights Commission's attempts to grapple with the reality of the women's liberation movement and its impact is just one example of a phenomenon characteristic of the entire governmental structure that has both resulted from and is contributing to the growth of women's issues as legitimate concerns of federal policy. What is emerging is a network of people in various agencies of the government, feminist organizations, and other private institutions, with a personal and professional commitment to improving the status of women. While the impact of the movement on the latter has not been dealt with here, suffice it to say that feminists and feminist concerns have emerged strongly within the media, some labor unions, many educational institutions and associations, and a few other places. Together the participants in this loosely structured network are forming a policy system on women's rights.

The idea of a policy system is one that has emerged sporadically in the scholarly literature and under various names. Ralph Huitt conceives of a set of "policy systems" in which:

> A particular policy is made by the people in the agencies, public and private, who are interested in and know about that policy area. There is an almost continuous interchange among committee members, their staff, the executive (that is, agency personnel, White House staff, and private persons appointed to "task forces" and the like) and representatives of private associations at almost every stage of the process,

---

116. See especially the symposium on "Sexism and Racism: Feminist Perspectives," *Civil Rights Digest*, Spring 1974, and "Women and Poverty," June 1974.

from the first glimmer of an idea to compromises in
conference and to administration of the act.[117]

Cater refers to such systems as "subgovernments" and attributes
them to:

an increasingly fragmented power structure trying to cope
with increasingly big and complicated problems. These are
working arrangements for the effective exercise of
governmental power. In modern government, that power
must be exercised.[118]

Such subgovernments are not all alike. They may be "small and
tightly ordered" like the sugar subgovernment, "largely manipu-
lated outside the formal offices of the federal government" like oil,
or an intricate complex like that of defense, "far-flung, comprising
a vast Executive bureaucracy, numerous committees in Congress,
and a formidable representation on the wider Washington
community." [119]

The best description was given by Griffiths in 1939 when he
argued that "government by whirlpools" was the prevalent mode:

One cannot live in Washington for long without being
conscious that it has these whirlpools or centers of activity
focusing on particular problems. The persons who are thus
active . . . are variously composed. Some are civil servants,
some are active members of the appropriate committees in
the House and Senate, some are lobbyists, some are unofficial
research authorities, connected perhaps with the Brookings
Institution or with one of the universities, or even entirely
private individuals. Perhaps special correspondents of
newspapers are included. These people in their various
permutations and combinations are continually meeting in
each other's offices, at various clubs, lunching together, and

117. Ralph K. Huitt, "Congress, The Durable Partner," in *Lawmakers in a
Changing World*, ed. Elke Frank (Englewood Cliffs, N.J.: Prentice-Hall, 1966), p.
19. I'd like to thank Henry Pratt of Wayne State University for alerting me to this
literature.

118. Douglass Cater, *Power in Washington* (New York: Random House, 1954),
p. 22.

119. Ibid., pp. 20–21.

participating in legislative hearings or serving on important but obscure committees set up within the departments.
Among such human beings interested in a common problem, ideas are bound to emerge—ideas for programs, ideas for strategy.[120]

It often takes years for such a policy system to develop; for the significant people in different institutions to emerge, become known to each other, and establish the pattern of meetings, conferences and mutual activities necessary to the creation of an informal network. While the policy system on women's rights is hardly complete, its rapid rise in part answers our original question on the relatively early, unstrenuous achievement of a good deal of policy in this area. There were a large number of "woodwork feminists" in the federal government. It could no doubt be shown that many women in the upper reaches of government had had a good deal of personal experience with sex discrimination and/or other personal reasons for immediate interest in this issue. As Wolman has pointed out, the influence of individual personalities and proclivities is a "recurring theme" throughout the policy process.[121]

These women thus created a potential "policy system" which only needed the proper conditions to jell. Such conditions were provided in general by the emergence of the women's liberation movement which legitimated an interest in this area. The movement also no doubt educated many women to feminism who were not already sensitive to its nuances. It was the movement, expressed through the actions of its adherents and the news coverage of the media, which created the environment for a new policy area. The policy system per se in turn was created by the specific issues which were attacked. Of these, the WEAL higher education campaign and the Equal Rights Amendment have stimulated the greatest efforts and the greatest interaction. It was via these issues and because of the sympathetic women within

---

120. Ernest S. Griffith, *The Impasse of Democracy* (New York: Harrison-Hilton Books, 1939), p. 182.
121. Wolman, *Federal Housing*, p. 80.

government that the movement could easily achieve effective access to key points of decision making—a major goal of any interest group.[122]

Nevertheless, the ideas of a changed environment and a new policy system alone are not sufficient to explain the new policies. Women, let alone feminists, are simply just not that powerful in government or in the private sector. The reason the women's liberation movement could achieve many hard-fought legislative goals of the civil rights movement so much faster than it did was because the civil rights movement preceded it. It is not for naught that almost all the women's rights legislation involves amendments to or parallels of minority civil rights legislation. The civil rights movement broke the ground. It both created a precedent for and a model of action in the area of sex discrimination. Once the main redistributive decision had been made about the addition of sex discrimination as an area of federal policy, all that was really necessary was pressure to apply it consistently. This major redistributive decision was made, as pointed out earlier, somewhat by accident, in 1964. While sex in Title VII was not at the time treated seriously, its existence prompted many latent feminists to create a pressure group to demand its adequate enforcement. This pressure group, NOW, helped stimulate a growing movement which in turn prompted more legislation, in a rapidly accelerating cycle.

One should be conscious, however, that coattail riding on another movement's achievements has its limits. First, those on the tails cannot usually control the direction of the coat. Many civil rights organizations have made it clear that they are very suspicious of their feminist offspring and not amenable to an easy alliance. Second, the feminist movement has several significant issues—child care, abortion, and especially the abolition of sex-role stereotypes and the traditional roles—on which there are no civil rights precedents. Here the movement will have to learn to fight its own battles, and will not find the going so easy.

---

122. Ibid., pp. 3–6; and Truman, *The Governmental Process*, p. 264, note 11.

7
Policy and Movement

$\mathbf{F}$ROM A SINGLE STUDY IT IS IMPOSSIBLE TO
advance firmly any theories about the relationship between social
movements and public policy. It is also impossible to reach any
definitive conclusions about the relation between the women's
liberation movement and women's rights policy at this early stage
of its development beyond the fact that there is one. Nonetheless,
some patterns of mutual effect have emerged which are entitled to
a few general and tentative reflections.

There is clearly a *symbiotic* relationship between feminists within
our governmental institutions, feminists operating in the private
sphere, and even feminists who are openly opposed to and/or
alienated from the American political system. This symbiosis
exists despite the fact that many individuals or groups within
these different spheres would consider such a relationship personally reprehensible if they were conscious of its presence. It is
maintained by several factors.

> 1. Most feminists, for reasons outlined earlier, share a set
> of common ideas and symbols which provide for a basic

unity. What ideological conflicts have emerged have been entirely within the younger branch of the movement and are not shared by all of it (e.g., whether one has to be a lesbian in order to be a feminist). While there are disagreements over strategy and priorities, such differences are usually viewed as mutually complementary or irrelevant rather than contradictory to one another. Unlike many sectarian leftist groups, different activities are seen more as a division of labor than as a means of divisiveness.

2. New ideas or activities are widely shared through both the feminist and commerical media. This keeps different segments from becoming totally isolated from one another.

3. There are interlocking informal communications networks throughout most of the movement through which information, ideas, contacts, and some resources are shared.

How this network operates is illustrated by a connection between an obscure radical feminist in California and the White House that occurred in late 1970. Largely as a result of the grand press blitz of that year, the White House received an average of three letters a week from women who wanted to know how they could join a women's liberation group. They were referred to the Women's Bureau who dutifully answered the queries, using chapter lists from NOW and WEAL, a list of primarily East Coast small groups printed in the *Ladies Home Journal* (in their special August 1970 insert on the women's movement agreed to after a hundred feminists held a sit-in in the publisher's office), and *The Mushroom Effect*. The latter was a sixteen-page tabloid directory produced by the efforts of a single woman in Albany, California, and of great value to the Women's Bureau because, unlike the other sources, it was mostly non-East Coast groups.[1] Copies of this directory had been taken by its compiler to a small Minneapolis women's liberation conference in September 1970. Among the people there to whom it was given was a Midwest feminist who was also in occasional contact with Catherine East. As East's

---

1. Interview with Jean Wells, economist at the Women's Bureau, Washington, D.C., 26 March 1973.

office was across the hall from the Women's Bureau, she was aware of their need and acquired a copy of *The Mushroom Effect* for them. Thus the work of a politically alienated feminist on the other side of the country was used to answer the White House's mail. While this incident is perhaps not the most significant exchange that has occurred in the movement, it is a graphic example of how the symbiosis operates without the participants necessarily being aware of each other or their mutual connections.

However, this symbiosis involves a great deal more than just an exchange of resources or occasional cooperation. The relationship between movement and policy is a dynamic system in which the actions of each affect the actions of the other. The traditional perspective on this relationship has seen it as a rather nebulous one-way pattern in which a social movement affects public opinion and that in turn affects policy. Specific influence was exercised through interest groups.[2] While this perspective is not exactly wrong, it is limited. The process is simply much more complicated than that. In general one can say that a social movement provides resources for those within government who are sympathetic to use in pursuit of common aims. The movement's ability to affect public opinion is just one of those resources. Information on problems, new ideas, skilled help, activities which generate publicity, and lots of warm bodies are some of the other resources. These resources can also be used to pressure those within government who are not sympathetic to the movement's aims to at least act as though they were; though these efforts will usually sway only the apathetic, not the active opponents. Unlike the resources of well-organized interest groups, however, these resources are not automatically available at the beck and call of a congressional representative or an administrative official. The resources that a social movement has to offer are largely people and their time, and they have to be carefully cultivated. Acting as liaison between policy makers and move-

---

2. Harmon Zeigler, *Interest Groups in American Society* (Englewood Cliffs, N.J.: Prentice-Hall, 1964). David B. Truman, *The Governmental Process* (New York: Alfred A. Knopf, 1951).

ment participants is one of the many functions of a movement's leadership, and thus a movement's effect on policy is in part a consequence of the ability and interest of that leadership.

Policy in turn has a major effect on a movement's political activities because it determines the shape of the political realm. According to Schattschneider, "A conclusive way of checking the rise of conflict is simply to provide no arena for it or to create no public agency with power to do anything about it." [3] It should be evident from much of American history that precluding a political arena does not preclude conflict, but merely its institutional expression. If the institutions that exist are incapable of channeling conflict it will not die, but will spill over into the private realm or violate the norms of political behavior. Policy channels conflict by creating institutions for its legitimate expression, by creating issues, and by affecting the structure of available opportunities for action. But its effects on a movement are not uniform. Not all movements, or all parts of a movement, will respond similarly to policy changes. A movement can respond only insofar as its particular resources fit the channels available and its values allow it to participate in those channels. Nor are the effects of policy all in the same direction. The correlation between movement strength and the development of policy in accord with its aims is at best a rough one. Sympathetic policy can destroy a movement by preempting it; and unsympathetic policy can strengthen a movement by creating a crisis which mobilizes its adherents.

The relationship between movement and policy can be more clearly seen by taking the effects of each on the other in turn as they have developed by and about women.

It is relatively easy to document the effects of the women's liberation movement on the development of women's rights public policy as was done in the last chapter. Simply put, prior to the movement there was very little policy on women's status and not much interest in generating more. After the movement had

---

3. E. E. Schattschneider, *The Semi-Sovereign People* (New York: Holt, Rinehart & Winston, 1960), p. 71.

achieved public prominence there was a great deal more. The relationship between movement and policy included several factors.

1. The movement generated a great deal of publicity on women and women's status. This publicity had the effect of legitimating women's rights as a relevant public concern. True, there was a good deal of ridicule by the media of women's liberation, but that ridicule did not obscure the hard realities of the situation.

2. Because the movement was raising some issues and making some demands that were within the American value structure, it created a climate of expectations that something would be done. Issues such as the abolition of marriage or the use of women as sex objects were not immediately transformable into valid public concerns, but those on educational and employment equality were. For the latter at least, to prove the problem was sufficient to demand a solution.

3. By making women's rights a public issue and expanding the area of conflict, the movement created a constituency for those "woodwork" feminists already within government. Many had been concerned with women's issues for years, but had been unable to impress those in positions of power with the priority of such issues. A public, politically active women's movement enabled them to say there was a popular demand for solution of such problems and thus strengthened their claims. As relationships between government officials and feminists developed, the former could also provide inside information to the latter about upcoming issues in which public pressure would be of mutual benefit. An organized movement was particularly valuable with elected officials, half of whose constituents were women. Especially on those issues for which there was no organized opposition, it could be argued that congressional support of women's issues would lead to electoral support by female constituents. While the reality of such claims was seldom put to the test, the defeat of staunch ERA foe Congressman Emanuel Celler by Elizabeth Holtzman and a couple other electoral victories was strong backing for them.

4. In addition to public support, the movement also

provided information, data, and testimony to feminists within Congress who were sponsoring relevant bills. Edith Green relied very heavily on Sandler and WEAL with their numerous contacts with academic women for data and testimony for her education bills. Similarly, many traditional issues raised by congressional opponents of the ERA were not able to be effectively controverted until after the rebirth of feminism. Only women of draft age could convincingly testify against using draft exemption to deny equal rights, and only blue-collar union women could deny the value of protective legislation.

5. In addition to grass-roots research, the movement also supplied grass-roots support. This support is especially manifested in constituent mail, but can also be inferred by meetings, conferences, and demonstrations. Such support provides a source of constant pressure which makes it difficult to ignore an issue even if it is low on an official's personal priority list.

6. The existence of a diverse movement spanning a wide spectrum of feminist attitudes pushed the leaders of the more respectable women's organizations to more strongly feminist positions. Leaders of the Business and Professional Women's Clubs, who in 1966 had disdained activity that might be labeled "feminist," found themselves lobbying actively for all the women's legislation of the Ninety-second Congress and urging their large membership to apply pressure in their home districts. The woman who was most responsible for splitting WEAL off from NOW in 1968 because of NOW's pro-abortion stand became the author of a 1973 satirical pro-abortion proposal.[4]

---

4. It was submitted as an amendment to pending congressional joint resolutions to reverse the Supreme Court decision on abortion and included the following provisions: "Provided that since women are, by virtue of this Amendment, subject to involuntary motherhood, they shall have the option at their sole discretion, of declaring the child which they are required to bear to be the financial responsibility of the state, whereupon responsibility for the support, nurturance and education of such child shall be assumed by the body politic. . . .

And also provided that the Congress of the United States shall establish a special fund for the support of such involuntarily-born children, to be administered by the Social Security Administration, to which male citizens from the age of

The support of women from such established and responsible organizations added an aura of respectability to feminism.

7. Their acceptability was increased by those groups labeled radical or revolutionary and ridiculed by the media. The latter groups provided a "radical flank" against which other feminist organizations and individuals could appear respectable. Without the more flamboyant and/or extremist groups, organizations like NOW and WEAL would have been open to being dismissed as too far out.

8. Administratively, a movement represents one organized expression of an enforcement agency's clientele. Clientele are those "groups whose interests [are] strongly affected by an agency's activities [and provide] the principal sources of political support and opposition." [5] As Zeigler has noted, administrators often gradually identify with the regulated clientele and adopt their perspective because of their long and intense association.[6] This is one of the ways in which an agency becomes "captured" by its clientele so that it no longer carries out its initial regulatory function.[7] However, this idea of cooptation presumes that there are specific organized interests that are supposed to be regulated in favor of a vague, unorganized public good. When instead a situation exists where one group is supposed to be regulated in the interest of another—as is often the case with redistributive policy—it is also possible for the favored group to do the capturing. Thus an agency can still maintain its original purpose if it is coopted by the right clientele. For example, the EEOC has as its clientele the industries which it is supposed to regulate and the minorities and women for whom it is supposed to regulate. So far, control of the EEOC has been kept well out of the hands of industry, which in part accounts for its sympathetic interpretations and findings. For

puberty onward shall contribute a pro-rata share as the Congress shall from time to time provide."

5. Herbert A. Simon, Donald W. Smithburg, and Victor A. Thompson, *Public Administration* (New York: Alfred A. Knopf, 1950), p. 461.

6. Zeigler, *Interest Groups*, pp. 292–93.

7. Philip Selznick, *TVA and the Grassroots* (Berkeley: University of California Press, 1949); Marver Bernstein, *Regulating Business by Independent Commission* (Princeton, N.J.: Princeton University Press, 1955).

a long time, it was largely under the control of and only sympathetic to the interests of minority groups—which is why it made so many interpretations adverse to women's interests. Over time it has incorporated the feminist perspective—and many feminist employees—into its operation and now cooperates with feminist groups in its enforcement efforts. Minorities and women did compete—and to a certain extent still do—for the limited time and attention of the EEOC. But it was not until the women's liberation movement that the EEOC even acknowledged that it ought to give equal time. HEW on the other hand, has hardly been captured by feminist groups. Instead, its civil rights enforcement agencies experience many cross-pressures which often leave them paralyzed.

9. Movement organizations can provide support for agencies as well as put pressure on them. Investigators for HEW have instructions to seek out and get information from women's groups on the campuses they visit. These groups have often provided them with inside knowledge and insights into the campus employment structure which are not readily available from the computer printouts the university provides. After the EEOC began to show interest in sex discrimination, NOW offered to testify in their behalf at appropriations committee hearings and also joined with minority organizations in lobbying for greater enforcement powers. Thus an organized clientele can be a resource for a regulatory agency if it's the right clientele.

It is a lot more difficult to document the effects of policy on the movement. Policy influences the range of alternatives for movement action, but since one can only imagine what the total range might be, one never knows exactly how policy has exercised its influence. It is easy to see what activity policy stimulates; it is hard to see what activity it precludes. To simplify our task, let us look at how two policy decisions, the ERA and Executive Order 11375, have influenced movement activity. We have already seen how the addition of "sex" to Title VII was in part responsible for stimulating the movement in the first place (though it is likely that it would have started anyway) by creating expectations which were not met by the EEOC.

The ERA provides an interesting example because it is unlikely that anyone would have thought of it if it was not waiting in the wings for the proper moment. There are not any acute problems women currently face which the ERA will solve. At best it will clear up some legal deadwood that might well be eliminated by judicial and legislative decisions without it. Its most valuable effect at this point will be the psychological victory it will provide of declaring women constitutionally equal with men. During the first years of the new feminist movement few people had heard of it and those that did did not give it much credence. Only the National Women's Party, the Business and Professional Women and a few sympathizers really believed in it.

Yet it existed, and so long as it existed, its failure to pass Congress was a nagging sore of defeat. In 1970 getting the ERA out of the House Judiciary Committee was the most easily available symbolic action in favor of women's rights. Since 1970 was the anniversary year of the Nineteenth Amendment, passage of the ERA was seen as an appropriate commemorative. And once in the public eye it quickly became a rallying point. Why it was such an attractive one to so many women was discussed earlier. The point is that if it had not existed, no one would have thought of it; but since it did exist, everyone had to support it. (Some feminists didn't but they were a very small, quiescent minority.)

The first effect of the ERA was to stimulate a lot of activity in Washington. NOW, WEAL, the BPW, and many individuals oriented themselves to Congress as they had seen no need to before. The aftereffects of this orientation can be seen in the following developments (though many of these might have occurred eventually):

    1. The creation of specific lobbying groups (The Women's Lobby Inc.) out of the Ad Hoc Committee as well as other lobbying groups within NOW and WEAL.

    2. The creation of an ERA coordinating committee in which women's groups began to learn how to work together and to utilize each other's resources.

    3. The incorporation of many nonfeminist women's groups into this committee, thus creating the opportunity to

educate them to feminism and demonstrate that not all feminists were the freaks that the media painted them as.

4. The development of contacts with several liberal and/or public interest organizations (like Common Cause) via this mutual interest which creates the possibility for future cooperation.

5. Provided an opportunity to develop contacts between feminist groups and congressional offices which could be used for other issues.

6. Gave many politically unaware women an excellent education in how Congress works, thus increasing their level of political skill.

Once passed, the ERA went to the states, where it had still further effects. Some states ratified it very quickly. In those which did not, the local effort to get it ratified affected the local movement in much the same way that congressional passage affected the national movement. In particular it stimulated state coalitions. ERA ratification efforts by NOW carried over into a general feeling within the organization that it ought to be organized by state instead of region (WEAL was already organized by state). Additionally, many women sensing the potential for political activity have advocated that substate organizations ought to be by congressional district. If this occurs, it will orient the feminist groups to electoral activity as a primary one. Awareness of the value of cooperation and increased political education were additional results. The impact of this experience has been to make activity within the traditional political realm appear more possible and more appealing than it was before. Now that people have done it, it is no longer quite so remote, nor does it seem quite so irrelevant. Many feminists who engaged in the ERA ratification drive found themselves thinking more in terms of legislation as a logical goal of movement action.

The ERA also provided an excellent opportunity for a lot of political education of nonfeminists. It gave people an excuse to make speeches and raise feminist issues. Women and men who previously might have had no more than a curious interest in the movement found themselves listening because the ERA was a major public issue.

It should be added that the ERA could also have an adverse effect on the movement by deflecting its energies from more important concerns. The specific legal consequences of the ERA itself are not really worth the effort that has been put into it. It is only the political opportunities it offers as a by-product, and its symbolic value, which are worthwhile. If ratification efforts drag on and on for years to the detriment of other activities, the ERA will turn out to be a losing proposition—especially if it is not ratified before the 1979 deadline. Just as the support it stimulated nationally influenced Congress to pass additional feminist legislation, failure to ratify can convince legislators that the movement has no political clout.

The existence of Executive Order 11375 combined with the educational exemption in Title VII can well be said to have fostered the WEAL higher education campaign. Of the many uses to which the Executive Order could be put, it is unlikely that the movement would have chosen to attack academia, as faculty women were a very small group whose problems were not perceived as being acute by any other than themselves. Concomitantly, if the educational exemption had not been part of Title VII, it is quite possible that Dr. Sandler would have filed a complaint with the EEOC for her personal case and done no more. But the Executive Order was the only outlet she had, and the very nature of its broad provisions demanded class action.

Once into motion, the higher education campaign had a very profound effect on the structure of available opportunities for action of academic women and student feminist groups. Previously, faculty women were agitating for change within their particular disciplines because these were the locations of their communications networks and professional identities. Students, as part of the younger branch of the movement, were largely involved in consciousness-raising groups and women's studies projects. Nonfaculty employees were rarely concerned with feminism at all. The higher education campaign gave all these groups of women something to do which promised a degree of effectiveness.

What it demanded of them in turn was that they engage in

such traditional political activity as writing their congressional representatives—a very unappealing action to student radicals; "betraying" their male colleagues to a government agency, and admitting "merit" was not the only criterion of academic success—normally reprehensible to professionally socialized academic women; and cooperation among students, faculty, and other employees to provide HEW investigators with information—something rarely experienced by any of these groups. While it is likely that campus women's liberation groups would have still existed without the higher education campaign, it is unlikely they would have strongly engaged in these activities. Certainly it was difficult for students, who often disdained the establishment, to find themselves assisting the government in law enforcement. It was also difficult for academic women used to operating on an extremely individualistic basis to generate the group solidarity necessary for a successful local investigation. The fact that women on many campuses were unable to do this accounts in part for some of the nonresults that occurred. It was the campuses with the most widespread and organized women's groups—Michigan, Columbia, Berkeley are just three—that got the most thorough and vigorous HEW action.

While the above examples illustrate situations in which the movement did respond to policy developments, there are many situations in which it did not. For example, the higher education campaign required many radically identified young women to operate "within the system." While many did so with reluctance, some could not do it at all. It violated their value structure too severely. The interference of a "revolutionary" value structure with traditional political activity is one that has marked much of the younger branch of the women's liberation movement—coming as it did out of the radical community. For the first two to three years it often led to what was called the radical paradox. Many politicos, viewing themselves as radicals, found repugnant the possibility of pursuing "reformist" issues which might be solved without altering the basic nature of the system, and thus they felt, only strengthen the system. However, their search for a sufficiently radical action and/or issue came to naught, and they found themselves unable to do anything out of fear that it might be counterrevolutionary. The structure of available opportunities for action did not provide any that were permitted by their value structure.

The "feminists" of that original split were not quite so affected by the radical paradox and thus found themselves occasionally able to operate within the political realm even though it was an alien environment for them. Female Liberation in Boston found themselves part of the New England Women's Coalition which had held a Congress to Unite Women in February of 1971. The coalition, which included NOW chapters, voted to hold a referendum on child care in Cambridge. As that was the primary location of Female Liberation, they found themselves spearheading a drive to collect 10,000 signatures on a petition and then running a campaign which won two to one in every ward. Unfortunately, there was no follow through to this victory because by the election Female Liberation was strongly dominated by the SWP who decided that abortion was *the* issue to which their energies should be devoted. The following year the New York Radical Feminists joined in a coalition with NOW and the NWPC to lobby the Albany legislature not to repeal the liberal abortion law. This involvement was contrary to their ideological opposition to lobbying as a reformist activity and was stimulated by the success of a repeal attempt in the Spring of 1972 which Governor Rockefeller vetoed. Desperation justified a change in tactics. (The Supreme Court decision on abortion was handed down before the 1973 legislature met so NYRF members did not actually have to go through with it.)

A movement's ability to respond to policy is limited not only by its values, but also by its resources. For example, a strategy of selected legal cases to develop a desired body of judicial opinion, such as that pursued by the NAACP, was impossible for the early movement because it simply did not have a cadre of volunteer lawyers available or the means of raising funds to pay them. Some organizations are now building this resource, but it has taken time. Additionally, women did not have the Constitutional basis for litigation blacks had, due to the Supreme Court's acceptance of sex as a legitimate basis for classification (see supra, p. 210).

In a similar vein, the younger branch of the movement developed many abortion counseling and referral groups during the time when such activity was illegal. To a certain extent they thus aided some doctors in financially exploiting women because the women did not have the skills to perform the abortions themselves. The Supreme Court decision legalizing most abortions obviated this activity.[8] Now these same groups are transforming themselves into public abortion and health clinics; they are doing social work instead of illegal work.

These and the other kinds of social service projects which predominate in the younger branch of the movement result in part because the small, autonomous groups lack the resources to engage in electoral and other political action. First, their members are rarely politically oriented (in the traditional sense) or politically skilled. Second, pressure-group activity is limited because the groups are rarely coordinated enough to stimulate and maintain a public campaign. Third, their members lack the "credentials" to make themselves credible to elected officials. Fourth, most of these groups' energies go to meeting group-maintenance needs, and service projects facilitate cohesiveness. And last but not least, small groups are just not large enough to operate in a normal-size political district. Those communities that are small enough to be a viable political arena for a small group are usually too conservative to support one. Very few communities in this country—Cambridge and Berkeley are two—are both small and liberally oriented. By contrast, the strategy of electing local officials was a logical one for blacks in small southern towns because they were often the majority of the population and many of their most immediate grievances could be dealt with on the local level.

The effect of policy on this branch of the movement can be less

---

8. *Roe* v. *Wade*, 410 U.S. 113; *Doe* v. *Bolton*, 410 U.S. 179. Several Constitutional amendments have been introduced into Congress which would nullify this ruling, and both state and federal laws have been passed to limit its applicability.

seen at the federal level than the local one. While the symbiotic relationship that is developing between national feminist organizations and varying federal agencies is at best nascent for the younger branch, some local groups have begun to work with city agencies. For example, antirape organizations in several cities have established an uneasy alliance with sex-crime units in their police departments to educate women in rape prevention and encourage them to work with the police to apprehend rapists.

Nonetheless, the continuing centralization of power in the federal government means that it is the national feminist organizations that will have the greatest impact on policy—and be most affected by it in turn. NOW and the other older branch organizations are thriving at this point because they have been able to use the institutional tools which our society provides for social and political change. Yet the "honeymoon" is over. The women's liberation movement caught the government by surprise, and it responded along the lines it had developed for civil rights policy. Now that the backlash has begun on several fronts, it remains to be seen whether the feminist groups can develop and mobilize their resources to maintain the momentum without getting so bogged down in the nitty-gritty politics of incremental success that they lose sight of their ultimate goals.

Bibliography

Abbott, Edith. *Women in Industry*. New York: D. Appleton, 1910.

Allen, Pam. *Free Space: A Perspective on the Small Group in Women's Liberation*. New York: Times Change Press, 1971.

Ash, Roberta. *Social Movements in America*. Chicago: Markham, 1972.

Baker, Elizabeth F. *Technology and Woman's Work*. New York: Columbia University Press, 1964.

Becker, Howard S. *Sociological Work: Method and Substance*. Chicago: Aldine, 1970.

———, and Geer, Blanche. "Participant Observation and Interviewing: A Comparison." *Human Organization*, 16 (1957): 28–32.

Berger, Caruthers Gholson. "Equal Pay, Equal Employment Opportunity and Equal Enforcement of the Law for Women." *Valparaiso Law Review* 5 (Spring 1970): 326–73.

Bernstein, Marver. *Regulating Business by Independent Commission*. Princeton, N.J.: Princeton University Press, 1955.

Bird, Caroline. *Born Female: The High Cost of Keeping Women Down*. New York: David McKay, 1968.

Blood, Robert O. "Long-Range Causes and Consequences of the Employment of Married Women," *Journal of Marriage and the Family* 27 (February 1965): 43–47.

————, and Wolfe, Donald M. *Husbands and Wives: The Dynamics of Married Living.* Glencoe, Ill.: Free Press, 1960.

Blumer, Herbert. "Collective Behavior." *Review of Sociology: Analysis of a Decade*, edited by Joseph B. Gittler. New York: John Wiley & Sons, 1957.

————. "Social Movements." In *New Outline of the Principles of Sociology*, edited by A. M. Lee. New York: Barnes & Noble, 1951.

Brown, Daniel. "Sex Role Development in a Changing Culture." *Psychological Bulletin* 54 (July 1958): 232–42.

Buck, Solon J. *The Agrarian Crusade.* New Haven, Conn.: Yale University Press, 1920.

Cain, Glen G. *Married Women in the Labor Force: An Economic Analysis.* Chicago: University of Chicago Press, 1966.

Cameron, William Bruce. *Modern Social Movements.* New York: Random House, 1966.

Cantril, Hadley. *The Psychology of Social Movements.* New York: John Wiley & Sons, 1963.

Carden, Maren Lockwood. *The New Feminist Movement.* New York: Russell Sage Foundation, 1974.

Cater, Douglass. *Power in Washington.* New York: Random House, 1964.

Chafe, William Henry. *The American Woman: Her Changing Social, Economic and Political Roles, 1920–1970.* New York: Oxford University Press, 1972.

Chesler, Phyllis. *Women and Madness.* Garden City, N.Y.: Doubleday, 1972.

Citizen's Advisory Committee on the Status of Women. *Women in 1970.* Washington, D.C.: Government Printing Office, 1970.

————. *Women in 1971.* Washington, D.C.: Government Printing Office, 1971.

Clark, Peter, and Wilson, James Q. "Incentive Systems: A Theory of Organizations." *Administrative Science Quarterly* 6 (June 1961): 129–66.

Clausen, Aage R. *How Congressmen Decide: A Policy Focus.* New York: St. Martin's Press, 1973.

Coleman, James. *Community Conflict.* Glencoe, Ill.: Free Press, 1957.

Currie, Elliott, and Skolnick, Jerome H. "A Critical Note on Conceptions of Collective Behavior." *Annals of the American Academy of Political and Social Science* 391 (September 1970): 34–45.

Dahrendorf, Ralf H. *Class and Class Conflict in Industrial Society.* Palo Alto, Calif.: Stanford University Press, 1959.

Davies, J. Clarence, III. *The Politics of Pollution.* Indianapolis: Bobbs-Merrill, 1970.

Dawson, C. A., and Gettys, W. E. *An Introduction to Sociology.* New York: Ronald Press, 1929.

Doely, Sarah Bentley, ed. *Women's Liberation and the Church.* New York: Association Press, 1970.

Dye, Thomas R. *The Politics of Equality.* Indianapolis: Bobbs-Merrill, 1971.

————. *Understanding Public Policy.* Englewood Cliffs, N.J.: Prentice-Hall, 1972.

Epstein, Cynthia Fuchs. "Positive Effects of the Multiple Negative: Explaining the Success of Black Professional Women." *American Journal of Sociology* 78 (January 1968): 912–35.

Equal Employment Opportunity Commission. *The Legislative History of Titles VII and XI of the Civil Rights Act of 1964.* Washington, D.C.: Government Printing Office, 1967.

————. *Toward Job Equality for Women.* Washington, D.C.: Government Printing Office, 1969.

Ferriss, Abbott L. *Indicators of Trends in the Status of American Women.* New York: Russell Sage Foundation, 1971.

Flexner, Eleanor. *Century of Struggle.* Cambridge, Mass.: Harvard University Press, 1959.

Freeman, Jo. "The Legal Basis of the Sexual Caste System." *Valparaiso Law Review* 5 (Spring 1971): 203–36.

Friedan, Betty. *The Feminine Mystique.* New York: Dell, 1963.

————. "NOW: How it Began." *Women Speaking*, April 1967.

Gamson, William A. *Power and Discontent.* Homewood, Ill.: Dorsey Press, 1968.

Gerlach, Luther P., and Hine, Virginia H. *People, Power, Change: Movements of Social Transformation.* Indianapolis: Bobbs-Merrill, 1970.

Gilman, Charlotte Perkins. *Women and Economics.* Boston: Small, Maynard, 1898; reprint ed., New York: Harper & Row, 1966.

Goode, William J. *World Revolution and Family Patterns.* Glencoe, Ill.: Free Press, 1963.

Griffith, Ernest S. *The Impasse of Democracy.* New York: Harrison-Hilton Books, 1939.

Gross, Edward. "Plus Ça Change . . . The Sexual Structure of Occupations Over Time." *Social Problems* 16 (Fall 1968): 198–208.

Gurr, Ted Robert. "A Causal Model of Civil Strife: A Comparative Analysis Using New Indices." *American Political Science Review* 42 (December 1968): 1104–24.

————. *Why Men Rebel.* Princeton, N.J.: Princeton University Press, 1970.

Gusfield, Joseph R. "Organizational Change: A Study of the WCTU." Ph.D. dissertation, Department of Sociology, University of Chicago, 1954.

Harbeson, Gladys E. *Choice and Challenge for the American Woman.* Cambridge, Mass.: Schenkman, 1967.

Hayden, Casey, and King, Mary. "A Kind of Memo." *Liberation,* April 1966.

Heberle, Rudolph. *Social Movements.* New York: Appleton-Century Crofts, 1951.

Henry, Alice. *The Trade Union Woman.* New York: D. Appleton, 1917.

————. *Women and the Labor Movement.* New York: George H. Doran, 1923.

Hole, Judith, and Levine, Ellen. *Rebirth of Feminism.* New York: Quadrangle Books, 1971.

Holtzman, Abraham. *The Townsend Movement: A Political Study.* New York: Bookman Associates, 1963.

Hovey, Marcia. "A Doughty Lady Turns 50." *Manpower,* March 1970.

Howard, John R. *The Cutting Edge: Social Movements and Social Change in America.* Philadelphia: Lippincott, 1974.

Huitt, Ralph K. "Congress: The Durable Partner." In *Lawmakers in a Changing World,* edited by Elke Franke. Englewood Cliffs, N.J.: Prentice-Hall, 1966.

Hyman, H. H. "The Psychology of Status." *Archives of Psychology,* no. 269, New York, 1962.

Irwin, Inez Haynes. *The Story of the Women's Party.* New York: Harcourt, Brace, 1921.

Jackson, Maurice; Petersen, Eleanora; Bull, James; Monsen, Sverre; and Richmond, Patricia. "The Failure of an Incipient Social Movement." *Pacific Sociological Review* 3 (Spring 1960): 40.

Jaquette, Jane. *Women in Politics.* New York: John Wiley, 1974.

Kanowitz, Leo. *Women and the Law.* Albuquerque, N.M.: University of New Mexico Press, 1969.

Killian, Lewis M. "Social Movements." In *Handbook of Modern Sociology*, edited by R. E. L. Faris. Chicago: Rand McNally, 1964.

King, C. Wendell. *Social Movements in the U.S.* New York: Random House, 1956.

King, Martin Luther Jr. *Stride Toward Freedom.* New York: Harper & Row, 1958.

Kissinger, C. Clark, and Ross, Bob. "Starting in '60: Or From SLID to Resistance," *New Left Notes*, 10 June 1968.

Knowles, Louis L., and Prewitt, Kenneth, eds. *Institutional Racism in America.* Englewood Cliffs, N.J.: Prentice-Hall, 1969.

Kornhauser, William. *The Politics of Mass Society.* Glencoe, Ill.: Free Press, 1959.

Kraditor, Aileen S. *The Ideas of the Woman Suffrage Movement 1890–1920.* New York: Columbia University Press, 1965.

Kramer, Daniel C. *Participatory Democracy: Developing Ideals of the Political Left.* Cambridge, Mass.: Schenkman, 1972.

Lang, Kurt, and Lang, Gladys. *Collective Dynamics.* New York: Crowell, 1961.

LaRue, Linda J. M. "Black Liberation and Women's Lib." *Trans-Action* 8 (November–December 1970): 59–64.

Lemons, J. Stanley. *The Woman Citizen: Social Feminism in the 1920s.* Urbana, Ill.: University of Illinois Press, 1973.

Lester, Richard A. *Antibias Regulation of Universities.* New York: McGraw-Hill, 1974.

Lewis, Linda, and Baideme, Sally. "The Women's Liberation Movement." In *New Left Thought: An Introduction*, edited by Lyman T. Sargent. Homewood, Ill.: Dorsey Press, 1972.

Lionberger, Herbert F. *Adoption of New Ideas and Practices.* Ames, Iowa: Iowa State University Press, 1960.

Lipset, Seymour M. *Agrarian Socialism.* Berkeley: University of California Press, 1959.

———. *Political Man: The Social Basis of Politics.* Garden City, N.Y.: Doubleday, 1960.

Lipsky, Michael. "Protest as a Political Resource." *American Political Science Review* 62 (December 1968): 1144–58.

Lowi, Theodore J. "Distribution, Redistribution and Regulation: The Functions of Government." In *Public Policies and Their Politics,* edited by Randall B. Ripley. New York: W. W. Norton, 1966.

————. *The Politics of Disorder.* New York: Basic Books, 1971.

Martin, Joanna Foley. "Confessions of a Non Bra-Burner." *Chicago Journalism Review* 4 (July 1971): 11.

Martin, Wendy, ed. *The American Sisterhood.* New York: Harper & Row, 1972.

McCall, George J., and Simmons, J. L. *Issues in Participant Observation.* Reading, Mass.: Addison-Wesley, 1969.

————. "The Nature of Participant Observation." *American Journal of Sociology* 67 (1962): 566.

McLaughlin, Barry. *Studies in Social Movements: A Social-Psychological Perspective.* New York: Free Press, 1969.

Messinger, Sheldon. "Organizational Transformation: A Case Study of a Declining Social Movement." *American Sociological Review* 20 (February 1955): 3–10.

Morgan, Robin, ed. *Sisterhood Is Powerful.* New York: Random House, 1970.

Morrow, William L. *Congressional Committees.* New York: Charles Scribner's Sons, 1969.

Myrdal, Gunnar. *An American Dilemma.* 2 vols. New York: Harper & Row, 1944. Vol. 2, Appendix 5: "A Parallel to the Negro Problem."

North, Sandie. "Reporting the Movement." *Atlantic Monthly,* March 1970.

O'Neill, William. *Everyone Was Brave: The Rise and Fall of Feminism in America.* Chicago: Quadrangle, 1969.

Oberschall, Anthony. *Social Conflict and Social Movements.* Englewood Cliffs, N.J.: Prentice-Hall, 1974.

Oppenheimer, Valerie K. *The Female Labor Force in the United States.* Population Monographs Series #5. Berkeley: University of California Press, 1970.

Pinard, Maurice. "Mass Society and Political Movements: A New Formulation." *American Journal of Sociology* 73 (May 1968): 682–90.

————. *The Rise of a Third Party: A Study in Crisis Politics.* Englewood Cliffs, N.J.: Prentice-Hall, 1971.

————; Kirk, Jerome; and Von Eschen, Donald. "Process of Recruitment in the Sit-In Movement." *Public Opinion Quarterly* 33 (Fall 1969): 355–69.

Polsby, Nelson. "Policy Analysis and Congress." In *American Politics and Public Policy*, edited by Michael P. Smith. New York: Random House, 1973.

President's Task Force on Women's Rights and Responsibilities. *A Matter of Simple Justice.* April 1970.

Proshansky, Harold, and Seidenberg, Bernard, eds. *Basic Studies in Social Psychology.* New York: Holt, Rinehart & Winston, 1965.

Ridley, Jeanne Clare. "Demographic Chance and the Roles and Status of Women." *Annals of the American Academy of Political and Social Science* 375 (January 1968): 15–25.

Rivers, Richard A. "In America, What You Do Is What You Are: The Equal Employment Opportunity Act of 1972." *Catholic University of America Law Review* 22 (Winter 1973): 460–62.

Rogers, Everett M. *Diffusion of Innovations.* New York: Free Press, 1962.

Rossi, Alice. "Equality Between the Sexes: An Immodest Proposal." In *The Woman in America*, edited by Robert J. Lifton. Boston: Beacon Press, 1964. Pp. 98–143.

————, and Calderwood, Anne, eds. *Academic Women on the Move.* New York: Russell Sage Foundation, 1973.

Runciman, W. G. *Relative Deprivation and Social Justice.* Berkeley: University of California Press, 1966.

Saltman, Juliet Z. *Open Housing as a Social Movement.* Lexington, Mass.: D. C. Heath, 1971.

Salisbury, Robert H. "An Exchange Theory of Interest Groups." *Midwest Journal of Political Science* 13 (February 1969): 1–32.

Schattschneider, E. E. *The Semi-Sovereign People.* New York: Holt, Rinehart & Winston, 1960.

Selznick, Philip. *TVA and the Grass Roots.* Berkeley: University of California Press, 1949.

Shapiro, Harvey D. "Women on the Line: Men at the Switchboard: Equal Employment Opportunity Comes to the Bell System." *New York Times Magazine*, 20 May 1973.

Shils, Edward. "Center and Periphery." *Selected Essays.* Chicago: Center for Social Organization Studies, Department of Sociology, University of Chicago, 1970.

Simon, Herbert; Smithburg, Donald W.; and Thompson, Victor A. *Public Administration*. New York: Alfred A. Knopf, 1950.

Skolnick, Jerome H. *The Politics of Protest*. A Task Force Report Submitted to the National Commission on the Causes and Prevention of Violence. New York: Simon & Schuster, 1969.

Smelser, Neil J. *Theory of Collective Behavior*. Glencoe, Ill.: Free Press, 1963.

Sovern, Michael I. *Legal Restraints on Racial Discrimination in Employment*. New York: Twentieth Century Fund, 1966.

Stouffer, Samuel A. *The American Soldier*, vol. 1: *Adjustment During Army Life*. Princeton, N.J.: Princeton University Press, 1949.

Tanner, Leslie, ed. *Voices from Women's Liberation*. New York: New American Library, 1970.

Thimmesch, Nick. "The Sexual Equality Amendment." *New York Times Magazine*, 24 June 1973.

Tocqueville, Alexis de. *The Old Regime and the French Revolution*. Translated by John Bonner. New York: Harper & Bros., 1856.

Truman, David B. *The Governmental Process*. New York: Alfred A. Knopf, 1951.

Turner, Ralph H., and Killian, Lewis M. *Collective Behavior*. Englewood Cliffs, N.J.: Prentice-Hall, 1957.

U.S. Commission on Civil Rights. *The Federal Civil Rights Enforcement Effort*. Washington, D.C.: Government Printing Office, 1971.

———. *The Federal Civil Rights Enforcement Effort—A Reassessment*. Washington D.C.: Government Printing Office, 1973.

———. *Jobs and Civil Rights*, by Richard P. Nathan. Clearinghouse Publication No. 16. Washington D.C.: Government Printing Office, 1969.

U.S. Congress, House. Special Subcommittee on Education of the Committee on Education and Labor. *Discrimination Against Women, Hearings on Section 805 of H.R. 16098*. 2 vols. 91st Cong., 2nd sess., 1970.

U.S. Congress, Senate. Subcommittee on Constitutional Amendments of the Committee on the Judiciary. *The "Equal Rights" Amendment*. 91st Cong., 2nd sess., 5–7 May 1970.

U.S. Department of Labor. *Trends in Educational Attainment of Women*. Washington, D.C.: Government Printing Office, 1969.

Ware, Cellestine. *Woman Power: The Movement for Women's Liberation.* New York: Tower Publications, 1970.

White, James J. "Women in the Law." *Michigan Law Review* 65 (April 1967): 1051–1122.

Wilkinson, Paul. *Social Movement.* New York: Frederick Praeger, 1971.

Witherspoon, Joseph. *Administrative Implementation of Civil Rights.* Austin, Texas: University of Texas Press, 1968.

Wolman, Harold. *The Politics of Federal Housing.* New York: Dodd, Mead, 1971.

Women's Bureau, U.S. Department of Labor. *Action for Equal Pay.* Washington D.C.: Government Printing Office, 1966.

————. *Handbook on Women Workers.* Washington, D.C.: Government Printing Office, 1969.

————. *Underutilization of Women Workers.* Washington, D.C.: Government Printing Office, 1971.

Wortis, Helen, and Rabinowitz, Clara. *The Women's Movement: Social and Psychological Perspectives.* New York: Halsted Press, 1972.

Zald, Mayer N., and Ash, Roberta. "Social Movement Organizations: Growth, Decay and Change." *Social Forces* 44 (March 1966): 327–40.

————, and Denton, Patricia. "From Evangelism to General Service: The Transformation of the YMCA." *Administrative Science Quarterly* 8 (September 1963): 214–34.

Zeigler, Harmon. *Interest Groups in American Society.* Englewood Cliffs, N.J.: Prentice-Hall, 1964.

Index